DATE DUB			
Jan 5 '71			
Oct 9 '75			

GAYLORD M-2   PRINTED IN U.S.A.

Experiments in Physical Organic Chemistry

Experiments in Physical Organic Chemistry

NEIL S. ISAACS

University of Reading

THE MACMILLAN COMPANY
COLLIER-MACMILLAN LIMITED, LONDON

Second Printing, 1969

Library of Congress catalog card number: 69-10025

The Macmillan Company
Collier-Macmillan Canada, Ltd., Toronto, Ontario

Printed in the United States of America

To Diane

Foreword

This book is the manifestation of an interesting pedagogic idea, namely, the integration in single exercises of practical work in the laboratory with the theory of organic chemistry. Gone are the days when a student could (or should) be content to practice at the bench the art of organic chemistry, aided by a book of recipes and such empirical experience as he might have built up, but leaving thought about underlying principles to be pursued, if at all, as a separate activity elsewhere. It is not disputed that to replace empiricism by rationality in the control chemical processes leads in practice to a great economy of time and effort. But our teaching has lagged behind the general appreciation of this situation. Teaching should be geared to produce more chemists who have learned the trick of thinking and working in coordination.

This is the aim of Dr. Isaacs's book. Its method is first to choose a number of recognized principles, having the theoretical support and a wide degree of general application, and then to bring to each such principle the vivid quality conferred on it by practical experience. This involves prescribing, in relation to each of the principles to be studied, one or more experiments dependent on it. They have to be, and are, very carefully edited, as experiments that a class of students can do with equipment that is likely to be available. In the description and discussion of each experiment, the principle being illustrated is first explained in simple terms, and its scope is indicated; then the illustrative experiment is described with adequate practical detail (the point of which can at once be understood); and finally some questions are added in order to spread the line of thought over a wider area than can be covered practically.

To me this approach appears to be one for which high hope may be entertained. It is an approach for which many university teachers of chemistry will feel an intrinsic sympathy.

Sir Christopher Ingold

Preface

The history of a natural science shows a progression from an initial qualitative phase in which the limitations of the subject are defined and the phenomena involved are described and classified, through a semiquantitative phase in which by the application of experiment and logic the bases of these phenomena are established, to the final flowering of a fully quantitative science able to account for the known facts and to predict new ones with complete accuracy.

Organic chemistry, often credited with a date of birth around 1828, corresponding to the synthesis of urea from ammonium cyanate by Wohler, can be fairly said to be well into the second phase of development with the emergence of physical-organic chemistry as a recognized branch of the subject during the last forty years or so. At the present, the development of organic chemistry continues on a broad front and important discoveries in preparative and descriptive chemistry together with increasingly successful excursions into theoretical chemistry accompany physical-organic studies.

Physical-organic chemistry may be said to encompass all studies of the mechanistic pathways of organic reactions and the systematic examination of the variables involved. The techniques used include rate and equilibrium measurements, stereochemistry, all forms of spectroscopy, and analytical methods besides preparative chemistry.

Nowadays it is a widespread practice to devote a considerable part of an organic course to the physical aspects or, indeed, to build the course around a core of physical-organic studies, a logical approach. It is for these reasons and for the success achieved in promoting understanding of the subject at the expense of memory work that we have attempted to bring a series of physical-organic experiments into the undergraduate laboratory. In this book are set forth instructions for carrying out experiments which illustrate some of the more important principles of the subject. Instrumental methods are freely used but as a means to solving a problem as in a research situation rather than as the purpose of the experiment itself. The experiments are grouped for convenience into three sections which utilize principally physical methods, spectroscopic methods, and preparative techniques and each is, as far as possible, arranged to be conducted during a normal four-hour laboratory period. However, it should be understood that this is only possible in some cases where by prior preparation on the part of the instructor, solutions, chemicals, and apparatus are provided ready for use. Methods of synthesis of materials which are not available commercially are given and the instructor may decide whether these preparations are actually carried out by the student.

My thanks are extended to my colleagues for the many helpful suggestions that were forthcoming; to Dr. Gilbert for the photo-chemistry experiment, to Dr. Hutchinson for the dipole moment measurement, to Mr. Neelakantan for the computer programs, and to Professor L. J. Clark for his encouragement in the initial writing of this course. I would also like to pay tribute to the many students who have willingly given of their time to iron out the problems in many of the experiments.

Reading   N. S. I.

Contents

xi

Physical Measurements

PART I

Measurement of Reactivities by the Competition Technique

The relative abilities of two compounds A and B to react with a common reagent X may be measured by allowing a mixture of A and B having known composition to compete for a small amount of X. The relative amounts of the products, AX and BX are measured, the ratio being proportional to the reactivities of A and B:

$$A + X \xrightarrow{k_A} AX$$

$$B + X \xrightarrow{k_B} BX$$

$$\frac{\text{Reactivity of } A}{\text{Reactivity of } B} = \frac{k_A}{k_B}$$

If $[A]_0 = [B]_0$[1]

$$\frac{k_A}{k_B} = \frac{-\dfrac{d}{dt}[A]}{-\dfrac{d}{dt}[B]} = \frac{\dfrac{d}{dt}[AX]}{\dfrac{d}{dt}[BX]} = \left(\frac{[AX]}{[BX]}\right)_{t \to 0}$$

Therefore, if the product analysis is conducted at the beginning of the reaction,

$$\frac{k_A}{k_B} = \frac{[AX]}{[BX]} \tag{1}$$

[1] This condition is not necessary, as long as $[A]_0/[B]_0$ is constant and known,

$$\text{when } \frac{k_A}{k_B} = \left(\frac{[AX]}{[BX]}\right) \bigg/ \left(\frac{[A]_0}{[B]_0}\right)$$

3

Two corrections may have to be made to this simple picture. It is obvious that the proportions of *A* and *B* in the reaction mixture should not change during the course of the reaction; otherwise, the relative reaction velocity of the more reactive compound falls as it becomes consumed and vice versa so that Eq. (1) will no longer hold. Since a change in the proportions of *A* and *B* is inevitable if the two compounds differ at all in reactivity, the effect is minimized by using a large excess of the compounds and allowing only, say, 5% of the reaction to occur. Then, even in the extreme case where k_A/k_B is very large, the change in concentrations during reaction will only approach 5%. The second correction is a statistical one and depends upon the compounds used in the experiment. Suppose *A* has only one site at which reaction with *X* may occur whereas *B* has two such identical sites. Since we are interested in the reactivity at each individual site, we must compare half the amount of *BX* with the total amount of *AX*. In general,

$$\frac{\text{reactivity of } A \text{ per reaction site}}{\text{reactivity of } B \text{ per reaction site}} = \frac{[AX]/n_A}{[BX]/n_B}$$

where n_A and n_B are the numbers of IDENTICAL reaction sites in *A* and *B* respectively.

Competitive reactions are convenient for comparing the reactivities of aromatic compounds towards electrophilic or free radical substitution. Benzene is usually considered as the standard compound to which others are referred, the reactivities then being known as *partial rate factors*. If a mixture of benzene and a monosubstituted benzene is nitrated it is possible to measure the amounts of nitrobenzene and of the *ortho-*, *meta-*, and *para*-nitro derivatives of the substituted compound and hence to determine whether a given substituent activates or deactivates each position of the benzene ring.

Experimental

ELECTROPHILIC NITRATION OF BENZENE AND TOLUENE

The mechanism of this reaction is usually expressed as follows:

$$HNO_3 + Ac_2O \rightleftharpoons NO_2^+ + AcO^- + AcOH$$

Mix 78 g (1 mole) of benzene and 92 g (1 mole) of toluene. Add 5 ml of conc. nitric acid and 5 ml of acetic anhydride, mix well, and allow to stand at room temperature for 30 min.[2] Other nitration mixtures may be used, such as nitric and sulfuric acids in which case the mixture must be shaken vigorously during the reaction. Place the solution in a separatory funnel and wash well with water and with 50 ml portions of 2 M sodium carbonate solution until no more carbon dioxide is evolved. Separate the organic layer and dry over anhydrous sodium sulfate for 10 min and then distill off as much as possible of the benzene and toluene using a simple distillation apparatus and, if desired, reducing the pressure. Analyze the residual nitro compounds by gas chromatography (see Appendix B). A six foot silicone column at 170°C has proven satisfactory in separating nitrobenzene, *ortho*-, *meta*-, and *para*-nitrotoluenes in that order of elution (Figure 1–1). Estimate the relative amounts of each by measuring the

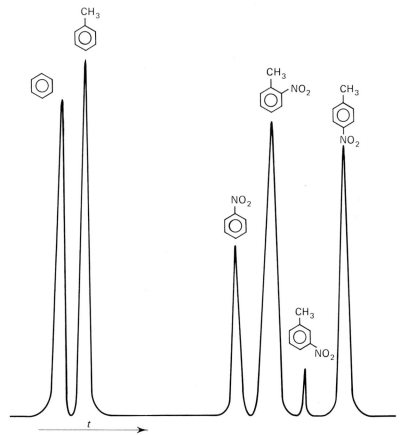

FIGURE 1–1 Typical gas chromatogram of nitration products of benzene and toluene.

[2] It is preferable not to mix nitric acid and acetic anhydride before adding since vigorous oxidation can occur.

area under each peak, or as a good approximation, the heights of the peaks and correct for the six identical positions in benzene ($n = 6$), two *ortho*, two *meta*, and one *para* position in toluene, ($n = 2,2$, and 1, respectively). To identify each peak, inject authentic samples of the four products and measure their respective retention times, since the order of elution given above may differ somewhat from column to column.

Discuss your results in terms of the amount of activation or deactivation of each position of toluene relative to benzene and suggest a mechanism by which the methyl group achieves this result.

Other aromatic compounds may be used in place of toluene, such as chlorobenzene. In such cases where deactivating substituents are present, the nitration is best carried out at a higher temperature, and the chromatographic analysis carried out under conditions determined by the column used.

Questions

1. Nitration of an equimolar mixture of benzene and *tert*-butylbenzene resulted in the following yields of products:

nitrobenzene	0.740 g
o-nitro-*tert*-butylbenzene	1.970 g
m-nitro-*tert*-butylbenzene	1.430 g
p-nitro-*tert*-butylbenzene	13.45 g

Calculate the partial rate factors for the o-, m- and p- positions of *tert*-butylbenzene.
2. Should the values obtained in Question 1 be applicable to other reactions such as bromination of *tert*-butylbenzene?
3. Predict the products to be obtained in major yield from mononitration of the following compounds:

HINT: Count the number of positions in the intermediate complex at which the positive charge may reside without disrupting the aromatic character of the second ring in examples *c–f*.

4. Why does N,N-dimethylaniline brominate to give 2,4,6-tribromo-N,N-dimethylaniline but nitrate to give *m*-nitro-N,N-dimethylaniline?

References

1. C. K. Ingold, *Structure and Mechanism in Organic Chemistry*, Bell, London, 1953, Chapter VI.
2. R. O. C. Norman and R. Taylor, *Electrophilic Substitution in Benzenoid Compounds*, Elsevier, London, 1965, p. 39.

A Linear Free Energy Relationship

EXPERIMENT 2

The mechanisms by which a nonreacting substituent group may affect the reactivity of a neighboring group are mainly of two types: it may affect the ease of approach of a reagent sterically or it may change the electron density at the reacting site by transmitting its own electronic requirements—donating or withdrawing electrons by inductive or mesomeric effects [1]. In terms of the transition state theory, the first mechanism may be said to affect the entropy of activation for the reaction while the second acts primarily by changing the free energy of activation. In order to study each quantitatively, it is most convenient to choose systems such that only one mechanism at a time is operating. For example, the *tert*-butyl group has great steric requirements but a relatively small electronic effect. The steric or entropy effect then is almost entirely responsible for the reduction in reactivity of methyl bromide when substituted by this group, forming *neo*-pentylbromide:

$$CH_3Br + OEt^- \xrightarrow{\text{EtOH}} CH_3OEt + Br^- \qquad k_2 = 34.4 \text{ liter.mole}^{-1} \text{ sec}^{-1}$$

$$CH_3-\underset{\underset{CH_3}{|}}{\overset{\overset{CH_3}{|}}{C}}-CH_2Br + OEt^- \xrightarrow{\text{EtOH}} CH_3-\underset{\underset{CH_3}{|}}{\overset{\overset{CH_3}{|}}{C}}-CH_2OEt + Br^-$$

$$k_2 = 8.26 \times 10^{-6} \text{ liter.mole}^{-1} \text{ sec}^{-1}$$

8

On the other hand, fluorine (covalent radius = 0.64 Å, H = 0.3 Å) [3] can have little steric effect but in view of its high electronegativity transmits a demand for electrons which is responsible for the enhancement of the acidity of acetic acid when substituted by this element:

$$CH_3C\overset{O}{\underset{OH}{\big\langle}} + H_2O \rightleftharpoons CH_3C\overset{O}{\underset{O^-}{\big\langle}} + H_3O^+ \qquad K = 1.7 \times 10^{-5}$$

$$\overset{\delta-}{F}-CH_2C\overset{O}{\underset{OH^{\delta+}}{\big\langle}} + H_2O \rightleftharpoons F-CH_2C\overset{O}{\underset{O^-}{\big\langle}} + H_3O^+ \quad K = 2.6 \times 10^{-3}$$

Steric effects are rather difficult to assess quantitatively, but where these may be ignored, the electronic effects may be compared quite accurately. The correlation between the effects of given substituents on two different reactions is known as a Linear Free Energy Relationship. The most successful of these was found by L. P. Hammett [4, 5] and relates the reaction rates or equilibria at a centre attached to a benzene ring to the electronic effects of substituents in the *meta* or *para* positions. The substituents are sufficiently removed from the reaction site for their steric effects to be negligible but electronic effects may be transmitted through the σ- or π-bond systems. In the following experiment, the effects of substituent groups on two equilibria— the dissociations of benzoic acids and anilinium ions—are to be examined to establish whether the effects are parallel in the two systems:

For the dissociation of a weak acid HX,

$$HX + H_2O \overset{K}{\rightleftharpoons} H_3O^+ + X^-$$

$$K = \left(\frac{[X^-][H_3O^+]}{[HX]}\right)\left(\frac{f_X \cdot f_{H_3O^+}}{f_{HX}}\right) \tag{1}$$

where K is the acid dissociation constant and f refers to the activity coefficients.

If conditions are arranged such that $[HX] = [X^-]$ as would be the case when exactly half of the acid added is neutralized with a strong base (since we may assume Na^+X^- to be 100% dissociated) and also assuming the activity coefficients to be unity,[1]

$$K = [H_3O^+] \quad \text{or} \quad pK = pH \quad (2)$$

Thus to estimate the pK for the acid it is only necessary to measure the pH of a dilute solution of the acid which has been exactly half neutralized with sodium hydroxide. A potentiometric titration of the acid permits a ready method of measuring the pH at half-neutralization.

Experimental

Materials required

Benzoic acid[2]	Anilinium chloride[4]
p-Toluic acid	*p*-Methylanilinium chloride
m-Toluic acid	*m*-Methylanilinium chloride
p-Chlorobenzoic acid	*p*-Chloroanilinium chloride
m-Chlorobenzoic acid	*m*-Chloroanilinium chloride
p-Hydroxybenzoic acid	*p*-Hydroxyanilinium chloride
p-Nitrobenzoic acid	*p*-Nitroanilinium chloride

Standard sodium hydroxide solution, $N/100$
Direct-reading pH meter, preferably with unit scale expansion[3]
Self-filling buret, 10 ml grade A
Magnetic stirrer

---

[1] The assumption that the activity coefficients are unity, a fact which is strictly true only at zero ionic strength, may be examined further by applying the limiting Debye–Hückel equation,

$$-\log f_{ion} = \mathscr{S}Z^2\sqrt{I}$$

where Z = ionic charge, $\mathscr{S}$ = constant = 0.51 for water at 25°, I = ionic strength. For acid concentrations of the order of 10^{-3} molar which will be used here, I at half neutralization is given by

$$I = \tfrac{1}{2}(2 \times [X^-] \times 1^2) = [X^-]_{1/2\,neut} \approx \frac{[X^-]init}{2} = 5 \times 10^{-4}$$

(assuming the residual acid is undissociated) then

$$\log f_{X^-} = \log f_{H_3O^+} = -0.51\sqrt{5 \times 10^{-4}} = -0.00011$$

$$f_{X^-} = f_{H_3O^+} = 0.999 \approx 1.$$

[2] Other pairs of acids may be added or substituted at the discretion of the instructor.
[3] See Appendix B.
[4] The anilinium chlorides may be prepared by passing dry HCl gas into anhydrous ethereal solutions of the corresponding anilines cooled in ice, filtering and recrystallizing the precipitated salts from ethanol.

Weigh accurately[5] approximately 50 mg of each acid separately into clean, 100 ml beakers. Dissolve the anilinium salts in 50 ml distilled water and the less soluble benzoic acids in the same volume of 10% ethanol warming to ensure complete solution if necessary. For each solution separately insert the glass and the calomel electrodes connected to the pH meter; arrange for magnetic stirring and titrate against $N/100$ sodium hydroxide. Take readings of pH against titer until the equivalence point is passed. Plot the titration curve as shown in Figure 2–1 and from it determine the neutralization equivalent and the pH at half-neutralization as indicated. Record the temperature at which the measurements are made and tabulate the values of K found [Eq. (2)] against the appropriate substituent group.

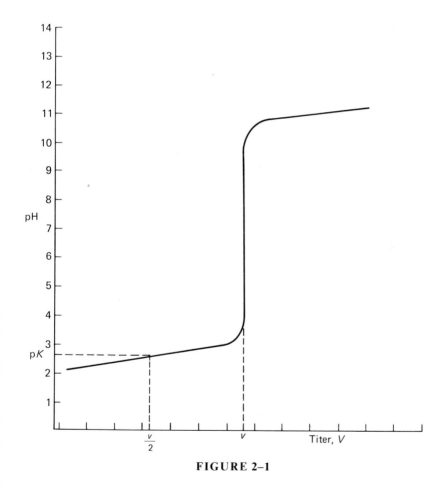

FIGURE 2–1

[5] For the purpose of the experiment, it is not necessary to weigh out each acid; it is suggested that this is done so that the molecular weight of each may be determined as a check on the titration.

Treatment of Results. Since we expect to find that the substituents operate on the free energy of activation, $\Delta F^{\ddagger}$, for the dissociation this should be manifest as a change in log K since

$$\Delta F^{\ddagger} = RT \ln K \tag{3}$$

(In this instance, being an equilibrium $\Delta F^{\ddagger}$ is the difference in free energies of activation for the forward and reverse reactions, but this does not affect the argument.) In order to make a comparison of substituent effects, a standard substituent, hydrogen, is chosen which is arbitrarily said to exhibit no electronic effects on the reaction. Benzoic acid and anilinium chloride are then the standard acids of the two series with dissociation constants K_0 and K'_0 respectively. If we now consider a substituted benzoic acid (K) and similarly substituted anilinium salt (K'), eg. p-chlorobenzoic acid and p-chloroanilinium chloride, we expect that the effect of p-Cl on the ionization of each acid will be in the same direction but not necessarily of the same magnitude, and may write

$$1/\rho_0\left(\log \frac{K}{K_0}\right) = 1/\rho\left(\log \frac{K'}{K'_0}\right) \tag{4}$$

where ρ_0, ρ' are reaction constants and express the relative susceptibilities of the two equilibria towards electronic effects. *For all other substituents, ρ_0, ρ will be the same.*

Further simplifications may be introduced to make the relationship more useful. If the ionization of benzoic acids at 25°C is taken as a standard reaction, ρ_0 may be made equal to unity and substituent effects on *this* equilibrium become the characteristic of the substituent only.
Hence,

$$\log \frac{K}{K_0} = \sigma \tag{5}$$

where σ is a substituent constant and K and σ refer to a *particular substituent and location in the ring.*

Therefore we may write

$$\log \frac{K'}{K'_0} = \rho\sigma \tag{6}$$

which is the relationship found experimentally by Hammett to fit many series of reactions at a benzene ring (see Appendix D).

1. Calculate values of σ for all the substituents considered using the dissociation constants of benzoic acids, Eq. (5).

2. Plot σ against $\log K'/K'_0$ for the anilinium salts. Draw the best straight line (least squares if possible) through the points and estimate ρ from the slope, Eq. (6).

Interpretation of results [6]. The dissociation of acids is enhanced by electron-withdrawing groups since the proton must depart leaving its bonding electrons behind:

Therefore from Eq. (5) σ will be positive for electron-withdrawing substituents (relative to hydrogen) ($\log K > \log K_0$) and negative for electron donors ($\log K < \log K_0$). Hence the magnitude of the electronic effect may be measured. Furthermore, if the transmission of the effect is purely by an inductive mechanism (polarization of σ-bonds), σ will be similar whether it refers to the *meta* or *para* position and is usually slightly greater from the *meta*, being nearer the reaction site. If, however, resonance structures contribute to charge transmission, the effect will be greater (positive or negative) from the *para* position.

The sign and magnitude of ρ is also informative, a positive value indicating that the reaction under consideration is more susceptible to electronic effects than the ionization of benzoic acids, and vice versa. Examine and discuss your values of σ and ρ interpreting them as completely as possible.

EXTENSION OF THE EXPERIMENT

Ortho substituents do not usually fit the Hammett equation well since steric effect are significant. Repeat the above experiment on *o*-chlorobenzoic acid and *o*-chloroaniline and verify this.

Questions

1. Suggest reasonable σ-values for the following substituents:

$$p\text{-}\overset{+}{\text{AsMe}}_3 \qquad p\text{-IO}_2$$

$$p\text{-OPh} \qquad m\text{-OPh}$$

$$p\text{-SnMe}_3 \qquad p\text{-}tert\text{-butyl}$$

2. Calculate the acid dissociation constants of *p*-nitrophenylboric and *p*-hydroxyphenylboric acids in water at 25°C (K for phenylboric acid, $PhB(OH)_2$, under the same conditions is 2×10^{-10}, $\rho = 2.15$).

3. Calculate the value of ρ for the acid dissociation of phenols in water at 25°C given the following information:

phenol	$K_A = 1.4 \times 10^{-10}$
p-methoxyphenol	$K_A = 3.5 \times 10^{-11}$
p-nitrophenol	$K_A = 6.4 \times 10^{-8}$

Suggest a reason why the value of ρ should differ from that for the dissociation of benzoic acids.

References

1. C. K. Ingold, *Structure and Mechanism in Organic Chemistry*, Bell, London, 1953.
2. I. Dostrovsky and E. D. Hughes, *J. Chem. Soc.*, 157, 161, 164, 166 (1946).
3. L. Pauling, *The Nature of the Chemical Bond*, 2nd Ed., Cornell U.P., Ithaca, N.Y., 1945, p. 164.
4. L. P. Hammett, *Physical Organic Chemistry*, McGraw-Hill, New York, 1940.
5. H. H. Jaffé, *Chem. Revs.*, **53**, 191 (1953).
6. J. Hine, *Physical-Organic Chemistry*, McGraw-Hill, New York (1962), Chapter 4.
7. L. N. Ferguson, *The Modern Structural Theory of Organic Chemistry*, Prentice-Hall, Englewood Cliffs, N.J., 1963, p. 411.

Kinetic Isotope Effects

Soon after the discovery of deuterium by Urey and coworkers [1], it was postulated that the two isotopes of hydrogen would not be chemically identical under suitable circumstances. This reasoning applies to any isotopes but the effect is particularly large for the isotopes of hydrogen where the relative mass difference is greatest. It was argued that a covalent bond to deuterium should be rather stronger than a similar one to protium (^{1}H) and that a reaction whose rate-determining step involved the breaking of such a bond would be slower when a deuterated compound was employed.

This is known as a *Primary Kinetic Isotope Effect* and is measured as the ratio of the rate constants for the two reactions, k_H/k_D, for which values are commonly of the order of 6 to 7. For example:

$$\frac{k_H}{k_D} \approx 7$$

The isotope effect is now well established and its presence is used diagnostically to indicate whether a bond to hydrogen is being broken in the transition state of a reaction. In the previous example therefore, a mechanism involving rate-determining removal of α-hydrogen is indicated as:

$$CH_3-\underset{\underset{H}{|}}{\overset{\overset{OH}{|}}{C}}-CH_3 \xrightarrow[2H^+,\ fast]{HCr^{VI}O_4^-} CH_3-\underset{\underset{H}{|}}{\overset{\overset{OCr^{VI}O_3^+H_2}{|}}{C}}-CH_3 + H_2O$$

isopropyl
chromate

$$CH_3-\underset{\underset{\overset{\nearrow H}{H_2O}}{|}}{\overset{\overset{OCrO_3^+H_2}{|}}{C}}-CH_3 \xrightarrow{slow} CH_3-\overset{\overset{O}{||}}{C}-CH_3 + Cr^{IV} + H_3O^+$$

The explanation for the greater stability of a bond to the heavier of any pair of isotopes is as follows. Each covalent bond in a molecule may be considered to act as an approximately independent oscillator and can vibrate at definite frequencies, v, in a number of modes such as stretching and bending (the origin of infrared spectra):

$$\overset{\longleftrightarrow}{-\overset{\diagdown}{\underset{\diagup}{C}}-H} \qquad \overset{\diagdown}{\underset{\diagup}{C}}-H$$

stretching mode   bending mode

The energy of vibration associated with a particular mode is quantized, that is, allowed only certain defined values and excluding zero. Hence, even in the lowest vibrational state (see experiment 18) the bond still possesses residual vibrational energy known as zero-point energy, E_0 (Figure 3–1). The zero-point energy, E_0 is given by

$$E_0 = \sum \tfrac{1}{2}hv_0$$

where h = Planck's constant and v_0 = frequency of vibration in the ground state, the summation being made over all modes of vibration in which the bond participates. The frequency in each mode is given by an expression such as

$$v_0 = \frac{h}{2\pi}\sqrt{\frac{k}{\mu}}$$

—a quantum-mechanical version of Hooke's Law—in which k is a force constant and μ is the reduced mass of the vibrating system, $= m_1 m_2 / m_1 + m_2$, and approximates to the mass of the light atom, i.e., hydrogen, where its mass,

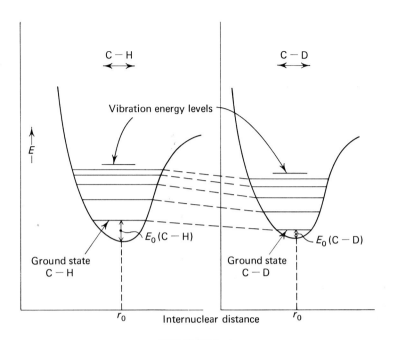

FIGURE 3–1

m_1, is much less than that of the rest of the molecule, m_2, thus

$$\frac{v_0(\text{C—H})}{v_0(\text{C—D})} \approx \sqrt{\frac{2}{1}} = 1\cdot414$$

and, since the vibration frequency depends upon mass, the zero-point energies will be related in the same way:

$$\frac{E_0(\text{C—H})}{E_0(\text{C—D})} \approx 1.414$$

This isotopic difference in vibrational energy decreases as the bonds are excited to progressively higher vibrational states until, in the limit the bond is broken as the stretching amplitude becomes sufficiently great and very little energy difference remains, Figure 3–1. The energy required for fission of the C—D bond, however, must have been greater than that for C—H since it started at the lower level. If the fission of this bond constitutes the activation process in a reaction, the activation energy will be greater and hence the rate less for the heavy isotope, Figure 3–2.

A second effect may also have to be considered when the isotopically substituted species is also the solvent in a reaction. The deuteronium ion, D_3O^+ is found to be a stronger acid than the hydronium ion, H_3O^+ and basic

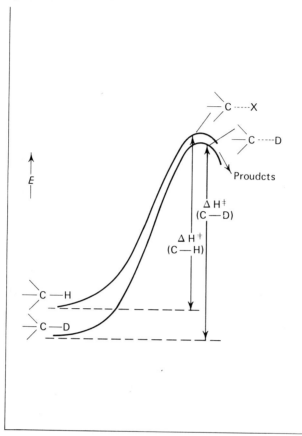

Reaction Parameter

FIGURE 3–2

dissociations in D_2O occur to a greater extent than in H_2O by a factor of about three:

$$B + H_3O^+ \underset{}{\overset{K_H}{\rightleftharpoons}} BH^+ + H_2O$$

$$B + D_3O^+ \underset{}{\overset{K_D}{\rightleftharpoons}} BD^+ + D_2O \qquad K_D > K_H$$

If a reaction involves a rapid protonation of a reagent followed by a rate-determining decomposition of the conjugate acid the latter will be in higher concentration in D_2O with consequent enhancement of the rate in this medium, hence $k_H/k_D < 1$:

$$B + H_3O^+ \underset{}{\overset{\text{rapid}}{\rightleftharpoons}} BH^+ + H_2O \xrightarrow[k'_H]{\text{slow}} \text{products}$$

$$B + D_3O^+ \underset{}{\overset{\text{rapid}}{\rightleftharpoons}} BD^+ + D_2O \xrightarrow[k'_D]{\text{slow}} \text{products}$$

$$[BD^+] > [BH^+],\ k'_H \geqslant k'_D \text{ depending on the reaction.}$$

The two isotopic effects may occur in conjunction as in the mutarotation of glucose which is a general acid-catalyzed reaction consisting of the conversion of either α-(I) or β-(II) D-glucose into an equilibrium mixture of the two. The postulated mechanism is as follows:

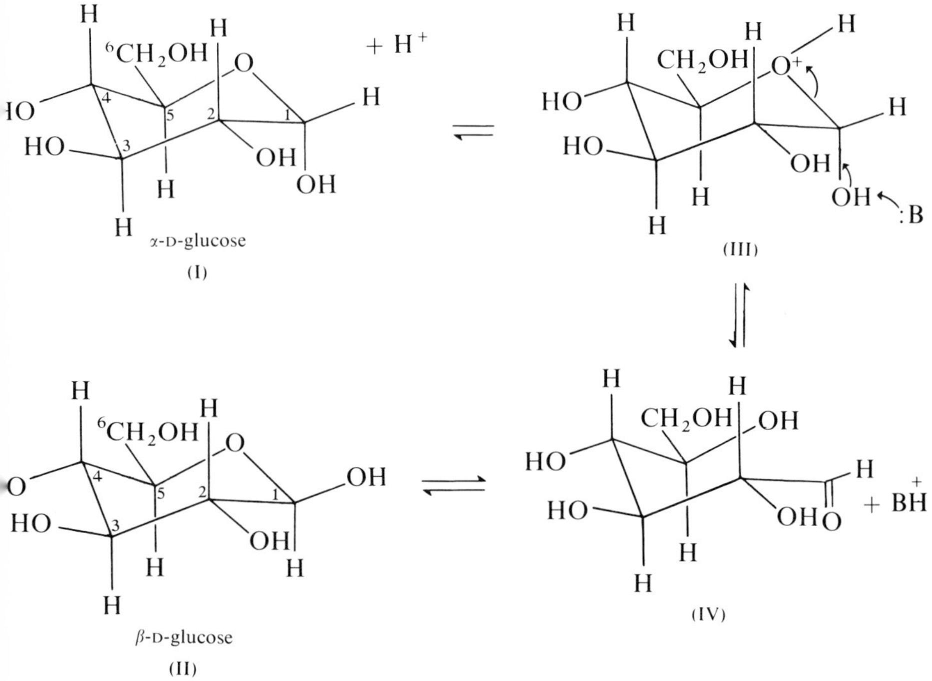

The slow step is expected to be the attack of the base B on the hydrogen of the anomeric hydroxyl group, since proton transfer from the solvent is very rapid.

In D_2O all the hydroxyl groups will rapidly exchange with deuterium and hence an O—D bond will have to be broken in step 2 leading to a normal kinetic isotope effect. This is offset by the increased concentration of conjugate acid (III) present in D_2O as a result of the greater acidity of D_3O^+. The expected value of the isotope effect will then be

$$\frac{k_H}{k_D} = 7 \cdot \tfrac{1}{3} \approx 2.3$$

Aromatic substitution reactions may or may not show kinetic isotope effects. For instance, nitrobenzene is nitrated at the same rate as the pentadeutero compound while diazocoupling with a phenol has been shown to be subject to the full seven-fold retardation by deuteration. Since both reactions proceed via a σ-complex intermediate, these observations point to differences in the relative velocities of the two stages:

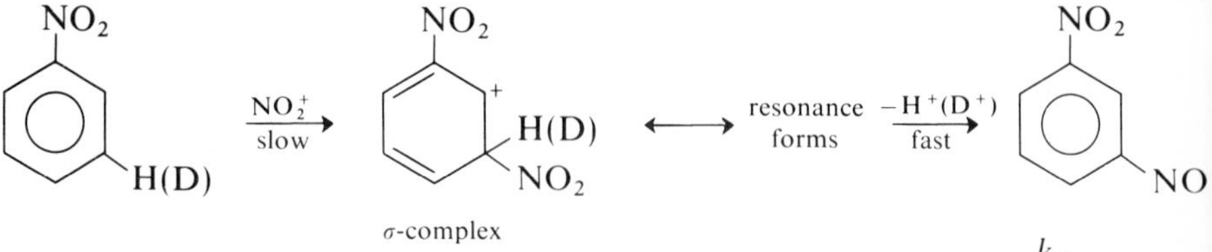

$$\frac{k_H}{k_D} \approx 1$$

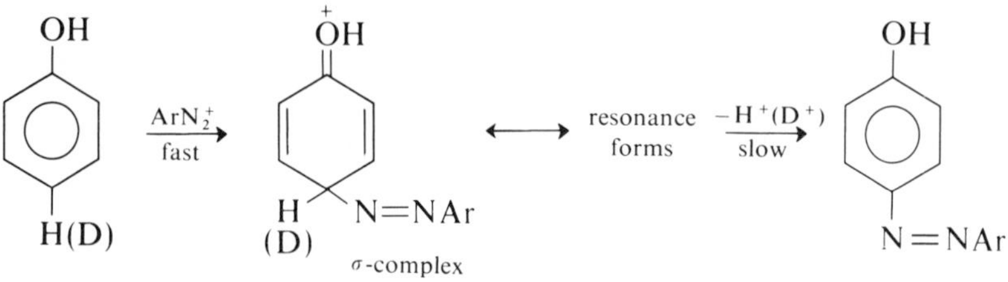

$$\frac{k_H}{k_D} \approx 7$$

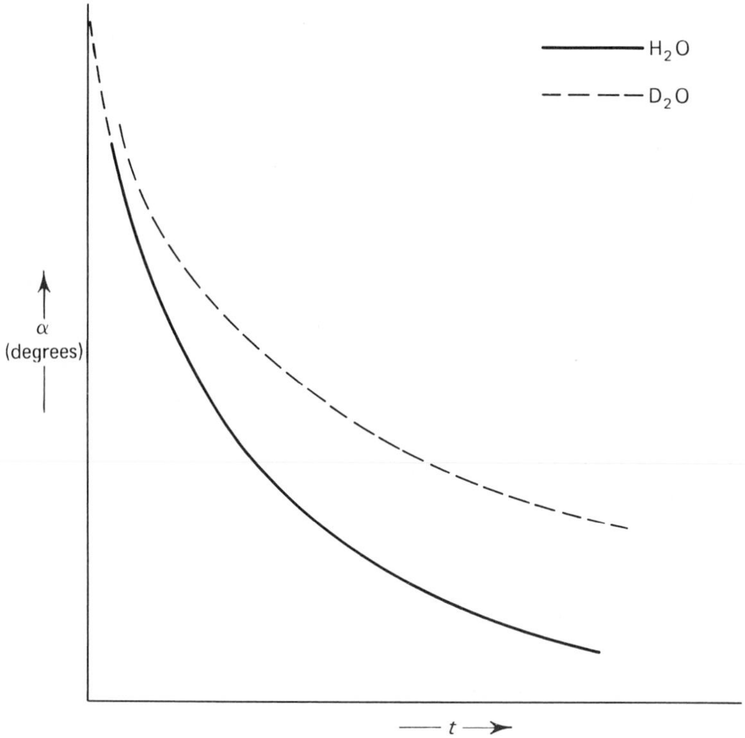

FIGURE 3–3

Experimental

ISOTOPIC EFFECTS ON THE MUTAROTATION OF GLUCOSE

Materials Required

> α-D-Glucose
> Deuterium oxide
> Polarimeter (reading to at least ±0.02°)

The Rate of Mutarotation in Water.[1] Weigh out 4.500 g pure α-D-glucose (dextrose) and add to a 25 ml volumetric flask containing 10–15 ml distilled water at ambient temperature, simultaneously starting a clock. Shake to dissolve the sugar, make up to the mark with water and mix the solution well. As quickly as possible fill a standard 10 cm polarimeter tube with the solution and measure the rotation as a function of time, taking readings every 10–15 min for about 2 hours and, if possible, a final reading the next day when equilibrium will have been reached. Plot the results graphically as in Figure 3–3.

The Rate of Mutarotation in Deuterium Oxide. In order to minimize the amount of D_2O used, the following apparatus may be constructed (Figure 3–4). A flask of calibrated volume 1.500 ml is made up from a B7 standard taper cup joint, drawn off and flattened about 5 cm below the joint, calibrated by weighing in the appropriate volume of water and marking the position of the meniscus. A semimicro polarimeter tube is constructed from a length of 2 mm glass tubing, cut and ground to 10.00 cm length and fitted with a side-arm in the middle. Two optically flat polarimeter plates are attached to the ends with epoxy cement and supports cut from two corks so that the tube is held in the correct position within the polarimeter. The tube is filled by means of a hypodermic syringe with a length of fine surgical polyethylene tubing attached to the needle and pushed down as far as possible into each limb successively so as to avoid leaving bubbles.

To measure the mutarotation, weigh 0.2700 g of α-D-glucose into the 1.5 ml flask, add a little under that volume of D_2O[2] and shake to dissolve, starting the clock at the same time. Make up to the mark with D_2O and transfer quickly to the semimicro polarimeter tube filling it completely. Observe the rotation as before over a period of two to three hours. This experiment may be carried out simultaneously with the H_2O experiment.

---

[1] It is, of course, equally valid to carry out the mutarotation in water using the semimicro polarimeter tube: the present arrangement is suggested so that the student can first become accustomed to the technique of taking frequent readings on the simplest apparatus and also so that the second experiment may be started when the first has slowed down but is not complete and alternate readings for the two experiments may be taken.

[2] The D_2O left at the end of the experiment may be recovered and reused only a little diluted with H_2O.

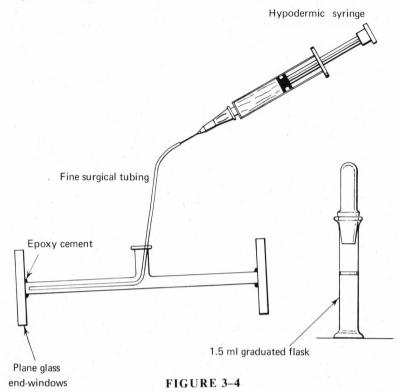

Hypodermic syringe

Fine surgical tubing

Epoxy cement

1.5 ml graduated flask

Plane glass
end-windows

FIGURE 3–4

Treatment of Results. Obtain the first-order rate constant for the mutarotation by plotting α against time and estimating the half-life, $t_{1/2}$ of the reaction (Figure 3–3):

$$k_1 = \frac{\ln 2}{t_{1/2}}$$

Alternatively, use the full rate expression or the FORTRAN Program (Appendix A) to evaluate k. Determine k_H/k_D and confirm the mechanism discussed.

An Isotope Effect on a Diazo Coupling Reaction

Materials Required

2-Naphthol-6,8-disulfonic acid, dipotassium salt
Deuterium oxide
4-Chloroaniline
Sodium nitrite
Buffer solution containing: sodium dihydrogen phosphate (0.78 g)
Disodium hydrogen phosphate (7.10 g)
Potassium chloride (3.73 g) in 1 liter water
Visible spectrophotometer

Preparation of 2-Naphthol-6,8-Disulfonic Acid-1-d. In a flask equipped with a glass stopper, place 1.6 g (0.005 mole) pure, dry 2-naphthol-6,8-disulfonic acid, dipotassium salt and add 10 ml (0.5 mole) deuterium oxide and approximately 50 mg sodium hydroxide. Seal the flask with a glass stopper and place in a thermostat bath at 70°–80° for 24 hours ensuring complete dissolution of the solid:

Neutralize the solution with 0.002 ml conc HCl using a *lambda* pipet then distill off the water (HDO) *in vacuo* for further use and dry the product. The yield is quantitative and provides sufficient phenol for up to 100 kinetic runs.

Rate Measurements on the Diazo Coupling Reaction.   Prepare a solution of diazotized *p*-chloroaniline by dissolving 0.127 g (0.001 mole) *p*-chloroaniline in 3 ml 1.0 M hydrochloric acid in a 50 ml volumetric flask, cooling to 0° and adding slowly a solution of 0.069 g (0.001 mole) sodium nitrite in 20 ml water. After adding water to bring the volume to 50 ml, store the flask in ice.

Dissolve 0.016 g (0.00005 mole) of 2-naphthol-6,8-disulfonic acid, dipotassium salt in about 20 ml of buffer solution in a 25 ml volumetric flask. Add by pipet 1.0 ml of the diazonium solution, starting a clock at the same time, quickly make up to the mark with buffer solution and transfer a sample of the mixture to a 1.0 cm spectrophotometer absorption cell and record absorbance as a function of time over a period of about 20 min at a wavelength of 520 mμ (this value of λ_{max} for the azo dye should be checked by a separate experiment).

Repeat the experiment using the same quantity of 2-naphthol-6,8-disulfonic acid-1-d dipotassium salt. Exchange of deuterium in water at this pH and this low temperature is too slow to be significant.

Treatment of Results.   Plot absorbance as a function of time and note the difference in reaction rates between deuterated and undeuterated phenols. Treat the kinetics as pseudo first-order,

$$\text{Rate} = k_1[\text{phenol}]$$

and estimate values of k_H and k_D (see Appendix A).

1. Calculate the value of the isotope effect, k_H/k_D.
2. Account for the value obtained using your knowledge of the mechanism of the diazocoupling reaction.

Questions

1. Suggest explanations of the following observed isotope effects:

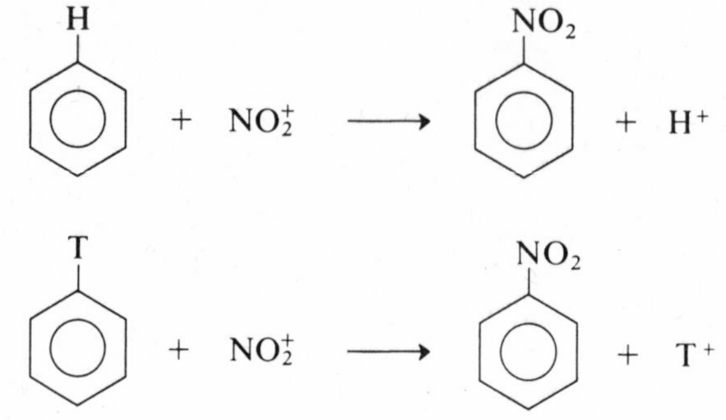

$$k_H/k_T = 1$$

where $T = {}^3H$

$$PhCHO \xrightarrow{MnO_4^-} PhCOOH$$

$$k_H/k_D = 7.5$$

$$PhCDO \xrightarrow{MnO_4^-} PhCOOH$$

$$CH_3COCH_3 \xrightarrow[H_3O^+]{Br_2} CH_3COCH_2Br$$

$$k_H/k_D = 0.48$$

$$CD_3COCD_3 \xrightarrow[D_3O^+]{Br_2} CD_3COCD_2Br$$

2. By considering the following reactions, estimate the magnitude of k_H/k_D where k_H refers to the unlabelled compounds.

a. $RCH{=}CD_2 + Br_2 \longrightarrow RCHBr\text{-}CD_2Br$

b. $\quad\quad\quad Ph_2C{=}N_2 \xrightarrow{D_3O^+} PhCD_2\text{-}N_2^+ \longrightarrow Ph_2CD^+ + N_2$ products

c. $\quad PhCD_2\text{-}ONO_2 \xrightarrow{EtO^-} PhCDO + NO_2^- + EtOD$

d. $\quad\quad\quad\quad\quad PhCTO \xrightarrow{MnO_4^-} PhCOOH$

$\quad (T = tritium, {}^3H)$

References

1. H. C. Urey, F. G. Brickwedde, and G. M. Murphy, *Phys. Rev.*, **39**, 164 (1932).
2. E. Pacsu, *J. Amer. Chem. Soc.*, **55**, 5056 (1933); *ibid* **56**, 745 (1934).
3. W. H. Hamill and V. K. La Mer, *J. Chem. Phys.*, **4**, 144 (1936).
4. R. P. Bell and P. Jones, *J. Chem. Soc.*, 88 (1953).
5. K. B. Wiberg, *Physical-Organic Chemistry*, Wiley, New York, 1964.
6. K. B. Wiberg, *Chem. Revs.*, 713 (1955).
7. H. Zollinger, *Experientia*, **X**, 481 (1954).

Molecularity of Substitution Reactions at Saturated Carbon

One of the most intensively investigated organic reactions has been the substitution by a nucleophilic species of a weaker nucleophile bound to a saturated carbon atom:

$$X: \quad \overset{|}{\underset{|}{C}} \overset{\frown}{} Y \quad \longrightarrow \quad X - \overset{|}{\underset{|}{C}} \quad :Y$$

The reaction is quite general; some familiar examples of X: and Y: are set out in Table 4–1, the former in decreasing order of nucleophilic power (the availability of an electron pair) and the latter in approximate increasing order of ease of displacement (readiness to accept an electron pair)—note the similarity of these orders.

TABLE 4-1.*

Nucleophiles, X:	Leaving Groups, Y:	Nucleophiles, X:	Leaving Groups, Y:
H^-		SR_2^-	$-OCOR$
R_3C^-		I^-, Br^-, Cl^-	$-I, -Br, -Cl$
NH_2^-		$RCOO^-$	$-Tos$
OR^-	$-OR_2^+$	F^-	$-Bros$
OH^-	$-NR_3^+$	Tos^-	$-OH_2^+$
NR_3^-	$-SR_2^+$	H_2O, ROH	
		$ClO4$	

* From C. K. Ingold, *Structure and Mechanism in Organic Chemistry*, Bell and Sons, London, 1953.

Working at University College, London, C. K. Ingold and E. S. Hughes [1] recognized two extreme types of mechanism for this reaction. The dissociation of Y may either occur, concurrently with the attack of X: on the carbon atom (S_N2 process, Figure 4–1a) or may precede the attack of X: in a two-stage process involving an intermediate solvated carbonium ion (S_N1 process; see Figure 4–1b).

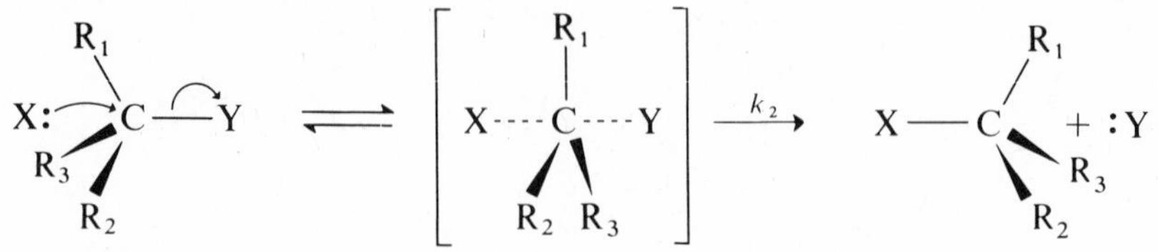

FIGURE 4–1a

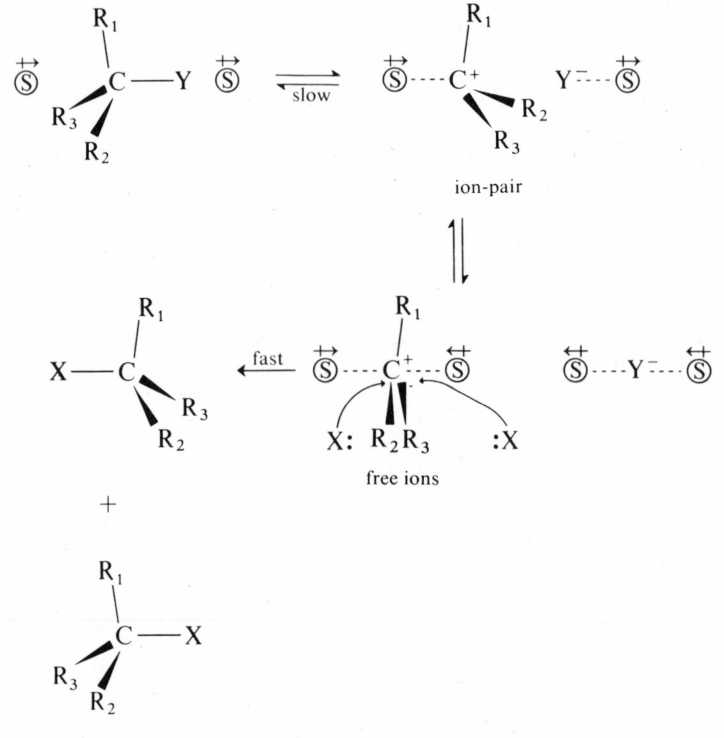

FIGURE 4–1b

The mechanism which is actually employed by a reacting system will be that which is energetically most favorable. Methyl and primary halides and esters usually react by the S_N2 mechanism (Figure 4–1, $R_1 = R_2 = H$), while circumstances which favor stabilization of the intermediate carbonium ion (see Experiment 31) will make the S_N1 process preferred. Thus reactions of tertiary halides and esters (Figure 4–2, $R_1 = R_2 = R_3 =$ alkyl) in highly polar solvents (p. 29) such as water, ethanol, acetic acid, provide examples of this mechanism. Two criteria which may be employed to distinguish which process is operating are, the stereochemistry of the product and the kinetic order of the reaction. The rate of the reaction under S_N2 conditions must be proportional to the concentrations of both nucleophile and substrate and should therefore exhibit second-order kinetics (Appendix A):

$$\text{Rate } (S_N2) = k_2[\text{X}:][\text{R}_3\text{C}-\text{Y}]$$

while S_N1 conditions only require the rate-determining ionization of the substrate which is independent of [X:], the reaction will thus be of the first-order:

$$\text{Rate } (S_N1) = k_1[\text{R}_3\text{C}-\text{Y}]$$

The following experiment permits a distinction to be made between mechanisms in the hydrolysis of *n*-butyl and *tert*-butyl bromides:

$$CH_3CH_2CH_2CH_2Br \xrightarrow{\ OH^-\ } CH_3CH_2CH_2CH_2OH + Br^-$$

$$CH_3-\overset{\overset{\displaystyle CH_3}{|}}{\underset{\underset{\displaystyle CH_3}{|}}{C}}-Br \xrightarrow{\ OH^-\ } CH_3-\overset{\overset{\displaystyle CH_3}{|}}{\underset{\underset{\displaystyle CH_3}{|}}{C}}-OH + Br^-$$

Experimental

Materials Required

        n-Butyl bromide, 1.0 *M* solution in 80% ethanol in water w/w
        tert-Butyl bromide, 1.0 *M* solution in 80% ethanol-water w/w
        pH Meter (Appendix B)
        Thermostat bath
        Clock or stop watch
        Sodium hydroxide, 1.0 *M*

THE HYDROLYSIS OF *n*-BUTYL BROMIDE

$$CH_3CH_2CH_2CH_2Br + OH^- \longrightarrow CH_3CH_2CH_2CH_2OH + Br^-$$

Half immerse a 100 ml beaker in a 55° water bath and arrange the glass- and calomel-electrodes of the pH-meter and a small glass stirrer paddle so that they reach almost to the bottom (Figure 4–2). Into a 50 ml volumetric flask also immersed in the thermostat bath pipet approximately 35 ml of solvent—80% ethanol–water, w/w—and 5.0 ml of 1 *M* sodium hydroxide. Allow the mixture to reach the temperature of the bath then add 5.0 ml of 1.0 *M* *n*-butyl bromide solution, starting a clock at the same time. Add solvent to bring the volume of liquid up to the mark, and mix well. Transfer the solution at once to the beaker

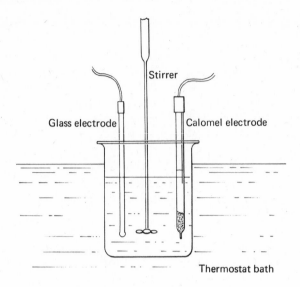

FIGURE 4–2 Apparatus for measuring the rate of hydrolysis of *n*-butyl bromide.

and begin taking readings of pH at measured times over a period of about 30 min stirring the solution gently meanwhile.

Repeat the above experiment with the beaker and flask immersed in an ice bath and using *tert*-butyl bromide as substrate:

$$(CH_3)_3C—Br + OH^- \longrightarrow (CH_3)_3C—OH + Br^-$$

Treatment of Results. Since hydroxide ion is consumed with the same stoichiometry in either a first- or second-order reaction, we are able to follow the reaction by measuring the fall in $[OH^-]$. This is achieved using the pH meter assuming that Eqs. (1) and (2) hold in the medium which is used:

$$pH = -\log_{10}[H^+] \tag{1}$$

$$[OH^-] = \frac{10^{-14}}{[H^+]} \tag{2}^1$$

The rate at time t of a second-order reaction:

$$RBr + OH^- \xrightarrow{k_2} \text{products}$$

is given by

$$\frac{-d}{dt}[RBr] = -\frac{d}{dt}[OH^-] = \frac{dx}{dt} = k_2[RBr][OH^-]$$

$$= k_2(a - x)(b - x)$$

---

[1] Strictly speaking this relationship is only rigorously true in pure water at 25°.

where k_2 = bimolecular velocity constant; a = initial alkyl halide concentration (mole/liter); b = initial hydroxide ion concentration (mole/liter); x = extent of reaction = number of moles per liter reacted at time t; $= (b - [OH^-]_t)$. Therefore

$$\frac{dx}{dt} = k_2(a - x)(b - x)$$

which upon integration gives (Appendix A),

$$k_2 = \frac{2.303}{t(a - b)} \log \frac{b(a - x)}{a(b - x)}$$

in the case that $a = b$ (as in the present experiment), reduces to

$$k_2 = \frac{1}{t}\left(\frac{x}{a(a - x)}\right)$$

Hence a plot of t against $x/a - x$ is linear with slope $= k_2 a$. The rate at time t of a first-order reaction:

$$RBr \xrightarrow{\text{slow}} R^+ \xrightarrow[\text{fast}]{OH^-} \text{products}$$

is given by

$$\frac{-d}{dt}[RBr] = \frac{-d}{dt}[OH^-] = \frac{dx}{dt} = k_1[RBr] = k_1(a - x)$$

where k_1 is a first-order velocity constant. Therefore

$$\frac{dx}{dt} = k_1(a - x)$$

and upon integration we obtain

$$k_1 = \frac{2.303}{t}\left(\log \frac{a}{(a - x)}\right) \text{ in units, (time}^{-1})$$

Hence a plot of t against $\log a/(a - x)$ will be linear with slope $= k_1/2.303$. For both reactions studied, make plots of $a/a(a - x)$ and $\log a/(a - x)$ against t. Determine which graph fits the data linearly and interpret your findings in terms of the reaction mechanisms.

An alternative though less rigorous treatment is as follows. Since the purpose of the experiment is to ascertain whether the concentration of hydroxide ion appears in the rate law (S_N2 process) or not (S_N1 process), a qualitative examination of this may be achieved by repeating the kinetic runs using 10 ml and 15 ml of the sodium hydroxide solution and keeping the total volume at 50 ml.

Comparison of the pH—time curves for each reaction will then indicate whether or not a reaction rate is sensitive to hydroxide ion concentration.

Explain your findings in terms of the structures of the two alkyl halides.

EXTENSION OF THE EXPERIMENT

The carbonium ion mechanism is much more prone to give olefin as by-product (E1 process) than the bimolecular displacement; (E2 process)

This may be demonstrated by running a gas chromatogram of both solutions after completion of reaction (silicone column, 30°) and noting the considerably larger olefin peak, which emerges first, from the reaction which shows first-order kinetics.

Questions

1. What reaction mechanisms would you expect the following systems to exhibit and what would be the product(s) in each case?
   a. R-2-bromo-2-phenylbutane and triethylamine in ethanol
   b. *Trans-4-tert*-butylcyclohexyl bromide and sodium hydroxide in aqueous acetone
   c. Styrene oxide and lithium aluminum hydride in ether
   d. Neopentyl iodide in hot formic acid
2. Arrange the following groups, R, in order of increasing ease of displacement of bromide in the reaction,

$$RBr + OH^- \longrightarrow ROH + Br^-$$

$R = cyclo\text{-}C_6H_{11}\text{-}, \quad Ph\text{-}, \quad PhCH_2\text{-}, \quad CH_3\text{-}CH=CH_2\text{-}$

$$CH_2=CH\text{-}CH_2\text{-}, \quad$$

3. Suggest mechanisms for the following nucleophilic displacements;

a. $Me_2C=CH-CH_2Br$ $\xrightarrow{OEt^-}$ $Me_2C-CH=CH_2$
    $\qquad\qquad\qquad\qquad\qquad\qquad\qquad\quad |$
    $\qquad\qquad\qquad\qquad\qquad\qquad\quad OEt$

b.

$-CH_2Br$ + CN^- $\longrightarrow$ $NC-$ $-CH_3$

c.

OBros $\xrightarrow{ACOH}$ OAc

Br   Br

l-trans   *dl-trans*

d. $R\text{-PhCH(OH)CH}_3$ $\xrightarrow{SOCl_2}$ $R\text{-PhCHClCH}_3$

References

1. C. K. Ingold, *Structure and Mechanism in Organic Chemistry*, Bell, London, 1953.
2. E. S. Gould, *Mechanism & Structure in Organic Chemistry*, Holt, Rinehart, and Winston, New York, 1959, p. 259–262.

Examination of Solvent
Effects on a Reaction

In order to describe accurately the energetics of a reaction occurring in solution all the interactions between solvent molecules, on the one hand, and the reagent molecules, intermediates and activated complexes on the other, must be taken into account. Attractive interactions will lower the potential energy of the system and vice versa and, since some sort of interaction will exist between any two molecules which are charged, polarized or polarizable, solvent often plays a profound role. To take two extreme examples, the Menschutkin reaction (quaternization of a tertiary amine by an alkyl halide) involves the separation of charge between initially uncharged molecules, the activated complex which represents the highest energy of the reacting system being a half-way stage:

$$R_3N \quad C—Br \longrightarrow R_3\overset{\delta^+}{N} \cdots C \cdots \overset{\delta^-}{Br} \longrightarrow R_3\overset{+}{N}—C \quad \overset{-}{Br}$$

A polar solvent (see Experiment 23) will interact with and lower the potential energy of the activated complex, to a greater extent than the reagents [1, 2]. A nonpolar solvent will interact only slightly with either. The energy profiles for the reaction may be drawn as shown in Figure 5–1 and compared to the hypothetical gas phase reaction in which no solvent interactions are present. The activation energy $E^{\ddagger}$, which determines the rate of the reaction is least in a polar solvent ($E_p^{\ddagger} < E_n^{\ddagger} \approx E_g^{\ddagger}$), hence the rate will be strongly influenced by

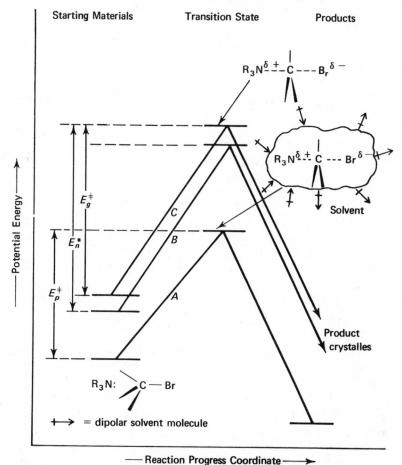

FIGURE 5–1 Schematic diagram of energetics of Menschutkin reaction carried out (*A*) **in a polar solvent;** (*B*) **in a nonpolar solvent; and** (*C*) **in the gas-phase.**

the medium. At the other extreme, a Diels-Alder reaction, such as the dimerization of cyclopentadiene (see Experiment 38) occurs by a concerted rearrangement

of electrons: no great charge separation is involved either in the product or activated complex. Reagents and activated complex are stabilized by solvent to roughly equal extents and the effect of solvent on the rate of the reaction is comparatively slight. Thus, the effects of solvents on reaction rates can yield information concerning the nature of the activated complex.

Experimental

Materials Required

> Benzyl bromide (50 ml, 1.00 M solution in 100% EtOH)
> Triethylamine (50 ml, 1.00 M solution in 100% EtOH)
> Benzene
> Aqueous silver nitrate solution, 0.02 M
> Thermostat bath

Transfer 5.0 ml of triethylamine solution by means of a pipet to a 50 ml volumetric flask placed in a thermostat bath at 70°. Add approximately 35 ml 100% ethanol and allow the mixture to come to thermal equilibrium. Pipet in 5.0 ml of the benzyl bromide solution, starting a clock simultaneously. Quickly make the solution up to the mark and mix well by shaking. Start sampling at once by withdrawing 5.0 ml aliquots of reaction mixture noting the time and dropping into a separatory funnel, containing 10 ml benzene and 10 ml water to quench the reaction. Stopper the funnel, shake well and allow the contents to settle. Separate the lower aqueous layer containing the ionic bromine and extract once more with a little water. Combine the aqueous layers and titrate the bromide in solution against standard 0.02 M silver nitrate using a fluorescent indicator such as dibromofluoroscein or eosin. Take samples every 5 min for 30–40 min after the start of the reaction. The extraction should be carried out immediately but the aqueous extracts may be left until the end of the reaction before being titrated.

Repeat this kinetic run replacing some of the solvent ethanol successively by 10, 15, 25, and 35 ml dry benzene. These reactions will be increasingly slow, so that the period between samples should be increased progressively, the final reaction being followed for about an hour.

Treatment of Results. The reaction is second order,

$$PhCH_2Br + NEt_3 \longrightarrow PhCH_2\overset{+}{N}Et_3Br^-$$

and is followed by extraction and titration of the ionic bromine. The value of the titer, V_t, is a measure of the extent of the reaction, x at time t.

For each run, calculate the specific rate constant, k_2 from the formula (Appendix A):

$$k_2 = \frac{1}{t}\left(\frac{x}{a(a-x)}\right)$$

where a = initial $[PhCH_2Br]$ = initial $[NEt_3]$

$$x = [Br^-] \quad \text{at time} \quad t = V_t$$

or plot t against $x/a(a-x)$, determining k from the slope of the best straight line.

One macroscopic property of the solvent which is often used to indicate solvent polarity (Experiment 25) is the dielectric constant which is a measure of the distribution and mobility of charge in the molecule and takes into account both molecular polarization and polarizability.

The solvent effect may be investigated in terms of an expression derived by Kirkwood [3] which relates the change in free energy ΔF experienced by a spherical dipolar molecule of radius r and dipole moment μ, on being transferred from a medium of unit dielectric constant to one of dielectric constant, D, as follows:

$$\Delta F = \frac{-\mu^2(D - 1)}{r^3(2D + 1)}$$

Since the reaction velocity is related to the free energy of activation by

$$\Delta F^{\ddagger} = -RT \ln k_2 + \text{constant}$$

we can expect a linear relationship to exist between $\log k_2$ and $(D - 1)/(2D + 1)$

$$\log k_2 = \frac{C(D - 1)}{(2D + 1)}$$

where C is a constant and D is the dielectric constant of the appropriate ethanol-benzene mixture.

Plot your values of $\log k_2$ against the dielectric constant function, taking values of D from Table 5–1.

TABLE 5–1. Dielectric Constants of Ethanol–Benzene Mixtures

% Benzene (w/w)	D	% Benzene (w/w)	D
0	25.80	60	10.80
10	23.20	70	8.60
20	20.60	80	6.50
30	18.00	90	4.30
40	15.50	100	2.28
50	13.10		

Show that the Kirkwood expression gives a reasonably good basis for the interpretation of this solvent effect.

Questions

1. Predict the effects on the rates of the following reactions produced by changing the medium from ethanol to water:

   a. $C_2H_5Br + OH^- \longrightarrow C_2H_5OH + Br^-$

   b. $CH_3Br + S(CH_3)_2 \longrightarrow {}^+S(CH_3)_3 \cdot Br^-$

c. $R\overset{+}{N}(CH_3)_3 + OH^- \longrightarrow ROH + N(CH_3)_3$

d. $PhCH_2CH_2Br + OH^- \longrightarrow PhCH=CH_2$

e. $CH_2\!-\!CH_2 + HNEt_2 \longrightarrow \underset{\underset{OH}{|}}{CH_2\!-\!CH_2\!-\!NEt_2}$

$\quad\quad\quad\quad\quad\overset{\diagdown\;\diagup}{O}$

f. $PhN_2^+ BF_4^- \longrightarrow PhF + N_2 + BF_3$

2. The relative rates of the Claisen rearrangement of *p*-anisylallyl ether in a number of solvents is as follows: cyclohexane, 1; phenyl cyanide, 1.6; benzyl alcohol, 6; ethylene glycol, 12; phenol, 29.
   The reaction is,

(* denotes a "labelled" carbon)

Explain these observations.

References

1. K. B. Wiberg, *Physical Organic Chemistry*, Wiley, New York, 1964, Chapters 2–6, 3–6.
2. K. J. Laidler, *Reaction Kinetics*, Vol. II, Macmillan, New York, 1963, Chapter 1.
3. J. G. Kirkwood, *J. Chem. Phys.*, **2**, 351 (1934).

Effect of pH on a Reaction Rate

Many reactions are known whose rates vary with the acidity or alkalinity of the media in which they are conducted. Two effects may be considered to account for this. In the first, hydronium ion or hydroxide ion is itself the reagent and its concentration obviously varies with pH.

For example, the hydrolysis of *n*-butyl bromide (Experiment 4) proceeds by attack of hydroxide ion on the alkyl halide:

$$C_4H_9Br + OH^- \longrightarrow C_4H_9OH + Br^-$$

for which

$$\text{rate} = k[C_4H_9Br][OH^-]$$

The rate of this reaction increases steadily with an increase in pH.

On the other hand, hydrogen isotope exchange at the aromatic nucleus involves the attack of hydronium ion and thus occurs more rapidly at low pH:

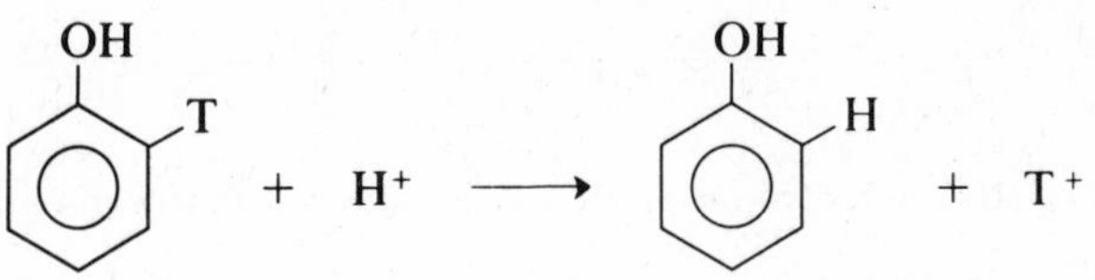

and

$$\text{rate} = k[\text{phenol}][H^+]$$

37

A second and more subtle effect of pH on a reaction rate may be brought about by changes in the nature of the reagent(s) upon accepting or donating a proton.

For example, ethyl acetate hydrolyzes only very slowly in pure water (pH 7), that is, ethoxide ion is displaced only reluctantly by a water molecule:

$$CH_3-\underset{\underset{H_2O}{}}{\overset{\overset{O}{\|}}{C}}-OC_2H_5 \xrightarrow{\text{2 steps}} CH_3-\overset{\overset{O}{\|}}{C}-OH + C_2H_5OH$$

In acidic solution the ester is significantly protonated thus permitting a molecule of ethanol to be displaced by water with comparative ease:

$$CH_3-\overset{\overset{O}{\|}}{C}-OC_2H_5 \underset{}{\overset{H^+}{\rightleftharpoons}} CH_3-\underset{\underset{H_2O}{}}{\overset{\overset{O}{\|}}{C}}-\overset{+}{\underset{H}{O}}C_2H_5 \xrightarrow{\text{2 steps}}$$

$$CH_3-\overset{\overset{O}{\|}}{C}-OH + C_2H_5OH + H^+$$

At high pH the rate again increases since the reagent now becomes OH^-, a more powerful nucleophile.

The hydrolysis of ethylene oxide to ethylene glycol shows a more complicated pH–rate relationship (Figure 6–1):

$$\underset{\underset{O}{\diagdown\diagup}}{CH_2-CH_2} + H_2O \longrightarrow CH_2OH-CH_2OH$$

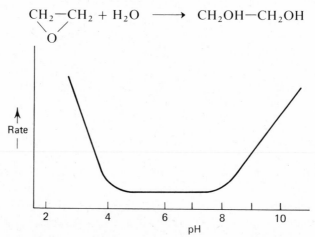

FIGURE 6–1 Hydrolysis of ethylene oxide as a function of pH

Three separate regions may be considered. The flat portion of the graph around the neutral point—a pH independent region—is evidently due to the hydrolysis by neutral water. At higher pH is superimposed with increasing importance the rapid hydrolysis by the stronger nucleophile, hydroxide ion:

$$CH_2-CH_2 + OH^- \longrightarrow CH_2-CH_2OH \xrightarrow[fast]{H_2O} CH_2-CH_2OH$$
$$\underset{O}{\diagdown\diagup} \qquad\qquad\qquad \underset{O^-}{|} \qquad\qquad\qquad \underset{OH}{|}$$

Catalysis at low pH is due to an increasingly significant proportion of the epoxide becoming protonated on oxygen, the resulting ion being much more readily attacked by water than the neutral epoxide:

$$CH_2-CH_2 \underset{}{\overset{H^+}{\rightleftharpoons}} CH_2-CH_2 \xrightarrow[fast]{H_2O} CH_2-CH_2OH + H^+$$
$$\underset{O}{\diagdown\diagup} \qquad\qquad \underset{\underset{+}{OH}}{\diagdown\diagup} \qquad\qquad \underset{OH}{|}$$

In Experiment 6, the rate of oxidation of formic acid by permanganate is studied in solution ranging from neutral to highly acidic. The equation may be written:

$$3\,HCOO^- + 2\,MnO_4^- + 5\,H^+ \longrightarrow 3\,CO_2 + 2\,MnO_2 + 4\,H_2O$$

but the following acid-base equilibria must be considered to explain the observations:

$$HCOO^- + H^+ \rightleftharpoons HCOOH \qquad pK_A = 3.0$$

$$MnO_4^- + H^+ \rightleftharpoons HMnO_4 \qquad pK_A = <0$$

The reactions are followed spectrometrically by observing the disappearance of the permanganate color with time.

Experimental

Materials Required
> Potassium permanganate
> Sulfuric acid
> Formic acid
> Dipotassium hydrogen phosphate, 1.0 M aqueous solution
> Potassium hydrogen phthalate, 1.0 M aqueous solution
> Visible spectrophotometer
> pH meter (optional)

The phosphate and phthalate solutions act as buffers of pH 7.0 and 4.0 respectively; that is, they are solutions which tend to persist at these values of pH despite the addition of small quantities of acid or base.

Prepare 0.03 M potassium permanganate solution by dissolving approximately 0.5 g of the solid in 100 ml distilled water and 0.1 M formic acid by weighing approximately 0.5 g and dissolving in 100 ml distilled water. Measure the wavelength of maximum absorbance of permanganate solution.

In a 50 ml graduated flask place about 40 ml distilled water and add 1 ml phosphate buffer and 4.0 ml formic acid solution by pipet. At zero time add 1.0 ml of permanganate solution, mix the solution and make up to the mark with water. Transfer this solution to the sample cell and place in the spectrophotometer. Measure the absorbance of the solution against pure water at the wavelength of maximum absorption as a function of time and continue to take readings until the absorbance has dropped considerably.

Repeat this experiment at pH 4 using potassium hydrogen phthalate buffer as the medium instead of water.

Repeat the experiment in the following media (increasing acidity):

0.01 M sulfuric acid	pH 2
1.0 M sulfuric acid	pH 0 $(=H_0 + 0.24)$
10% sulfuric acid in water	$H_0 - 0.16$[1]
30% sulfuric acid in water	$H_0 - 1.54$[1]

Treatment of results.   Since formic acid is in excess, each kinetic measurement is of first order to a good approximation,

$$\text{rate} = k[\text{permanganate}]$$

Plot absorbance against time and estimate the rate constant in each case (see Appendix A). Plot the rate constant against pH (H_0) and relate your points by a curve.

The mechanism of the permanganate oxidation of formic acid probably involves a rate-determining hydrogen atom transfer

followed by a rapid electron transfer with the formation of CO_2.

$$^{IV}Mn + Mn^{VI} \text{ etc.}$$

Give an explanation of your observed relationship between rate and pH in terms of this mechanism and the protonation equilibria of the reagents.

[1] pH (defined as $-\log[H_3^+O]$) ceases to be a useful measure of acidity in highly acidic media since the hydronium ion becomes less and less important as the source of protons, being replaced in concentrated sulfuric acid solutions by the undissociated H_2SO_4 molecule itself. The acidity is then best measured by an operational method based on the extent of dissociation of a weak base, B, dissociation constant K_A. The new scale H_0, the Hammett acidity function, is given by $H_0 = pK_A + \log[B]/[BH^+]$. For the purposes of this experiment, H_0 may be taken as an extension to the pH scale applicable below pH 0.

Questions

1. Explain the following rate-pH curves for the diazocoupling reactions of aromatic amines and phenols.

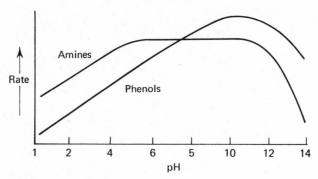

The equations for the reactions are:

$$X = -OH, -NR_2$$

2. Predict the effect of changing pH on the rates of the following reactions:

a. $CH_3C(=O)OEt + H_2O \longrightarrow CH_3C(=O)OH + EtOH$

b. $PhCH(OEt)(OEt) + 2 H_2O \longrightarrow PhCHO + 2 EtOH$

c. $PhNH_2 + PhCHO \longrightarrow PhN = CHPh + H_2O$

References

1. K. B. Wiberg and R. Stewart, *J. Amer. Chem. Soc.*, **78**, 1214 (1955).
2. R. Stewart, *Oxidation in Organic Chemistry,Part A*, ed. K. B. Wiberg, Academic Press, New York, 1965, p. 65.

Cryoscopic Evidence for a Carbonium Ion

Concentrated sulfuric acid is an extremely acidic solvent, that is, it has a great tendency to protonate solutes, and frequently brings about the complete ionization of weak bases such as alcohols which in turn may give rise to carbonium ions by loss of H_2O:

$$ROH + H_2SO_4 \rightleftharpoons R\overset{+}{O}H_2 + HSO_4^-$$

$$R\overset{+}{O}H_2 \rightleftharpoons R^+ + H_2O$$

$$H_2O + H_2SO_4 \rightleftharpoons H_3O^+ + HSO_4^-$$

overall
$$ROH + 2H_2SO_4 \rightleftharpoons R^+ + H_3O^+ + 2HSO_4^-$$

Such dissociations may be inferred from cryoscopic measurements since the depression of the freezing point of sulfuric acid is proportional to the sum of the molalities of all different solute species present (including its own conjugate base). Thus, the observed depression of freezing point brought about by addition of an alcohol to sulfuric acid is greater by a factor i than that which would be predicted on the basis of no dissociation of the solute. The van't Hoff factor, i is numerically equal to the total number of particles produced in the dissociation, and is a whole number if the dissociation is complete.

For example,

$$B + H_2SO_4 \rightleftharpoons BH^+ + HSO_4^- \qquad i = 2$$

$$ROH + 2H_2SO_4 \rightleftharpoons R^+ + H_3O^+ + 2HSO_4^- \qquad i = 4$$

The following relationship holds,

$$\Delta T = \frac{10^3 k_s a}{Mbi} \tag{1}$$

where ΔT is the observed depression of freezing point, a = weight of sulfuric acid, b = weight of solute (here, triphenyl carbinol) and M its molecular weight, k_s is the cryoscopic constant for the medium.

Experimental

Materials Required

> Sulfuric acid, 98%
> Oleum
> Triphenylcarbinol
> *p*-Nitrotoluene

Construct the cryoscopic apparatus shown in Figure 7–1. The lip of the tube is made so that the shoulder of the Beckmann thermometer will rest on it with the bulb of the thermometer 1–2 mm from the bottom of the tube. This arrangement minimizes the danger of breakage. Prepare 100% sulfuric acid by adding carefully 100 g oleum (containing 30% SO_3) to 338 g conc sulfuric acid. The product should melt at 8–10°C, (pure H_2SO_4 melts at 10.49°). Store in a desiccator. While ordinary conc sulfuric acid may be used for the experiment, the higher

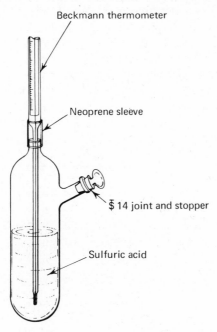

Beckmann thermometer

Neoprene sleeve

$\bar{\text{S}}$ 14 joint and stopper

Sulfuric acid

FIGURE 7–1 Cryoscopic apparatus.

melting points exhibited by solutions in the 100% acid permit easier freezing. Obtain the approximate freezing point of the 100% sulfuric acid using a 0–100° thermometer and set the Beckmann thermometer so that the mercury is near the top of the scale at that temperature.

Weigh the clean, empty cryoscopic tube and fill with the 100% sulfuric acid to a depth of about 7–8 cm. Reweigh, taking care to avoid excessive contact with air. Insert the Beckmann thermometer and attach to a neoprene sleeve (the finger of a surgical rubber glove is admirable) with a length of copper wire at each end so as to form an airtight seal.

Cool the acid by bringing up a beaker containing acetone-dry ice or an ice-salt freezing mixture and stir carefully with the Beckmann thermometer so that uniform freezing occurs. Freezing may take place on immersion in an ice bath but super-cooling is likely to be noted, especially at the first freezing. Now bring up a one liter beaker of water at a temperature about 5°C below the expected freezing point, and allow the acid to warm slowly, stirring as soon as partial thawing occurs.

Note the temperature on the Beckmann thermometer at which the last crystal of sulfuric acid melts. Repeat until consistent results are obtained. Now add, by way of the side-arm, a weighed amount (about 0.1 g) of dry p-nitro-toluene (a nonelectrolyte for which $i = 1$), in pellet form if possible. Allow this to dissolve in the sulfuric acid (warming and stirring may be necessary). Determine the freezing point of the solution as before. From this, the molal depression of freezing point, k_s may be determined from Eq. (1) for the particular sample of sulfuric acid used. Add to the same solution, a weighed portion (about 0.1 g) of triphenylcarbinol. Determine the new freezing point and measure the depression from that of the p-nitrotoluene solution. Apply this value to Eq. (1) using the above value of k_s and obtain i. Write an equation for the dissociation of triphenylcarbinol which satisfies the value found. A more accurate technique is to add successively several portions of both the p-nitrotoluene and triphenyl-carbinol and plot ΔT against a to obtain from the slopes k_s and i respectively.

Measure the ultraviolet spectrum, between 300 and 700 mμ of a dilute solution of triphenylcarbinol in conc sulfuric acid. Compare it with the spectrum of triphenylmethyl fluoroborate (Experiment 31).

Questions

1. The i factors observed for a number of compounds in sulfuric acid are listed below. Write equations rationalizing these values.

$$CH_3COOH \qquad i = 2$$

$$CH_3COCH_3 \qquad i = 2$$

$$C_2H_5OC_2H_5 \qquad i = 2$$

$$Cl_2CHCOOH \qquad i = 1.6$$

$i = 2.4$

$i = 1.3$

CH_3OH $i = 3$

$(CH_3CO)_2O$ $i = 4$

$C_6H_5COOCH_3$ $i = 2$, increasing to 3 on standing

HNO_3 $i = 4$

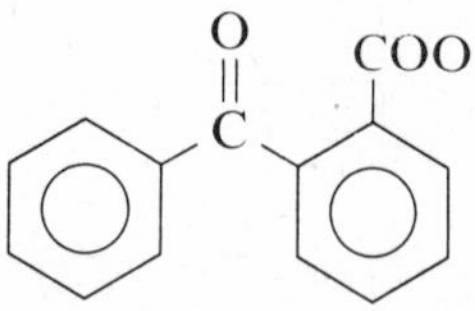

$i = 4$

2. Mesitoic acid (2,4,6-trimethylbenzoic acid) may not be esterified, nor may its esters be hydrolyzed, by the usual methods. Interconversion of the acid and ester is, however, readily achieved by solution in conc sulfuric acid followed by addition of either alcohol or water. Explain these reactions:

$$(CH_3)_3C_6H_2COOH \underset{\substack{(1)\ H_2SO_4 \\ (2)\ H_2O}}{\overset{\substack{(1)\ H_2SO_4 \\ (2)\ ROH}}{\rightleftarrows}} (CH_3)_3C_6H_2COOR$$

1. Explain the fact that proton exchange occurs between benzene and conc sulfuric acid when mixed, as shown by deuterium labelling:

$$C_6H_6 + D_2SO_4 \longrightarrow C_6H_5D + DHSO_4 \text{ etc.}$$

References

1. L. P. Hammett and A. J. Deyrup, *J. Amer. Chem. Soc.*, **55**, 1800 (1933).
2. A. Hantzsch, *Z. Physik. Chem.*, **61**, 253 (1907); *ibid.*, **65**, 41 (1908); *ibid.*, **68**, 1782 (1909); *Chem. Ber.*, **55**, 953 (1922); *ibid.*, **63**, 1782 (1930).
3. E. S. Gould, *Mechanism and Structure in Organic Chemistry*, Holt, Rinehart, and Winston, 1959, p. 98.

Structural Effects on Elimination Reactions

It has long been known that where a β-elimination reaction may in principle give two or more olefinic products, one is usually produced preferentially to the others. For example, the treatment of 2-bromobutane with ethoxide yields a mixture of 1-butene and 2-butene, 70% to 30% respectively:

$$CH_3-CH-CH-CH_2$$
$$\overset{|}{Br}$$

$$EtO \rightsquigarrow H \qquad\qquad H \rightsquigarrow OEt$$

$$CH_3-CH=CH-CH_3 \qquad\qquad CH_3CH_2CH=CH_2$$

2-Butene, 70%   1-Butene, 30%

Saytzeff's Rule [1] predicts that *the olefin formed in major yield is the most highly substituted ethylene.* The rule is obeyed where the leaving group is halogen, tosylate, acetate, or xanthate. The interpretation usually given is that the energy of the system in the transition state, which contains the partly formed double

bond, is lowered by conjugation with unsaturated groups, or, if none are present,
by hyperconjugation[1] with alkyl groups.

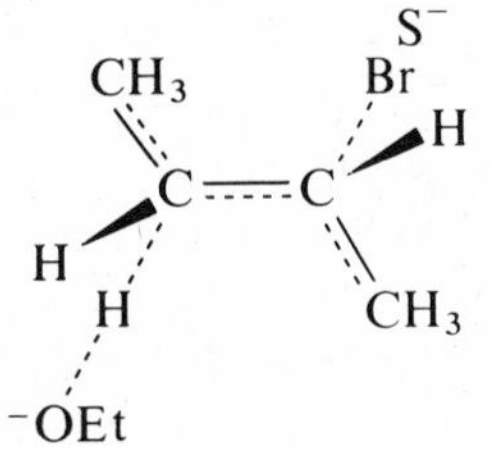

a. more favorable 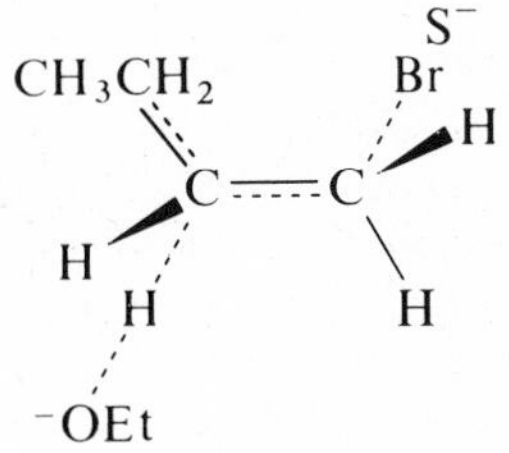   b. less favorable

An important exception to Saytzeff's Rule is found where the leaving group
is positively charged nitrogen or sulfur; for these cases Hofmann's Rule [3]
applies which states that, *the olefin formed in major yield from eliminations of
quaternary ammonium or tertiary sulfonium ions is the **least** substituted ethylene.*

For example, 2-butyltrimethylammonium hydroxide on heating forms
1-butene and 2-butene, but now in the ratio of 25% to 75% respectively:

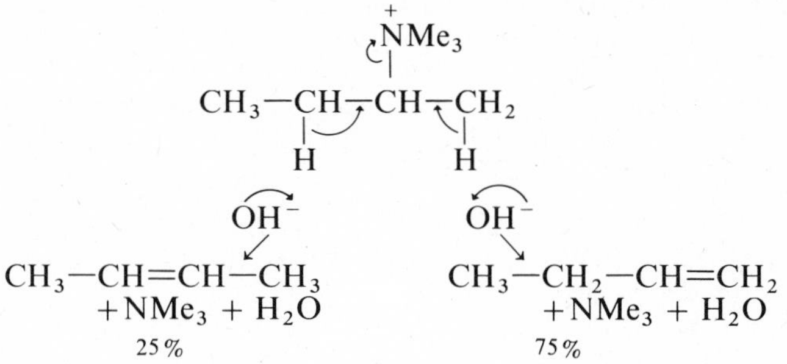

$$CH_3-CH=CH-CH_3 \qquad CH_3-CH_2-CH=CH_2$$
$$+NMe_3 + H_2O \qquad +NMe_3 + H_2O$$
25%   75%

Ingold has suggested that the reason for this reversal of the product ratio
might be the weakening of the acidity of the 3-hydrogen by electron donation

---

[1] Hyperconjugation [2] is the name given to the weak overlap of a π-orbital with molecular
orbitals of an adjacent alkyl group. It is best represented by the participation of valence-bond
structures of the type:

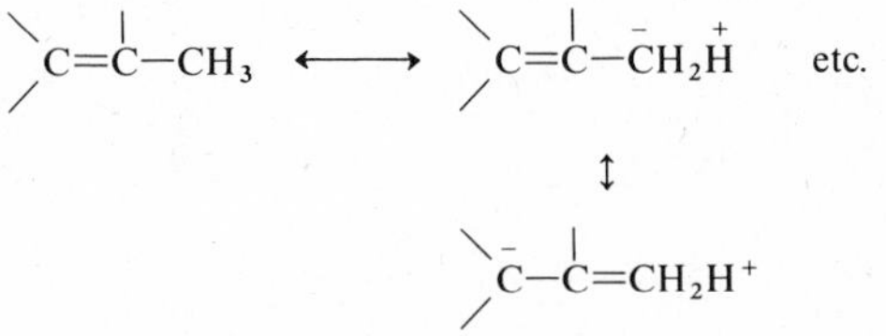

Its effects are similar to conjugation in character but much less in degree and result in electron
donation by the alkyl group, if the potential energy of the system is thereby lowered. The effect is
greatest with a methyl substituent, followed by primary, secondary, and tertiary alkyl groups.

from the attached methyl group hence making the 1-hydrogen easier to remove. This does not readily explain why Saytzeff- or Hofmann-type elimination depends on the leaving group and has been discounted by Schramm [5] and by H. C. Brown [6]. Their explanation is that hyperconjugative stabilization always acts but steric factors override this in eliminations from 'onium ions. They showed that an increase in the steric requirements of substituents adjacent to the incipient double bond, or of the base, or of the leaving group, all tended to increase the proportion of least substituted ethylene, the Hofmann product.

Experimental

Materials Required

> *tert*-Amyl bromide
> *tert*-Amyltrimethylammonium iodide[2]
> Gas chromatograph

THE DEHYDROBROMINATION OF *tert*-AMYL BROMIDE

Place 50 ml of 25% potassium hydroxide solution in ethanol in a 100 ml flask fitted with a fractionating column, condenser set for distillation, and ice-cooled receiver. Add 5 ml *tert*-amyl bromide and distill at such a rate that the head temperature does not exceed 80°. Dry the distillate over calcium chloride and analyze by gas chromatography using a six foot silicone column at room temperature or a silver nitrate column. Identify the two olefin peaks and measure their relative areas.

---

[2] Preparation of *tert*-Amyltrimethylammonium iodide:

tert-Amylamine [7].   Mix, in a flask, 25 ml acetic acid, 16.6 g *tert*-amyl alcohol and 10.0 g sodium cyanide. Add a mixture of 50 g concentrated sulfuric acid in 25 ml acetic acid over a half-hour period keeping the temperature between 50° and 60°, and the flask in the fume hood. Stopper the mixture and allow to stand overnight then pour onto 500 g ice, neutralize with 20% sodium hydroxide and extract with ether. Dry the ethereal solution and remove the ether to obtain *N-tert-amyl-formamide*. (12–14 g). Without further purification, hydrolyze by refluxing with 25 g sodium hydroxide in 150 ml water for 4–5 hours. Cool the mixture and extract with ether. Dry the ethereal solution over KOH and remove the ether to obtain *tert-amylamine*, bp 78°.

tert-Amyldimethylamine [6].   In a 100 ml flask, suspend 25 g paraformaldehyde in 50 ml 100% formic acid and add 10 g *tert*-amylamine. Insert a condenser and allow the exothermic reaction to proceed. When evolution of heat ceases reflux for a further 30 min then pour into water. Cautiously make strongly alkaline with 25% sodium hydroxide cooling the solution in ice. Extract the basic solution with ether, dry over sodium hydroxide pellets and distill, collecting *tert*-amyldimethylamine at 120°, 160 mm.

tert-Amyltrimethylammonium Iodide.   Dissolve 5 g *tert*-amyldimethylamine in ether and add 7.0 g methyl iodide. Allow the mixture to stand for 30 min, then filter off the white precipitate of *tert*-amyltrimethylammonium iodide (decomposes 225°), wash with ether and dry in the air.

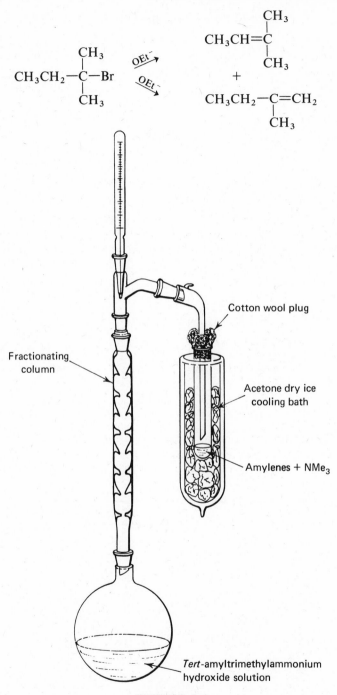

FIGURE 8–1

The Hofmann Elimination of *tert*-Amyltrimethylammonium Hydroxide [7]

Dissolve 5.1 g (0.02 mole) *tert*-amyltrimethylammonium iodide in water and add the solution with stirring to an equivalent amount of silver oxide prepared from 3.4 g silver nitrate precipitated with excess sodium hydroxide decanted and washed with water. Shake or stir vigorously for a few minutes then filter the yellow silver iodide precipitate. Add 6.0 g sodium hydroxide and distill the mixture through a good fractionating column allowing the temperature at the head to rise only to about 80° and trapping the products in a dry ice cooled trap (Figure 8–1). Allow the distillation to proceed for 2–4 hours then analyze the product on the gas chromatograph as before. Because of the small quantity used, it is better to inject the sample as vapor into the chromatograph using the microsyringe and filling with the vapor in the trap. Identify two olefin peaks and compare their areas with those of the product from *tert*-amyl bromide. If authentic samples of 2-methyl-2-butene or 2-methyl-1-butene are available, identify the product peaks by comparison of the retention times.

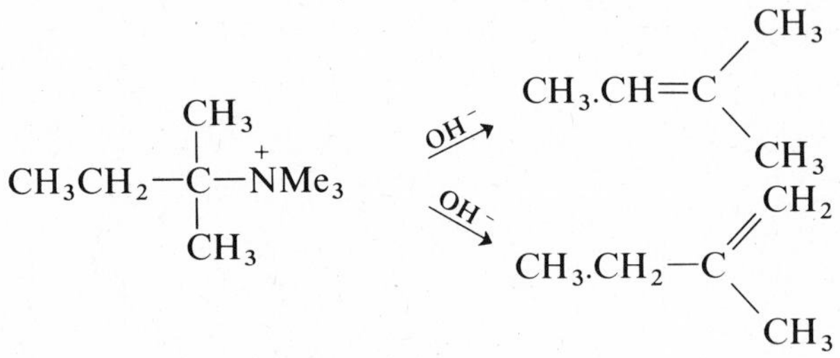

Questions

1. Write structures for the major products of the following reactions giving reasons for your choice in each case:

   a. $Me_2CH.CHBr.CH_2COOH + OH^-$

   b.

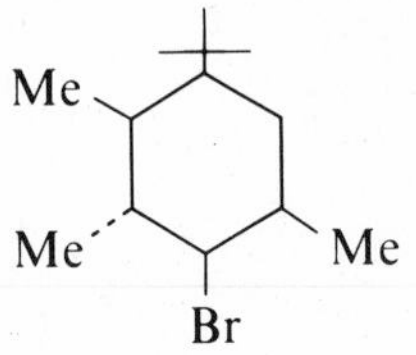

$$+OH^- \longrightarrow$$

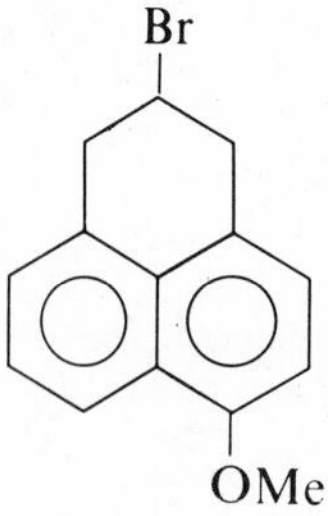

   c.

$$+OH^- \longrightarrow$$

d.

$$CH_2CHBrCH_2$$

OMe   NO$_2$ $+ OH^-$ $\longrightarrow$

e. $CH_3CH_2CHClCH_3 + Ag^+/EtOH \longrightarrow$

f. $CH_3CH_2CHCH_3 + OH^- \longrightarrow$
                    |
                    SO_2Me

g. $(CH_3)_2CH-C(CH_3)_2 + H_2SO_4 \longrightarrow$
                        |
                        OH

h.

OCOPh $+ OH^-$ $\longrightarrow$

OCOPh

2. The same basic reagent may bring about both elimination (E) and substitution (S_N) to an alkyl halide, RBr. Some values of E/S_N ratios are given below. Discuss the structural factors which influence this ratio.

R	E/S_N	R	E/S_N
Et	0.01	2-Bu	0.82
n-Pr	0.09	2-Am	0.81
n-Bu	0.10	3-Am	0.88
n-Am	0.09	PhCH$_2$CH$_2$	0.94
iso-Bu	0.59	tert-Bu	0.97
iso-Pr	0.80		

3. Write structures for all the isomeric 1,2,3,4,5,6-hexachlorocyclohexanes and predict the number of moles of HCl each would readily lose on treatment with sodium hydroxide.

References

1. A. Saytzeff, *Liebigs' Annalen*, **179**, 296 (1875).
2. J. Hine, *Physical Organic Chemistry*, McGraw-Hill, New York, 2nd ed., 1964, p. 18.
3. A. W. Hofmann, *Liebigs' Annalen*, **78**, 253 (1851); *ibid.*, **79**, 11 (1851).

4. C. K. Ingold, *Structure and Mechanism in Organic Chemistry*, Bell, London, 1953, Chapter VIII.
5. R. M. Schramm, *Science*, **112**, 367 (1950).
6. H. C. Brown and I. Moritani, *J. Amer. Chem. Soc.*, **78**, 2203 (1956).
7. J. J. Ritter and J. Kalish, *J. Amer. Chem. Soc.*, **70**, 4048 (1948).

The Baker-Nathan Effect

EXPERIMENT 9

The Baker-Nathan Effect is a reactivity order that suggests the order of electron release from substituent alkyl groups to be Me > Et > Pr^i > Bu^t. Thus in most, but not all, aromatic substitution reactions by electrophilic species, (reactions which are known to be accelerated by electron donation to the ring), the *para* position of toluene is more reactive than that of *tert*-butylbenzene. This occurs despite the fact that the inductive effects due to permanent bond polarizations are in the reverse order, Bu^t > Pr^i > Et > Me. Some examples of reactions which exhibit the Baker-Nathan order, as well as some which exhibit the inductive order of reactivities, are shown in Table 9–1. Several explanations have been put forward to account for the Baker-Nathan effect. Perhaps the one most consistent with the facts involves an alternative mechanism for electron release known as hyperconjugation.[1] In valence bond theory terms, the description of the methyl group attached to an aromatic ring has to include some weight from 'no bond' structures (I), (II) which can release electrons into the ring. This is known as carbon-hydrogen hyperconjugation. Analogous structures may be written for the other alkyl groups in which successive hydrogen atoms are replaced by methyl. In *tert*-butylbenzene which has no α-hydrogen atoms, only carbon-carbon hyperconjugation is possible. This is believed to be less effective than carbon-hydrogen hyperconjugation in relaying electronic

[1] See also footnote, p. 47.

charge to the ring, therefore structures III, IV are less important than I, II:

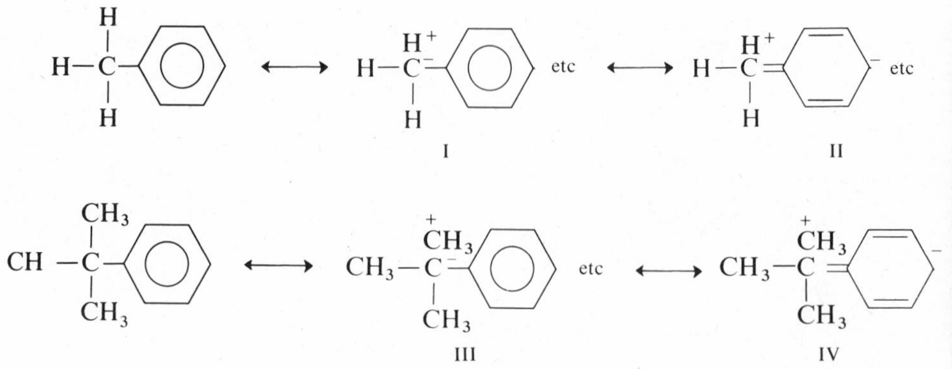

I

II

III

IV

By this mechanism there should be a smooth gradation of electron-releasing capability in the Baker-Nathan order. Other theories proposed include the view that the normal inductive effects are overshadowed by steric hindrance towards solvation of the charged intermediate in the reaction (Figure 9–1).

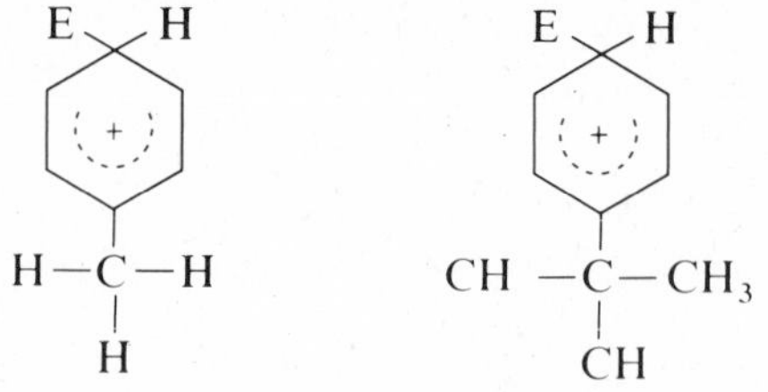

FIGURE 9–1

This would have the effect of increasing the potential energy of the *p-tert*-butyl intermediate and the activation energy to its formation thus resulting in a retardation of reaction relative to *p*-methyl.

Although several theories can account for the Baker-Nathan order of release it is not so easy to see why it does not always apply. It is probably significant to note that the reactions displaying the inductive order are those which are relatively insensitive to electron release—that is, have a low ρ-value (Experiment 2) and thus do not need the hyperconjugative electron release at the expense of hindrance to solvation for the reaction to proceed readily.

Experimental

Materials required

Toluene, pure
tert-Butylbenzene, pure
Acetic acid (glacial)

Bromine
Visible spectrophotometer or colorimeter.

TABLE 9–1. Examples of Baker-Nathan and Inductive Reaction Orders

Reaction		Relative Rates	
	p-H	p-Me	p-Bu^t
A. Me > Bu^t			
1. Benzoylation (Friedel-Crafts reaction)	1	589	430
2. Hydrolysis of ArCMe$_2$Cl	1	26	14
3. Alcoholysis of ArCH$_2$Cl	1	1.6	1.5
4. Halogen exchange, ArCH$_2$Br + iodide ion	1	1.5	1.4
5. Solvolysis of ArCH$_2$Br in formic acid	1	58	28
6. Beckmann rearrangement of ArC(CH$_3$)=NOH	1	1.9	1.8
B. Bu^t > Me			
1. Nitration of benzenes	1	58	75
2. Mercuridesilylation of benzenes	1	10.6	14.0
3. Acid cleavage of aryl germanes	1	5.7	7.0

Note: The fact that rates for both alkyl substituents in all reactions are greater than those for the parent benzenes (R = H) confirms that electron release facilitates the reactions since it is known that this is less from hydrogen than from alkyl.

Place a test tube, approximately 6–8 inches long, fitted with standard taper glass stopper in a large beaker of boiling water so that it is three parts immersed, the top projecting through a cover over the beaker. Add 25.0 ml of a solution containing 5.0 ml each of 1.0 M toluene and 1.0 M bromine solutions in acetic acid, diluted to 50.0 ml with acetic acid, starting a clock at the moment of addition. Take 1.0 ml samples at approximate intervals 1, 3, 5, 10, 20, 40, 60 min, dilute each with acetic acid to 25.0 ml in a volumetric flask and measure the absorbance of each solution at the wavelength of maximum absorption of bromine in 1 cm stoppered cuvets; the experiment may be repeated or a duplicate run performed simultaneously using the other half of the prepared solution. Repeat the experiment using *tert*-butylbenzene in place of toluene, adjusting the sampling times as required in order to follow the reaction to 60–70% completion.

Plot absorbance against time for each reaction and compare the graphs to decide whether the Baker-Nathan effect is operating. Alternatively, convert the absorbance readings to concentration using the Beer-Lambert Law:

$$\varepsilon = A/bc$$

where

ε = extinction coefficient for bromine

A = absorbance

b = cell thickness in cm

c = molar concentration of bromine

and calculate the second-order rate constants (see Appendix A), assuming that the solutions increase in volume by 10% at 100°C.

Questions

1. How is the Baker-Nathan reaction order reflected in the Hammett ρ-values? [Refer to Jaffé, *Chem. Revs.*, 191 (1953).]
2. What tests could be applied to examine the postulate that the Baker-Nathan reaction order is the result of the steric inhibition of solvation by the larger groups?

References

1. J. W. Baker and W. S. Nathan, *J. Chem. Soc.*, 1844 (1935).
2. R. O. C. Norman, *Quantitative Aspects of Aromatic Substitution*, Royal Institute of Chemistry Lecture Series No. 2, 1963 p. 26.
3. E. Berliner and M. M. Chen, *J. Amer. Chem. Soc.*, **80**, 343 (1958); E. Berliner, *Tetrahedron*, **5**, 202 (1959).
4. H. C. Brown, J. D. Brady, M. Grayson and W. H. Bonner, *J. Amer. Chem. Soc.*, **79**, 1897 (1957).
5. R. A. Benkeser, T. V. Liston, and G. M. Stanton, *Tetrahedron Letters*, **15**, 1 (1960).

The Brønsted Salt Effect

A technique which is sometimes of use in investigating reaction mechanisms and one which is rather similar in principle to the solvent effects described in Experiment 5, employs nonreacting ions in the medium. Under certain circumstances, quite dramatic changes in rates may be observed when inert salts are added to the medium, which thereby becomes more polar in character, owing to changes in the stabilization of the transition state with respect to the reagents [1]. Consider the general second-order reaction, in which,

$$A + B \;\rightleftharpoons\; AB^{\ddagger} \;\longrightarrow\; \text{products}$$

reagents A and B pass through an activated complex or transition state, $AB^{\ddagger}$ before conversion to products (Figure 10–1). The activation energy for the reaction, $\Delta F^{\ddagger}$, in a medium of zero ionic strength $(I = 0)$, (see Eq. (15)) is given by:

$$\Delta F^{\ddagger} = F_{AB^{\ddagger}} - (F_A + F_B) \tag{1}$$

where F_A, F_B and $F_{AB^{\ddagger}}$ are the free energies of A, B and $AB^{\ddagger}$ respectively. If now the ionic strength of the medium is increased to I, the free energies of A, B and $AB^{\ddagger}$ will all change by amounts ΔF_A, ΔF_B and $\Delta F_{AB^{\ddagger}}$ each depending on the nature of the species. Hence,

$$\Delta \Delta F^{\ddagger} = \Delta F_{AB^{\ddagger}} - (\Delta F_A + \Delta F_B) \tag{2}$$

The rate constant of the reaction is related to the activation energy by the

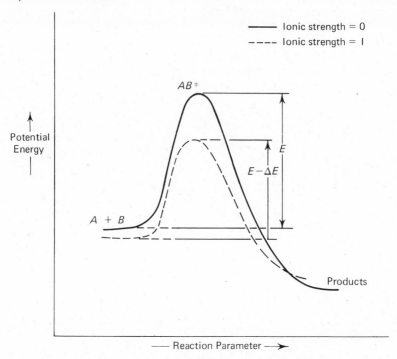

FIGURE 10–1 Medium effect on a reaction pathway.

Arrhenius Equation. The rates k_0 and k at $I = 0$ and $I = I$ respectively are therefore given by

$$k_0 = Ae\frac{-E_A}{RT} \equiv Ae^{-\Delta F^\ddagger/RT} \qquad I = 0 \tag{3}$$

where $E_A \equiv \Delta F^\ddagger$

$$k = Ae^{\frac{-(\Delta F + \Delta\Delta F^\ddagger)}{RT}} \qquad I = I \tag{4}$$

from which

$$\log\frac{k}{k_0} = \frac{-\Delta\,\Delta F^\ddagger}{RT} = \frac{(\Delta F_A + \Delta F_B - \Delta F_{AB\ddagger})}{RT} \tag{5}$$

Assuming ideal behavior of the solutions at zero ionic strength,

$$F_A = RT \ln f_A$$

where f_A etc. refers to the activity coefficient,

$$F_B = RT \ln f_B$$

and,

$$F_{AB\ddagger} = RT \ln f_{AB\ddagger} \tag{6}$$

therefore,

$$\frac{k}{k_0} = \frac{f_A f_B}{f_{AB\ddagger}} \tag{7}$$

The Debye-Hückel expression for the activity coefficient [2] of an ion is:

$$-\log f_{ion} = \mathscr{S}z_{ion}^2 F(I) \tag{8}$$

where $\mathscr{S}$ is a constant for the medium ($=0.509$ for water at $25°$) $z =$ charge on the ion and $F(I)$ may be taken as $\sqrt{I}$ in the limiting case of very dilute solutions. Substituting Eq. (8) in Eq. (7) and writing $z_{AB\ddagger} = z_A + z_B$ since charge must be conserved:

$$\log \frac{k}{k_0} = 2\mathscr{S}z_A z_B F(I) \tag{9}$$

We therefore have a theoretical expression with which to test measured changes in rate for reactions between ions ($z_A, z_B \neq 0$) in relation to the total ionic strength of the medium. It will be seen that if z_A and z_B are of the same sign, $\log k/k_0$ will be positive indicating an increase in rate with ionic strength or a positive primary salt effect. If z_A, z_B are of opposite sign $\log k/k_0$ will be negative and increasing the ionic strength will retard the reaction, a negative primary salt effect. Most reactions between ions are too fast for their rates to be measured. One which is conveniently slow is the "bleaching" of the triphenylmethane dye, crystal violet (I) by hydroxide ion to form the colorless carbinol (II). Since crystal violet is a cation, a negative salt effect would be predicted.

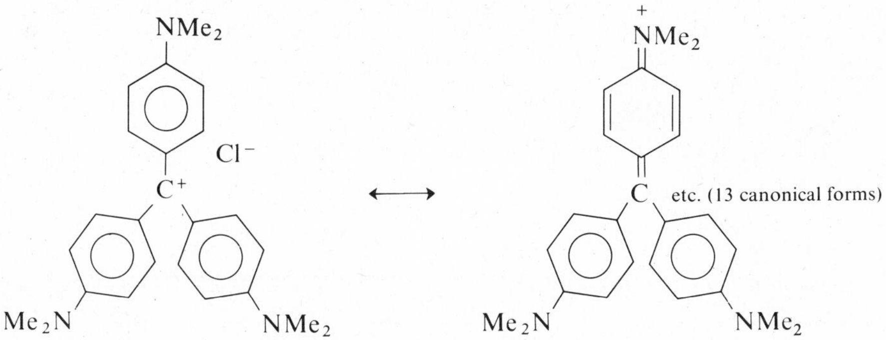

crystal violet, I

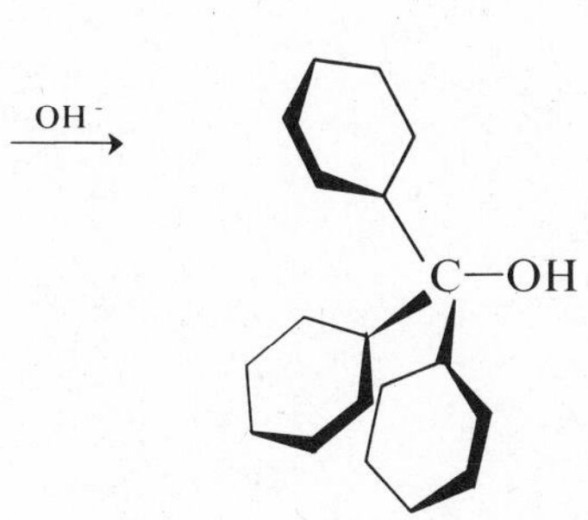

colorless, II

The salt which will be used is lithium sulfate which is inert as far as the reaction is concerned and, to a good approximation, ideal with respect to the Debye-Hückel relationship.

Experimental

Materials Required
Crystal violet chloride solution $(1.5 \times 10^{-4} M)$ in distilled water, stored in a polyethylene bottle.
Sodium hydroxide solution, 0.5 M
Lithium sulfate solution, 0.5 M
Thermostat bath (or large beaker at ambient temperature)
Visible spectrophotometer

Record the visible spectrum of crystal violet using the stock solution diluted ten times and 10 mm absorption cells with water as reference. Determine the absorption maximum,[1] λ_{max}. Pipet 5.0 ml of crystal violet solution into a 50 ml volumetric flask, add approximately 40 ml distilled water and place in a thermostat bath at 25°. Add 0.20 ml of sodium hydroxide solution starting a clock simultaneously and mix the solution thoroughly by shaking. Remove samples of the solution at intervals spaced about 5 min apart and measure the absorbance in a 10 mm spectrophotometer cell at the wavelength of maximum absorption.

It is necessary to take a fresh sample of reaction mixture for each reading and to rinse the cell with methanol and then water between samples, since the dye is strongly adsorbed on glass. For this reason, the stock solution is stored in a polyethylene bottle.

Repeat the experiment, adding successively 1, 2, 5, 10 ml of lithium sulfate solution to the reaction mixture. For each run, draw a graph, plotting absorbance against time.

Treatment of Results.   The reaction has been shown by LaMer [4] to be bimolecular:

$$CV + OH^- \xrightarrow{k_2} \text{Carbinol}$$

[1] Lewis [3] has interpreted this as being due to the excitation of the symmetric "propellor" form of the ion and the shoulder on the short wave length side as due to excitation of the antisymmetric form also present.

Symmetric propellor

Antisymmetric propellor

Therefore,

$$\text{Rate} = \frac{-d}{dt}[CV] = \frac{-d}{dt}[OH^-] = \frac{d}{dt}[\text{Carbinol}] = k_2[CV][OH^-] \quad (10)$$

However, under the conditions used,

$$\frac{[CV]}{[OH^-]} \approx 10^{-3}$$

hence effectively,

$$\frac{-d}{dt}[OH^-] = 0$$

and the reaction becomes pseudo first-order, (Appendix A)

$$k_2[CV][OH^-] = \underbrace{k_2[OH^-]}_{k_1}[CV] = k_1[CV]$$

$$\text{Rate} = \frac{-d}{dt}[CV] = k_1[CV] \quad (11)$$

hence,

$$k_1 = \frac{2.303}{t} \log \frac{x}{(a-x)} \quad (12)$$

where a = initial concentration of crystal violet, $[CV]_0$
$(a - x)$ = concentration of crystal violet at time, $[CV]_t$

But the absorbance (optical density) A, of a species is related to its concentration by the Beer-Lambert Law [Eq. (13)]:

$$\log \frac{I}{I_0} = A_{CV} = [CV] \times \varepsilon \times b \quad (13)$$

where

I_0 = intensity of light incident on absorption cell
I = intensity of light transmitted through cell
A_{CV} = measured absorbance of crystal violet solution
ε = molar extinction coefficient of crystal violet (constant)
b = optical path length

hence,

$$[CV] = \text{Constant (A)}$$

substituting in Eq. (12):

$$k = \frac{2.303}{t} \log \frac{A_0}{A_t} \quad (14)$$

Plot $2.303 \log(A_0/A_t)$ against t for each run and obtain the rate constants in each case or utilize the computer programme in Appendix A; a quicker but less rigorous procedure is to estimate the time taken for the absorbance to fall to half its initial value (half-life), since for a first-order reaction:

$$k = \frac{2.303 \log 2}{t_{1/2}}$$

To examine further the Brønsted relationship, Eq. (9), compute values of the ionic strength, I, of each medium from Eq. (15) taking into account every species of ion present:

$$I = \tfrac{1}{2} \sum^i [i]z_i^2 \tag{15}$$

$$I = \tfrac{1}{2}([CV] \times 1^2) + ([Cl^-] \times 1^2) + ([OH^-] \times 1^2)$$
$$+ ([Na^+] \times 1^2) + ([Li^+] \times 1^2) + ([SO_4^=] \times 2^2)$$

Plot I against k_1 and extrapolate the graph to $I = 0$ to determine k_0, the theoretical rate constant at zero ionic strength. Plot $\log k_1/k_0$ against $\sqrt{I}$ [Eq. (9)] and examine the linearity of the plot. If some curvature is noted, replace the ionic strength function, $\sqrt{I}$ by the more exact expression:

$$F(I) = \frac{\sqrt{I}}{1 + 1.56\sqrt{I}}$$

which is applicable to higher values of I than the simpler function. The observation of a salt effect in the predicted direction and in accordance with the Debye-Hückel electrolyte theory may be used to provide evidence concerning the movement of charge in a reaction in certain cases.

Questions

1. The specific rate constant for the hydrolysis of *tert*-butyl chloride in water appears to increase as the reaction proceeds, as manifested by an upward trend in the plot of $\log(a/(a - x))$ against time (see Appendix A). Explain this observation.

2. The hydrolysis of trityl chloride (triphenylmethyl chloride) in aqueous acetone is accelerated by added lithium perchlorate but retarded by addition of lithium chloride. Explain.

3. Discuss the observed salt effects given for the following reactions;

strong positive
(by NaN_3)

PhCHOBros $\xrightarrow{\text{AcOH}}$ PhCHOAc
|
CH$_3$ moderate, positive
                                      (by LiClO$_4$)

CHBrCOO$^-$
| $\xrightarrow{\text{OH}^-}$
CHBrCOO$^-$

$$\begin{array}{c}
\text{H} \qquad \text{COO}^- \\
\diagdown \quad \diagup \\
\text{C} \\
\| \\
\text{C} \\
\diagup \quad \diagdown \\
^-\text{OOC} \qquad \text{Br}
\end{array}$$

Rate increased by Na$^+$, K$^+$ but decreased by Ca^{++}, Mg^{++}.

References

1. C. W. Davis, *Progress in Reaction Kinetics*, Vol. I, Pergamon Press, London, 1961, p. 163.
2. E. A. Moelwyn-Hughes, *Physical Chemistry*, 2nd ed., Pergamon Press, London, 1957.
3. G. N. Lewis, T. T. Nagel, and D. Lipkin, *J. Amer. Chem. Soc.*, **64**, 1774 (1942).
4. J. C. Turgeon and V. K. LaMer, *J. Amer. Chem. Soc.*, **74**, 5988 (1952).

A Saturation Effect

It is frequently found that the effect produced on a rate or equilibrium by a given substituent is not duplicated by a second identical substituent and the effect of a third is less still. This decreasing efficacy of substituents is referred to as a saturation effect. It reflects the increasingly steep potential gradient for polarization of the bonds by which the effect is transmitted to the reaction site. Care must be taken, however, when interpreting effects in this way that they are not due to increasing steric hindrance at the reaction site. In the example which follows, the ionization of the acids should not be very sensitive to steric factors because of the small size and mobility of the proton.

Experimental

Materials Required

Acetic acid	Trichloroacetic acid
Chloroacetic acid	Sodium hydroxide (carbonate free), 0.010 M pH meter
Dichloroacetic acid	

By the method detailed in Experiment 2, determine the dissociation constants of the four acids weighing out approximately 0.0002 mole of the acid for each titration.

Calculate the factors by which the acidities of acetic, monochloroacetic and dichloroacetic acids are enhanced by substitution of chlorine for hydrogen as

$$\frac{K_{CH_2ClCOOH}}{K_{CH_3COOH}}, \quad \frac{K_{CHCl_2COOH}}{K_{CH_2ClCOOH}} \quad \text{and} \quad \frac{K_{CCl_3COOH}}{K_{CHCl_2COOH}},$$

respectively, and explain your results according to the above discussion.

Questions

1. By reference to the literature determine whether saturation effects are evident in spectroscopic data. Suitable series of compounds to examine for changes in the C—H stretching frequency or the NMR chemical shift might be, CH_3Cl, CH_2Cl_2, $CHCl_3$ and CH_3NO_2, $CH_2(NO_2)_2$, $CH(NO_2)_3$.
2. The dissociation constants (pK_A) for a series of aliphatic amines are $MeNH_2$, 10.6: Me_2NH, 10.73: Me_3N, 9.75 (measured in water at 25°). Discuss the reasons for this sequence of values.

Measurement of
Resonance Energies

Two localized π-orbitals, each connecting a pair of atoms, when adjacent and able to adopt a coplanar configuration, will interact to form a new set of molecular π-orbitals embracing all four atoms which are thereby said to become conjugated, Figure 12–1. The driving force behind this rearrangement of electrons is provided by the release of energy since the total potential energy of the electrons in the conjugated orbitals is less than the sum of those in the localized orbitals [1, 2]. This energy which may be considered to be released is known as the delocalization or resonance energy, DE. In the example shown in Figure 12–1, the DE of 1,3-butadiene is given by:

$$DE = 2(2E_{\psi_0}) - (2E_{\psi_1} + 2E_{\psi_2}) \tag{1}$$

where the terms E_{ψ_1}, E_{ψ_2} refer to the energy of an electron in the 1st and 2nd bonding orbitals of butadiene and ψ_0 to the bonding π-orbital of ethylene.

A method for the determination of delocalization energies involves measuring the heat of formation or destruction of a conjugated π-system by a chemical reaction, compared to the value for a localized system. For instance, the heats of hydrogenation of localized and conjugated olefins may be analysed as follows:

$$\diagup\!\!\diagdown C\!=\!C\diagup\!\!\diagdown + H_2 \longrightarrow \diagup\!\!\diagdown \underset{H\ \ H}{C\!-\!C} \diagup\!\!\diagdown + \Delta H_1$$

$$\Delta H_1 = 2E_{C-H} - E_{H-H} - E_{C\pi C} \tag{2}$$

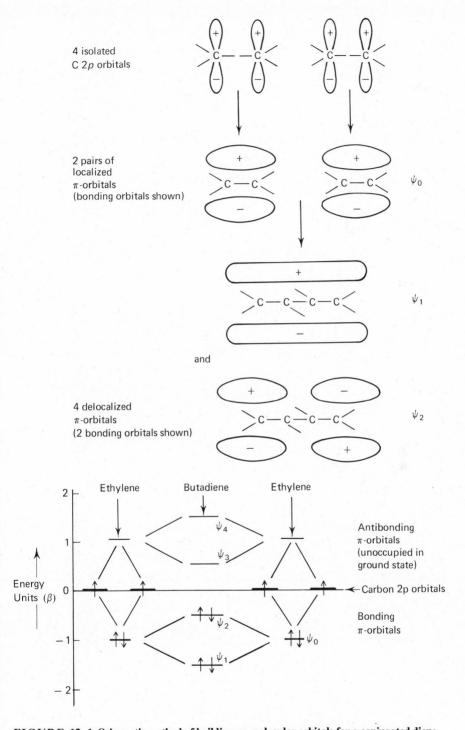

FIGURE 12–1 Schematic method of building up molecular orbitals for a conjugated diene.

$$\underset{/}{\overset{\backslash}{C}}=\underset{\backslash}{\overset{/}{C}} \quad + \; 2H_2 \quad \longrightarrow \quad \underset{H}{\overset{|}{-}}\underset{H}{\overset{|}{C}}-\underset{H}{\overset{|}{C}}-\underset{H}{\overset{|}{C}}-\underset{}{\overset{/}{C}}- \;+\; \Delta H_2$$

$$\Delta H_2 = (4E_{C-H} - 2E_{H-H} - 2E_{C\pi C}) - DE$$

$$= 2\Delta H_1 - DE \tag{3}$$

where E_{C-H}, E_{H-H}, $E_{C\pi C}$ are the dissociation energies of a C—H, H—H, and C—C—π bond respectively. Since ΔH_1 and ΔH_2 can be measured by calorimetry, DE can be calculated.

Some typical results obtained from hydrogenation experiments are given in Table 12–1.

TABLE 12–1. Heats of Hydrogenation of Some Simple and Conjugated Olefins[a]

Substrate	$-\Delta H$ (kcal/mole)	DE (kcal/mole)
$CH_2{=}CH_2$	32.8	—
$CH_3{-}CH{=}CH_2$	30.1	—
$C_5H_{11}CH{=}CH_2$	30.1	—
	Average $\Delta H_1 = 31.0$	
$CH_2{=}CH{-}CH{=}CH_2$	57.1 (2H$_2$)	4.9
	49.8 (3H$_2$)	43.2

[a] G. B. Kistiakowsky *et al.*, *J. Amer. Chem. Soc.*, **57**, 65, 876 (1935); **58**, 137, 146 (1936); **59**, 831 (1937).

The measurement of heats of hydrogenation offers considerable difficulties to the student because the reactions are heterogeneous—involve a solid catalyst, liquid olefin and gaseous hydrogen, and are somewhat slow. Experiment 12 utilizes the homogeneous reduction of the carbonyl group (I) by sodium borohydride [4].

$$\underset{/}{\overset{\backslash}{C}}{=}O + BH_4^- \xrightarrow{\text{ROH}} \left(\underset{H}{\overset{|}{-}}\overset{|}{C}{-}O \right)_4 B^- \xrightarrow{\text{MeOH}} \underset{H}{\overset{|}{-}}\overset{|}{C}{-}OH + (MeO)_3B$$

$$+ \; MeO^-$$

The reaction is considerably exothermic and the reduction is confined specifically to the carbonyl function, carbon-carbon double bonds being unaffected. Therefore, only the delocalization energy between the carbonyl group and the remainder of the π-system will be measured. The carbonyl group may be conjugated with an attached vinyl group (II) and to an even greater extent with an aromatic ring (III):

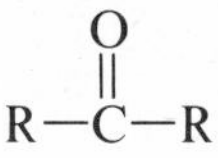

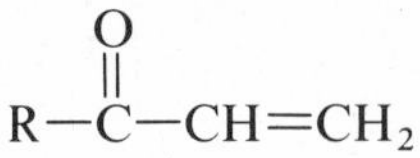

The diarylketone (IV) is interesting since the two aryl groups can become conjugated only through the carbonyl function (cross conjugation), and, if the rings can be coplanar without too much steric stress, should contain a considerable amount of delocalization energy.

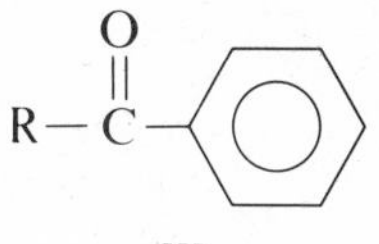

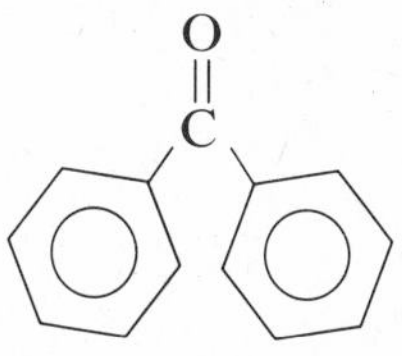

Experimental

Materials Required

Sodium borohydride	Benzophenone
Diethyl ketone	Dewar flask, 250 ml
Acetophenone	Thermometer, 0–50° graduated in 0.1°C
Vinylmethyl ketone	

All the solvents and substrates should be dried and free of traces of acid. Prepare a solution of 8.0 g sodium borohydride in 400 ml of 1:1 mixture of methanol and tetrahydrofuran; the latter solvent is added to suppress the methanolysis of borohydride which generates heat. Filter the solution and store in an ice bath until used.

Fit a clean dry Dewar flask of about 250 ml capacity with a thermometer, stirrer, and electrical heating coil as shown in Figure 12–2. Remove about 60 ml of borohydride solution, allow to warm to room temperature and pipet 50.0 ml into the Dewar flask. Commence taking readings of temperature with time. Because of the slow reaction between methanol and borohydride, a gradual increase in temperature is found at this stage. Introduce an accurately weighed sample of diethylketone through the funnel, wash it in with 2 ml of tetrahydrofuran and, by placing a rubber bulb over the funnel wash all the ketone into the flask. Give a few turns to the stirrer by hand to ensure good mixing and continue to take temperature readings until the mercury ceases or almost ceases to rise (about 5 min).

Plot temperature against time and measure the temperature rise, ΔT (Figure 12–3). Repeat the experiment using successively, methyl vinyl ketone, acetophenone and benzophenone.

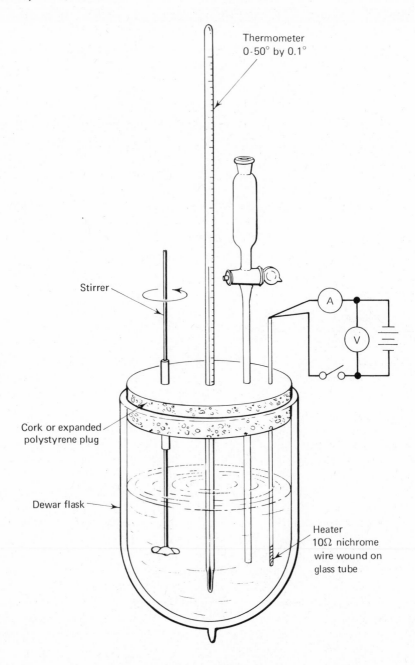

Thermometer
0-50° by 0.1°

Stirrer

Cork or expanded
polystyrene plug

Dewar flask

Heater
10Ω nichrome
wire wound on
glass tube

FIGURE 12–2 Apparatus for measuring heats of reduction by borohydride.

Measure the heat generated in the experiment by placing 53 ml 1 : 1 methanol-tetrahydrofuran at room temperature in the flask and applying a 6 volt potential to the heater leads, while stirring the liquid. Note the current and voltage of the heater and plot a temperature versus time graph to calibrate the calorimeter.

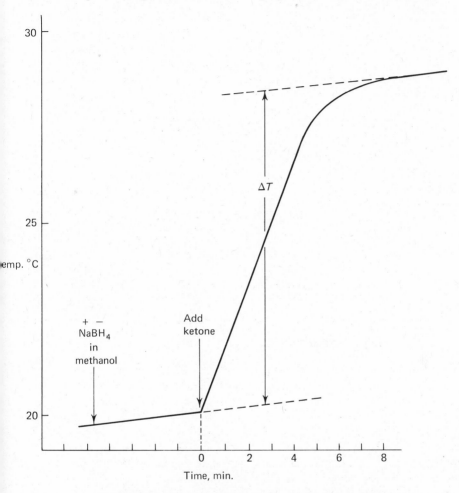

FIGURE 12–3 Typical graph for heat of reduction of a ketone.

Treatment of Results.   The heat, W, generated by the electric heater is given by:

$$W = \frac{Vi}{4.18} \text{ cal sec}^{-1} \tag{4}$$

where V = applied voltage, i = current.

Using the calibration curve, measure the heat generated by each of the reactions studied, ΔH where

$$\Delta H = \frac{Vit}{4.18} \tag{5}$$

t = number of seconds for heater to raise liquid the appropriate $\Delta T°$

Convert each value to kcal per mole of ketone. Compare the values of ΔH obtained and calculate DE for the conjugated ketones, using diethyl ketone as the unconjugated reference compound ($DE = 0$). Discuss the results obtained in terms of the size of the conjugated system in each case.

Extension of the Experiment.   In addition to the carbonyl compounds set out above, others such as acetone, cyclohexanone, butan-2,3-dione etc. may be included at the instructor's discretion.

Questions

1. Discuss the effects of the methyl group on the energy of an ethylenic double bond system as shown by the following heats of hydrogenation:

	ΔH (kcal mole^{-1})
$CH_2{=}CH_2$	-32.8
$CH_2{=}CHMe$	-30.1
$CH_2{=}CMe_2$	-28.4
$CHMe{=}CMe_2$	-26.9
$CMe_2{=}CMe_2$	-26.6

2. The heat of hydrogenation of allene,

$$CH_2{=}C{=}CH_2 + 2H_2 \longrightarrow CH_3{-}CH_2{-}CH_3;$$
$$\Delta H = -71.3 \text{ kcal mole}^{-1}$$

is high compared to that of butadiene (57.1 kcal mole^{-1}). Discuss the reasons for this difference.

3. From the following combustion data, calculate the total π-energy of benzene:

			kcal mole^{-1}
$C_6H_6 + \tfrac{15}{2}O_2$	$\longrightarrow$	$6CO_2 + 3H_2O;$	$\Delta H = -782.3$
$C \text{ (graphite)} + O_2$	$\longrightarrow$	$CO_2;$	$\Delta H = -94.0$
$H_2 + \tfrac{1}{2}O_2$	$\longrightarrow$	$H_2O;$	$\Delta H = -57.1$
$C \text{ (graphite)}$	$\longrightarrow$	$C \text{(gas)};$	$\Delta H = 170$
H_2	$\longrightarrow$	$2H;$	$\Delta H = 102$

Assume the energy of a C—C single bond to be 80 kcal mole^{-1} and a C—H bond to be 98 kcal.

References

1. L. Pauling, *The Nature of the Chemical Bond*, 2nd ed., Cornell Univ. Press, Ithaca, New York, 1945, p. 217.
2. A. Streitweiser, *Molecular Orbital Theory for Organic Chemists*, Interscience, New York, 1961, Chapter 2.
3. G. B. Kistiakovsky *et al.*, *J. Amer. Chem. Soc.*, **57**, 65, 976 (1935); **58**, 137, 146 (1936); **59**, 831 (1937).
4. N. G. Gaylord, *Reduction with Complex Metal Hydrides*, Interscience, New York, 1956, p. 283.

Measurement of Neighboring Group Participation

The departure from a carbon atom of a group X: together with its bonding electrons—nucleophilic displacement—may be brought about or facilitated by a nucleophilic substituent Y, located in the same molecule in such a way that it may approach the rear side of the reaction site [4]. This constitutes an internal S_N2 reaction and gives rise initially to a cyclic product, which may be isolable, or may be rapidly opened in a second nucleophilic displacement reaction, the substituent Y now being the leaving group:

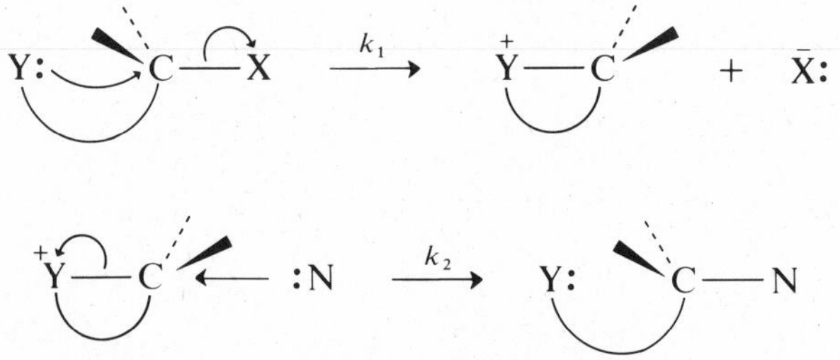

An example in which the intermediate is stable is the hydrolysis of a chlorohydrin to the glycol via an epoxide (Experiment 29):

Frequently however, the intermediate is not isolable since $k_2 \gg k_1$ but three criteria may be applied to detect the extent of participation of the neighboring group Y in the reaction.

(1). The ring-opening of the intermediate may proceed in a different direction to that of the cyclization giving rise to a recognizable rearrangement, the migration of Y,

An example of this behavior is found in the interaction of the phenyl group during acetolysis of the toluenesulfonate (I) leading to two products as a result of attack by acetic acid at both α- and β-carbons of the intermediate phenonium ion (II) [1]

(2). Since two Walden inversions are involved in an assisted displacement, the net stereochemistry will be retention of configuration. Retention is observed, for instance, in the hydrolysis of α-bromopropionate to lactate [2] through the nonisolable α-lactone (III):

D-α-bromopropionate   III   D-lactate

(3). The rate of the displacement is always increased by neighboring group participation and a properly conducted kinetic study can be the most sensitive technique for observing this phenomenon. If the neighboring group is only one or two bonds removed from the reaction center the observed change in rate is a composite effect of electronic and steric influences in addition to the neighboring group participation but with more remote groups, the latter only is important. Compare, for example, the relative rates of ethanolysis of a series of methoxyl-substituted alkyl *p*-bromobenzenesulfonates (ROBros) [3]:

$$ROBros + EtOH \longrightarrow ROEt + BrosOH$$

TABLE 13-1

R	Rel. Rate	Comments
$CH_3(CH_2)_2CH_2-$	1	Standard, no anchimeric assistance
$MeOCH_2CH_2-$	0.25	Electronic effect of MeO- group
$MeO(CH_2)_2CH_2-$	0.67	Electronic effect lessening
$MeO(CH_3)_3CH_2-$	20.4	Participation of MeO-, five-membered ring intermediate formed
$MeO(CH_2)_4CH_2-$	2.84	Less participation, six-membered ring formation less favorable
$MeO(CH_2)_5CH_2-$	1.19	Hardly any assistance from MeO-

The methoxyl group is in an optimum position to displace the brosylate ion when it is four carbon atoms removed from it, since the intermediate has a sterically favorable five-membered ring:

In a further example, the rates of acetolysis of the *anti-* and *syn*-norbornenyl toluenesulfonates, IV and V, respectively are in the ratio $10^7 : 1$! The *anti*-isomer receives assistance from the π-electrons situated at the rear side of the leaving group giving a "nonclassical" carbonium ion (VI) whereas no such participation is possible in the *syn*-isomer:

anti, IV   VI

Syn, V

These neighboring group effects have been named *anchimeric assistance* by Winstein and *synartetic acceleration* by Ingold, the latter term applying mainly to assistance imparted by σ-electron systems such as the phenonium system (II) while the former is of general application.

In Experiment 13 the relative rates of solvolysis of a series of chlorhydrins, $HO(CH_2)_n$—Cl, are measured

$$HO(CH_2)_nCl + H_2O \longrightarrow HO(CH_2)_nOH + HCl$$

and the stereochemistry of the deamination of an aminoacid [5] is examined:

$$\underset{\text{COOH}}{\overset{\displaystyle RCHNH_2}{|}} \longrightarrow \underset{\text{COOH}}{\overset{\displaystyle RCHN_2^+}{|}} \longrightarrow \underset{\text{COOH}}{\overset{\displaystyle RCHOH}{|}}$$

In both cases, the results are interpreted as examples of anchimeric assistance.

Experimental

Materials Required

n-Butyl chloride	Standard NaOH soln, 10^{-3} *M*
3-Chloropropan-1-ol	L-Alanine
4-Chlorobutan-1-ol	Polarimeter
5-Chloropentan-1-ol	

Note : If the chlorohydrins are not available, they may be readily prepared as follows:

3-CHLOROPROPAN-1-OL

$$2 HO(CH_2)_3OH + SOCl_2 \longrightarrow 2 HO(CH_2)_3Cl + SO_2 + HCl$$

To 76 g trimethylene glycol (1 mole, excess) in an equal volume of CCl_4 gradually add 20 g (0.16 mole) thionyl chloride in the fumehood mixing thoroughly after each addition. When the reaction has subsided, remove the solvent on the rotary evaporator and distill the residue collecting three fractions:
1. 1,3-dichloropropane bp 120–125° approx. 3–5 g
2. 3-chloropropan-1-ol bp 160–165° approx. 10 g
3. residue, trimethylene glycol bp 216°

Redistill the chlorohydrin taking the middle fraction for use.

4-CHLOROBUTAN-1-OL

This compound may be prepared in an analogous fashion from tetramethylene glycol (butan-1,4-diol), but the acid catalyzed cleavage of tetrahydrofuran is more convenient. Pass a rapid stream of hydrogen chloride gas, generated by the action of a mixture of sulfuric acid on sodium chloride in a gas generator, into a 100 ml flask half filled with tetrahydrofuran boiling under reflux. Arrange for a thermometer to dip below the surface of the boiling liquid and observe the temperature as 4-chloro-1-butanol accumulates according to the equation:

Continue passing HCl until the liquid temperature reaches 100–103° then distill the product collecting 4-chlorobutan-1-ol, bp 80–90°/15 mm.

5-CHLOROPENTAN-1-OL

Prepare this compound as for 3-chloropropan-1-ol, starting from pentamethylene glycol. Collect the following fractions;

1. 1,5-dichloropentane, bp 175–180°
2. 5-chloropentan-1-ol, bp 112°–12 mm
3. residue, pentamethylene glycol, bp 230–240°

KINETICS OF HYDROLYSIS OF THE CHLOROHYDRINS

Prepare a 2-liter beaker full of gently boiling water,[1] covered with a lid or copper rings with a hole in the center through which is clamped a stoppered

---

[1] Alternatively use a thermostat bath at about 80°, which is rather more convenient for the faster reactions.

flask of about 50 ml capacity immersed in the bath and containing 25.0 ml of water. In separate experiments, add to the flask 0.25 g of each chlorohydrin and of *n*-butyl chloride, starting a clock at the time of addition. Withdraw 1.0 ml aliquots by pipet at the following time intervals;

n-butyl chloride: 1, 5, 10, 15, 20, 30, 40, 50, 60 min
3-chloropropan-1-ol: 1, 5, 10, 15, 20, 30, 40, 50, 60 min
4-chlorobutan-1-ol: 0.5, 1, 1.5, 2, 2.5, 3, 4, 5 min[2]
5-chloropentan-1-ol: 1, 3, 6, 10, 15, 20, 25, 30 min

Drop each aliquot into 20 ml ice-water and titrate against 10^{-3} *M* sodium hydroxide solution as soon as possible, using phenolphthalein as indicator.

$$RCl + H_2O \longrightarrow ROH + HCl$$

Treatment of Results.   Plot for each reaction titer against time and draw a series of reaction progress curves through these points. Estimate the rate constants, which are first-order since the water is in large excess (pseudo unimolecular), either by estimating the half-lives of the reactions or using the first-order rate expression (Appendix A); titer is proportional to the extent of reaction, *x*.

Taking *n*-butyl chloride as "standard"—a reaction in which no neighboring group participation is possible—compare its rate of hydrolysis with those of the chlorohydrins and express the amount of anchimeric assistance observed as *A*, where,

$$A = \frac{k(\text{chlorohydrin})}{k(n\text{-BuCl})}$$

A value greater than unity indicates participation of the hydroxyl group in the displacement of chloride ion. Suggest structures for the transition states of each reaction, both assisted and nonassisted.

EXAMINATION OF THE REACTION PRODUCTS

Cool the remaining solution from the hydrolysis of 4-chlorobutan-1-ol and extract with two 10 ml portions of ether. Dry the extract over a little sodium sulfate, decant the solution and carefully remove most of the ether on a warm water bath. Examine the residue by gas liquid chromatography using a silicone column at room temperature and observe a peak eluted a little after that of ether, due to tetrahydrofuran, the product of this reaction. Check the identity of the compound by measuring the retention time of an authentic sample of tetrahydrofuran under the same conditions.

Observation of this cyclic ether is confirmatory evidence of the involvement of the hydroxyl group in the hydrolysis of 4-chloro-1-butanol.

---

[2] It is advisable to have a helper to note sample times when following this fast reaction.

The Deamination of L-Alanine

Dissolve 2.0 g L-alanine in 5 ml water and filter the solution if turbid. Add 5.0 g of sodium nitrite (a considerable excess) and cool the solution in ice. Add conc hydrochloric acid dropwise over a period of about 30 min until the solution is just acidic and allow it to stand at room temperature for a further 30 min or until the evolution of nitrogen ceases. Remove the water on the rotary evaporator keeping the temperature in the region of 30–35° and extract the solid residue with two portions of hot ethanol. Filter the extract and remove the ethanol on the rotary evaporator. Take up the syrupy residue in ether and filter any residual amino acid which is still present. Nonfilterable turbidity at this stage is probably a little water. Remove the ether by evaporation to obtain a sample of lactic acid as a viscous oil.

Weigh the product and dissolve it in the minimum of ethanol or water necessary for measuring its optical rotation, α, in a polarimeter. Express this as the specific rotation, $[\alpha]_D^t$ where

$$[\alpha]_D^t = \frac{100\,\alpha}{lc}$$

l = length of polarimeter tube (dm): c = weight of solute per 100 g solution.

Treatment of Results. The absolute configuration and sign of rotation of alanine and lactic acid are:

L-(+)-Alanine
dextrorotatory, $[\alpha]_{15}^D = +14.7°$
(In HCl)

L-(+)-Lactic Acid
dextrorotatory, $[\alpha]_{15}^D = +3.8°$

The experiment allows a distinction to be made between three possible mechanisms for this reaction; it may be assumed that diazotization involves no change of configuration.

1. Bimolecular substitution (S_N2) leading to *inversion*

L(+)-Alanine
diazonium ion

D(−)-Lactic Acid

2. Anchimerically assisted displacement leading to *retention*

3. Unimolecular dissociation of the diazonium ion leading to racemization with, perhaps, some inversion:

From the rotation of the lactic acid prepared above, determine which mechanism is operating.

Questions

1. Discuss *critically* the various criteria by which neighboring group participation may be recognized.
2. Which one of the following pairs of compounds would you expect to react faster towards solvolysis:

   a. $MeSCH_2CH_2$—OTos   or $MeOCH_2CH_2$—OTos

   b. $MeNH(CH_2)_4$—OTos   or $PhNH(CH_2)_4$—OTos

   c. ICH_2CH_2—OTos   or $BrCH_2CH_2$—OTos

   d.

e.

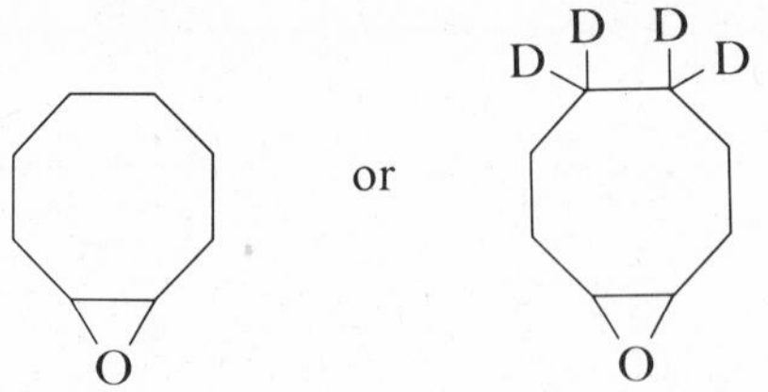

or

f.

or

(treatment with H_2SO_4)

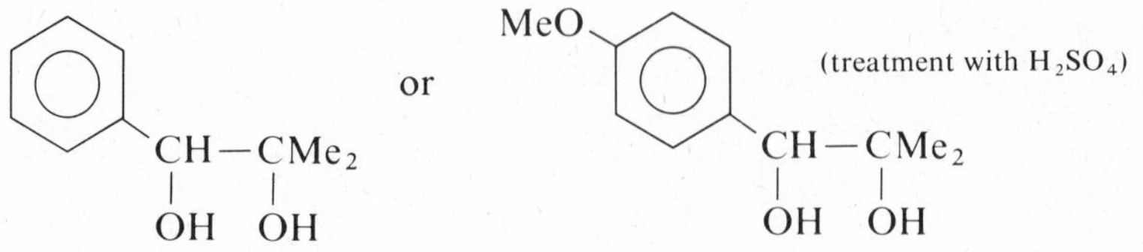

3. Draw in as full detail as possible the electronic arrangement of the intermediate species involved in phenyl participation (the *phenonium ion*). What sort of stability would you expect it to have? Would you expect an anion of similar structure to be more or less stable? If more stable, give examples of rearrangements in which its existence might be postulated.

References

1. D. J. Cram, *J. Amer. Chem. Soc.*, **71**, 3875 (1949); **74**, 2159 (1952).

2. W. A. Cowdrey, E. D. Hughes, and C. K. Ingold, *J. Chem. Soc.*, 1208 (1937).

3. S. Winstein, E. Allred, R. Heck, and R. Glick, *Tetrahedron* **3**, 1 (1958).

4. B. Capon, *Quart. Revs.*, **18**, 45 (1964).

5. P. Brewster, E. D. Hughes, C. K. Ingold, and P. A. D. S. Rao, *Nature*, **166**, 178, 179 (1950).

Structure Determination
Using Dipole Moments

EXPERIMENT 14

Because of electronegativity differences, covalent bonds between dissimilar atoms are polarized, that is, the centers of gravity of positive and negative charge are not coincident (Figure 14–1a). If the magnitude of the charges of opposite sign are denoted by q, and distance of separation d, the bond dipole moment μ_{bond} is given by

$$\mu_{bond} = q\mathbf{d} \qquad (1)$$

The net dipole moment μ of a molecule is given by the vector sum of the individual bond dipoles (Figure 14–1b), and the molecule will behave as a dipole

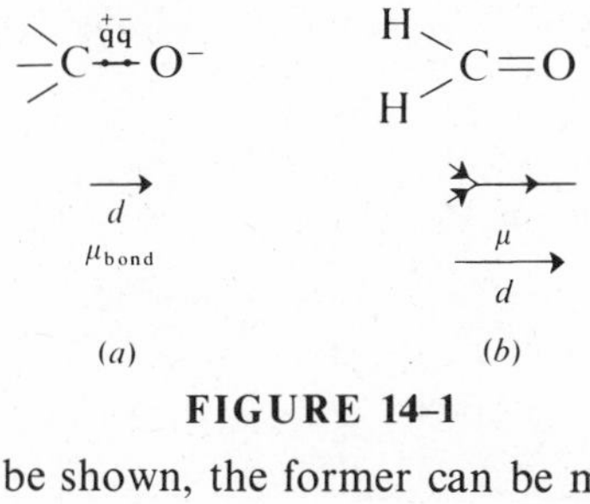

(a)　　　　(b)

FIGURE 14–1

if $\mu > 0$. Since, as will be shown, the former can be measured experimentally and the latter are approximately constant for each bond type, it is clear that structural information can be inferred from a knowledge of the dipole moment of a compound. Some examples are summarized in Figure 14–2.

83

$$O=C=O$$

$\mu = 0$
linear

$\mu = 1.85$
nonlinear

$\mu = 1.87$

$\mu = 1.54$

$\mu = 1.02$

$\mu = 0$

$\mu = 1.71$

$\mu = 1.97$

NO_2

—OMe

ortho $\mu = 4.83$
meta $\mu = 4.55$
para $\mu = 5.26$

CH_2

$\mu = 2.7$

$\mu \approx 1.04$

FIGURE 14–2

The experimental determination of dipole moments, which stems largely from the work of P. Debye, involves only the measurement of dielectric constant and density. The derivation of the necessary relationships is given in the following section.

Measurement of Dipole Moment

If an electric field, **E**, is applied to an assembly of electric dipoles, the dipoles tend to align themselves with the field:

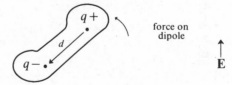

force on dipole

E

The macroscopic manifestation of this effect is the increase in capacitance of a capacitor when the polar substance is placed between its plates, since the partial alignment of the molecules stores energy in the system. The increase in capacitance (dielectric constant) then, is related to the dipole moment of a single molecule. This would seem to indicate that symmetric substances with zero dipole moment (Table 14–1) should not increase the capacitance (unit dielectric constant) but this is not found to be the case and another effect must also be considered namely polarization. Any molecule, when placed in an electric field **E** at any orientation, suffers a distortion or polarization of its electrons in the direction of the field and the generation of an induced dipole, independent of the *permanent dipole* discussed above. The *electric polarization* **P** is defined as the dipole moment per unit volume. Another useful vector field in the theory of electrostatics is the dielectric displacement **D** where,

$$\mathbf{D} = \mathbf{E} + 4\pi\mathbf{P} \tag{2}$$

D is connected with an enhancement of the applied electric field in a material medium.[1]

In an isotropic medium, **D**, **E** and **P** are all parallel; the dielectric constant, ε, of the medium is then defined as

$$\mathbf{D} = \varepsilon\mathbf{E} \tag{3}$$

or the factor by which the applied field is enhanced in the medium, relative to a vacuum.

It follows immediately that **P** and **E** are related according to Eq. (4):

$$\mathbf{P} = \frac{\varepsilon - 1}{4\pi}\mathbf{E} \tag{4}$$

When an electric field is applied to a material consisting of polar molecules, the permanent molecular dipoles will tend to align themselves with the field. In addition, a dipole moment will be induced in each molecule because the positive charges are displaced in the field direction and the negative charges in the opposite direction. The local electric field **E'** felt by a molecule consists of the applied field **E** plus that due to neighboring molecular dipoles. It can be shown[2] that **E'** is related to **E** and the polarization, **P** by Eq. (5),

$$\mathbf{E'} = \mathbf{E} + \frac{4\pi}{3}\mathbf{P} \tag{5}$$

If the density of polar molecules is low (gaseous sample), the *total* dipole moment for a molecule, **p**, is given by Eq. (6):

$$\mathbf{p} = \left(\frac{\alpha + \mu^2}{3kT}\right) \cdot \mathbf{E'} \tag{6}$$

[1] Gaussian (cgs) units are used throughout in this discussion.
[2] See H. A. Lorentz, *The Theory of Electrons*, Dover Press, New York, (1952), p. 305—Note 54.

where T is the absolute temperature, k is the Boltzmann constant, α is the molecular polarizability, responsible for the induced dipole moment, and μ is the permanent dipole moment, a constant for the molecule (at higher concentrations intermolecular interactions cause deviations from this simple picture).

$$\text{Now} \quad \mathbf{P} = N\mathbf{p}$$

where N is the number of molecules per unit volume, hence, it follows that:

$$\mathbf{P} = \frac{N[\alpha + (\mu^2/3kT)]}{1 - (4\pi/3)N[\alpha + (\mu^2/3kT)]} \cdot \mathbf{E} \tag{7}$$

and from Eqs. (4) and (7) one obtains:

$$\frac{4\pi}{3}N\left[\alpha + \frac{\mu^2}{3kT}\right] = \frac{\varepsilon - 1}{\varepsilon + 2} \tag{8}$$

N is obtainable in terms of Avagadro's number, N_0, the molecular weight, M, and the density of the material, ρ, thus,

$$N = \frac{\rho N_0}{M} \tag{9}$$

hence,

$$N = \frac{4\pi}{3}N_0\left(\alpha + \frac{\mu^2}{3kT}\right) = \frac{M}{\rho} \cdot \frac{\varepsilon - 1}{\varepsilon + 2} \tag{10}$$

This quality is sometimes referred to as the *molar polarizability*, P, something of a misnomer since it contains both induced and permanent dipole terms.

$$P = \frac{4\pi}{3}N_0\left(\alpha + \frac{\mu^2}{3kT}\right) \tag{11}$$

Most dipole moment determinations are carried out not in the gaseous phase but in dilute solution in a nonpolar solvent (i.e., $\mu_{\text{solvent}} = 0$). The derivation of the polarization of the solution P_s is obtained in a method analogous to the one previously outlined but contains terms for the polarizability of the solvent. Thus

$$P_s = \frac{N_1\alpha_1 + N_2[\alpha_2 + (\mu_2^2/3kT)]}{1 - (4\pi/3)N_1\alpha_1 - (4\pi/3)N_2[\alpha_2 + (\mu_2^2/3kT)]} \tag{12}$$

where subscript s refers to solution, 1 refers to solvent, and 2 refers to solute.

It will be seen that Eq. (12) is simply the summation of induced and permanent dipole contributions of the solute and induced dipole contribution of solvent. It follows that

$$\frac{4\pi}{3}N_1\alpha_1 + \frac{4\pi}{3}N_2\left(\alpha_2 + \frac{\mu_2^2}{3kT}\right) = \frac{\varepsilon_s - 1}{\varepsilon_s + 2} \tag{13}$$

If X_1 and X_2 are the mole fractions of solvent and solute respectively, the number, N_1, of solvent molecules per unit volume and the number, N_2, of solute molecules per unit volume are related to the total number, N_s, of molecules per unit volume:

$$N_1 = X_1 N_s \qquad N_2 = X_2 N_s \tag{14}$$

and if M_s is the average molecular weight of the solution,

$$M_s = X_1 M_1 + X_2 M_2$$

then

$$N_s = \frac{\rho_s N_0}{M_s} \quad \text{[see Eq. (9)]} \tag{15}$$

$$N_s = \frac{\rho_s N_0}{X_1 M_1 + X_2 M_2} \tag{16}$$

Now defining the molar polarizabilities of solvent and solute as before (Eqs. (11) and (12)), we have:

$$X_1 P_1 + X_2 P_2 = P_s = \frac{X_1 M_1 + X_2 M_2}{\rho_s} \cdot \frac{\varepsilon_s - 1}{\varepsilon_s + 2} \tag{17}$$

The molar polarizability P_2 of the solute can be written

$$P_2 = \frac{P_s - X_1 P_1}{X_2} \tag{18}$$

and for a sufficiently dilute solution, dielectric constant and density can be assumed to vary linearly with mole fraction:

$$\varepsilon_s = \varepsilon_1 + a X_2$$

$$\rho_s = \rho_1 + b X_2 \tag{19}$$

where the constants a and b are to be determined experimentally. Then combining Eqs. (11), (17), (18), and (19) we have:

$$P_2 = \frac{1}{X_2} \frac{(1 - X_2)M_1 + X_2 M_2}{\rho_1 + b X_2} \cdot \frac{\varepsilon_1 + a X_2 - 1}{\varepsilon_1 + a X_2 + 2} - (1 - X_2) \frac{M_1}{\rho} \cdot \frac{\varepsilon_1 - 1}{\varepsilon_1 + 2} \tag{20}$$

If $X_2 \to 0$, the limiting value

$$P_2^0 \doteq \frac{1}{\rho_1} \left(M_2 - \frac{M_1}{\rho_1} b \right) \frac{\varepsilon_1 - 1}{\varepsilon_1 + 2} + \frac{3 M_1 a}{(\varepsilon_1 + 2)^2 \rho_1} \tag{21}$$

is obtained by application of L'Hôpital's Rule. Also, from Eq. (11):

$$P_2^0 = \left(\frac{4\pi}{3} N_0 \alpha_2 + \frac{4\pi}{2} N_0 \right) \left(\frac{\mu_2^2}{3kT} \right) \tag{22}$$

The permanent molecular dipole moment of the solute, μ_2, which is the value sought can now be calculated by equating Eqs. (21) and (22). One term, however, must be found independently, namely α_2, the polarizability of the solute. This may be calculated from a consideration of the interaction of light with the molecule. The passage of light through a material medium is slowed up on account of interactions between the electric vector of the light wave (behaving like a very high frequency electric field) and the electrons of the molecule which are accordingly polarized at the same frequency. Since this frequency is so high (10^{15} sec^{-1}), the permanent dipoles cannot align themselves rapidly enough on account of the inertia of the molecules so their effect is cancelled and the effect on the light beam is due to polarizability only. Refractive index is a measure of the velocity of light through the medium relative to that *in vacuo* and it is found that at "optical" frequencies:

$$\varepsilon_2 = n_2^2 \qquad (23)$$

where n = refractive index
whence

$$\frac{4\pi}{3} N_0 \alpha_2 = \frac{n_2^2 - 1}{n_2^2 + 2} \qquad (24)$$

(from Eqs. (23) and (8) $\mu = 0$)

Assuming that α_2 is independent of frequency—i.e., is the same at "optical" frequencies as at that at which the dielectric constants are determined—we obtain from Eqs. (21), (22), and (24),

$$\mu_2^2 = \frac{9kT}{4\pi N_0} \left\{ \frac{1}{\rho_1} \left(M_2 - \frac{M_1}{\rho_1} b \right) \left(\frac{\varepsilon_1 - 1}{\varepsilon_1 + 2} + \frac{3M_1 a}{(\varepsilon_1 + 2)^2 \rho_1} - \frac{M_2}{\rho_2} \right) \left(\frac{n_2^2 - 1}{n_2^2 + 2} \right) \right\} \qquad (25)$$

If cgs units are strictly adhered to,

$$\mu_2 = 0.0128 \sqrt{T \left\{ \frac{1}{\rho_1} \left(M_2 - \frac{M_1}{\rho_1} b \right) \left(\frac{\varepsilon_1 - 1}{\varepsilon_1 + 2} + \frac{3M_1 a}{(\varepsilon_1 + 2)^2 \rho_1} - \frac{M_2}{\rho_2} \right) \left(\frac{n_2^2 - 1}{n_2^2 + 2} \right) \right\}}$$

debyes

$$\qquad (26)$$

where 1 debye = 10^{-18} esu.

For comparison, a dipole consisting of two charges each with the magnitude of the electronic charge, separated by 1 Å would have a dipole moment of 4.80 debyes. It can be seen that one requires to measure only a and b: the constants in Eq. (26) may be obtained from tables. The constant a is given as the slope of the (linear) plot of dielectric constant of solution versus concentration. The dielectric constant, ε, of a medium, is given by

$$\varepsilon = \frac{C_\varepsilon}{C_1} \qquad (27)$$

where C_1 is the capacitance of a capacitor with air between its plates (as dielectric) and C_ε the capacitance of the same capacitor with the given medium as dielectric. Capacitances are measured with a high frequency bridge [1, 2]. The constant b is the slope of the (linear) plot of density of solution versus concentration.

Experimental

Materials Required

o-Dichlorobenzene	Benzene, pure
m-Dichlorobenzene	Oscillometer or capacitance bridge (Appendix B)
p-Dichlorobenzene	

The dielectric constant measurements consist in measuring the capacitance by means of an accurate bridge working at a frequency of a few kc/sec, of a capacitor whose dielectric may be varied. Some suggested designs for capacitance cells are given in ref [2].

Calibrate the oscillometer by measuring the values obtained with standard liquids as set out in Table 14–1, applying Eq. (27). If the instrument gives a linear response, about four points is sufficient for calibration; more are desirable if nonlinear.

TABLE 14–1. Dielectric Constants of Standard Liquids

	ε	$T°C$
Cyclohexane	2.015	20
Carbon tetrachloride	2.238	20
Benzene	2.284	20
Diethyl ether	4.335	20
Chloroform	4.806	20
Chlorobenzene	5.708	20
1,2-Dichloroethane	10.65	20

TABLE 14–2. Densities of Dichlorobenzenes in Benzene, ρ_{20}

M	gml^{-1}
0.01	0.8848
0.02	0.8898
0.03	0.8949
0.04	0.9004

Determine the dielectric constants of solutions of the three dichlorobenzenes in benzene at concentrations 0.01, 0.02, 0.03, 0.04 M. The corresponding densities for these solutions are given in Table 14–2. Plot ε and ρ against concentration and obtain the constants a and b from Eq. (19). Insert these values into Eq. (26) using the following constants to calculate the dipole moment of each isomer;

Density of benzene $= 0.8790$ gml$^{-1}(20°C)$
Dielectric constant of benzene $= 2.284$ (20)
Refractive index of o-dichlorobenzene $= 1.5518$
$\qquad\qquad\qquad\quad$ m-dichlorobenzene $= 1.5457$
$\qquad\qquad\qquad\quad$ p-dichlorobenzene $= 1.5210$
Density of o-dichlorobenzene $= 1.3048$ gml^{-1}
$\qquad\quad$ m-dichlorobenzene $= 1.2880$
$\qquad\quad$ p-dichlorobenzene $= 1.4581$

By treating the results for the o- and m-isomers as the resultants of two vectors at 60° and 120° respectively, obtain the value for the bond moment of the chloro group.

Questions

1. The dipole moments of some substituted benzenes, Ph-X, are as follows;

X	H	CH$_3$	Br	I	Cl	NO$_2$
$\mu(D)$	O	$+0.4$	-1.52	-1.3	-1.55	-3.95

($+$ and $-$ indicate the direction of the dipole, towards and away from the ring respectively.)
Calculate the dipole moments of the following compounds.

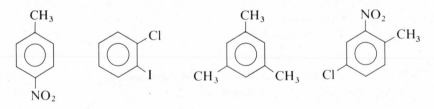

2. If the dipole moment of

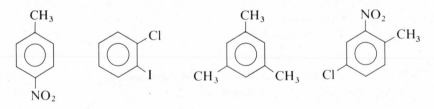

is 1.65 D, what is that of

?

3. The electronegativities of carbon, hydrogen and nitrogen are 2.5, 2.1 and 3.0 respectively on the Pauling scale. Would you expect the dipole moments of the series, NH_3, NH_2Me, $NHMe_2$, NMe_3, to increase or decrease? Check your answer from the literature.

References

1. C. P. Smyth, *Techniques of Organic Chemistry Vol 1, Part 3.*, Ed. A. Weissberger, Interscience, New York, 1960; L. E. Sutton, *Determination of Organic Structures by Physical Methods Part I*, Ed. E. A. Braude and F. C. Nachod, Academic Press, New York, 1953; J. W. Smith, *Electric Dipole Moments*, Butterworth, London, 1955.

2. P. Bender, *J. Chem. Ed.*, **23**, 179 (1946).

The Boltzmann
Distribution Law

EXPERIMENT 15

The behavior of a large aggregate of molecules, ie., an ordinary macroscopic sample, may be examined statistically. For example, a sample of a gas at constant temperature (above absolute zero) and pressure contains molecules moving with a range of velocities. We cannot tell at what speed a given molecule is moving and indeed this will change at every collision, but we can measure and predict the average speed and the distribution of speeds of the molecules, values which remain constant with time under these conditions. In this example, the distribution of speeds and hence energies of the molecules is given by the Maxwell Distribution Law which is applicable when the particles can have energies occurring over a continuous range of values. A slightly different distribution law applies when the energy states are discontinuous—restricted by quantization. In this case, the Boltzmann Distribution Law is applicable and may be expressed as follows:

$$\frac{n_I}{n_{II}} = e^{-(\varepsilon_I - \varepsilon_{II})/kT}$$

where n_I and n_{II} are numbers of molecules in energy states associated with energies ε_I and ε_{II} respectively, k is the Boltzmann Constant (the gas constant per single molecule), and T, the absolute temperature.

Experimental

Materials Required

Cyclohexane Infrared spectrophotometer
Carbon tetrachloride

92

Run the infrared spectrum of cyclohexane (or any saturated hydrocarbon) either as a thin film of pure liquid or in dilute solution in carbon tetrachloride. Identify the C—H stretching band [the only strong band which occurs above 2000 cm^{-1} (below 5 microns)] and measure the energy of this transition which corresponds to excitation of a C—H bond from the ground to first excited vibrational state.

Calculate from the Boltzmann Law the proportion of molecules which exist in the excited state (1) at room temperature and (2) at 500°C.

Run the infrared spectrum of carbon tetrachloride in dilute solution in cyclohexane. Identify the C—Cl stretching band (the strong band occurring at the low energy end of the spectrum) and measure its energy. Calculate the proportion of molecules in equilibrium in the excited state at room temperature.

Calculate the proportions of molecules

a. In ground and excited spin states of the unpaired electron of a radical in a magnetic field of 3.6 kilogauss (see Experiment 24).
b. In ground and excited *electronic* states of benzene ($\lambda_{max} = 250 \ m\mu$).

The following relationships will be of value.

$$k = 1.38 \times 10^{-16} \text{ ergs mole}^{-1} = 1.99 \text{ cal deg}^{-1} \text{ mole}^{-1}$$

$$\varepsilon = h\nu = \frac{hc}{\lambda} = hc\bar{\nu} \text{ ergs}$$

$$= \frac{hc}{\lambda J} = \frac{hc\bar{\nu}}{J} \text{cal}$$

$$= \frac{hcN_0}{\lambda J} = \frac{hc\bar{\nu}N_0}{J}$$

where

$h = $ Planck's constant $= 6.625 \times 10^{-27}$ erg sec
$c = $ velocity of light $= 3 \times 10^{10}$ cms sec^{-1}
$\lambda = $ wavelength of light (cm)
$\bar{\nu} = $ wavenumber of light (cm^{-1})
$\nu = $ frequency of light (sec^{-1})
$J = $ mechanical equivalent of heat $= 4.2 \times 10^7$ ergs cal^{-1}
$N_0 = $ Avogadro's number $= 6.023 \times 10^{23}$ mole^{-1}

Questions

1. a. Derive an expression for the equilibrium constant for a tautomeric pair of compounds in terms of the difference in energy between the tautomers.
   b. Acetylacetone, $CH_3COCH_2COCH_3$, exists as 80% enol, 20% keto forms; Calculate their difference in energy.

c. If the following bond energies are applicable, what is the energy of the hydrogen bond which stabilises the enol form?

$$C-C \qquad 80 \text{ kcal mole}^{-1}$$
$$C=C \qquad 140$$
$$C-H \qquad 98$$
$$C-O \qquad 78$$
$$C=O \qquad 170$$
$$O-H \qquad 110$$

Spectroscopic Measurements

PART II

Measurement of Substituent Effects by Infrared Spectroscopy

The elastic properties of a covalent bond depend on the distribution of electrons in the bond and so will be dependent on substituents which alter the electron density by any means. When a covalent bond is excited to a higher vibrational state a certain amount of charge separation occurs if the vibration is an infrared-active one. Withdrawal of electrons from the bond by neighboring substituents will make it harder for such charge separation to occur and more energy will be needed to raise the bond to a higher vibrational level. Thus, the infrared band corresponding to this transition will fall at higher wavenumber (shorter wavelength):

$$\overset{\longleftrightarrow}{\bar{v}}$$

$$
\begin{array}{c}
\text{C--X} \\
| \\
\text{H}
\end{array}
\qquad
\begin{array}{c}
\text{C--X} \\
\downarrow \\
\text{Y}
\end{array}
$$

$$\bar{v}' > \bar{v}$$

The extent of this spectral shift should give a measure of the electronic influence of the substituent. In the following experiment, the effect of substituents, Y, on the stretching frequency of the carbonyl group is measured:

$$
\begin{array}{c}
\text{--C=O} \\
| \\
\text{Y}
\end{array}
$$

The mechanism by which these electronic interactions are transmitted may be a combination of inductive (polarization of the σ-bonds) and mesomeric effects (overlap of neighboring orbitals) since conjugation between unshared pairs on Y and the carbonyl π-electrons can occur (Figure 16–1). Effects due to the bulk of the substituent should be small, though hydrogen-bonding may cause considerable discrepancies.

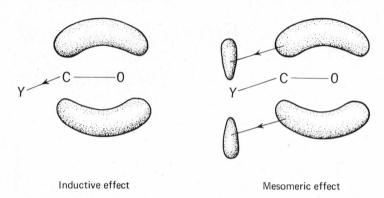

Inductive effect   Mesomeric effect

FIGURE 16–1 Mechanisms of electron-displacement. The direction of polarization depends on the nature of Y.

Experimental

Materials Required[1]

Acetaldehyde	Ethyl acetate
Acetone	Acetophenone
Methyl ethyl ketone	Acetamide
Methyl isopropyl ketone	Acetic acid
Methyl *tert*-butyl ketone	Infrared spectrophotometer
Acetyl chloride	

Measure as accurately as possible the position of maximum absorption of the carbonyl band in the neighborhood of 1700 cm^{-1} (6μ), using 5% solutions of each compound in carbon tetrachloride and a 0.1 mm fixed path cell.

Determine $\Delta\bar{\nu}$ for each substituent Y, which is defined as the spectral shift relative to acetaldehyde (Y=H).

Investigate the correlation between values of $\Delta\nu$ and the corresponding σ-values for each substituent (Experiment 2) and the Taft σ^* values, which are appropriate to aliphatic systems (see Appendix D).

[1] The above compounds are suggested as suitable: any may be omitted or other compounds CH$_3$CO—Y added at the discretion of the instructor.

Question

1. The energy of the C—H stretching frequency increases in the order —CH_3 < Ar—H < —C≡C—H. Suggest an explanation.

References

1. D. G. O'Sullivan and P. W. Sadler, *J. Chem. Soc.*, 4144 (1957).
2. L. J. Bellamy and R. L. Williams, *J. Chem. Soc.*, 2463 (1958).

Hydrogen Bonding

As far back as 1920, Latimer and Rodebush [1] proposed that many of the properties of water could be explained by assuming the liquid to be composed of large aggregates of molecules in a state of continual interchange. They suggested that a hydrogen atom may be chemically held to two saturated oxygen atoms and constitute a weak bond between them [2]:

$$-H\cdots\ddot{O}-H \qquad \ddot{O}-H \;\rightleftharpoons\; \ddot{O}-H\cdots\ddot{O}-H$$

It is now recognized that a hydrogen atom bound covalently to fluorine, oxygen or, to a lesser extent, nitrogen experiences a weak attractive force towards another electronegative atom in its vicinity. This effect is known as a *hydrogen bond* or *hydrogen bridge* and its strength is usually of the order 1 to 6 kcal mole^{-1} (compare covalent bonds, between 40 and 100 kcal mole), and length, somewhat variable, between 1.2–1.5 Å. The interaction is represented by a dotted line between donor and acceptor (hydrogen) in the examples which are shown in Table 17–1. Experiment 17 explores various aspects of hydrogen bonding.

TABLE 17–1. Some Examples of Hydrogen Bonding

1. Structure of Ice and Water

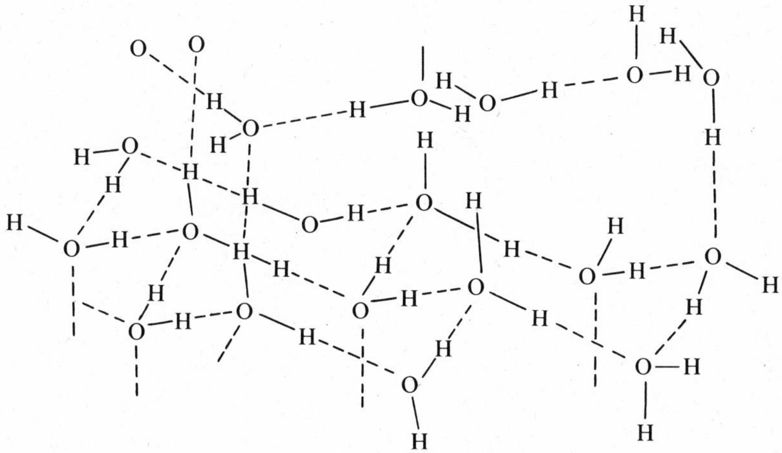

2. Bifluoride ion $K^+(F\cdots H\cdots F)^-$

3. *o*-Nitrophenol

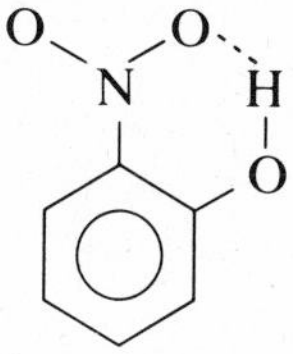

4. Carboxylic acid dimer

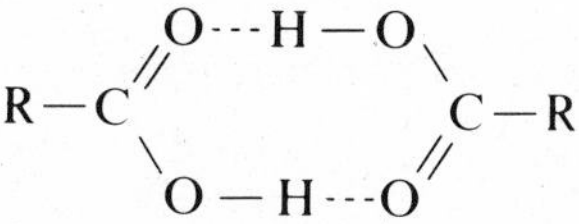

5. Ethyl acetoacetate enol

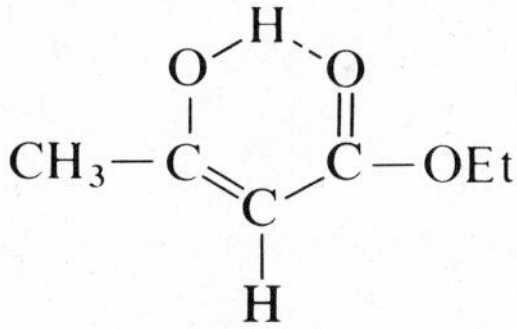

TABLE 17–1. (Continued)

6. Double-stranded nucleic acids
   (e.g. D.N.A.)

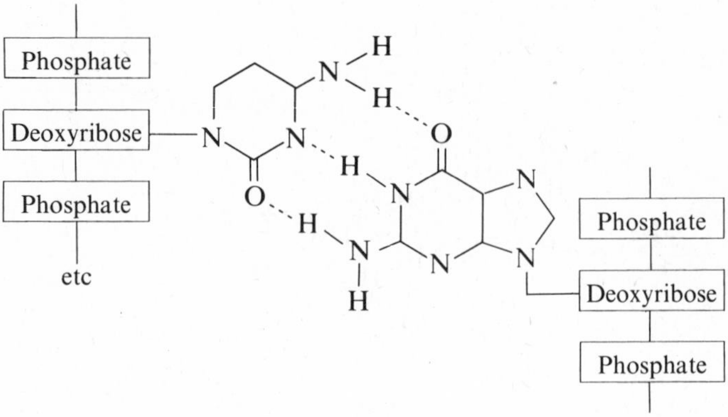

7. Indigo

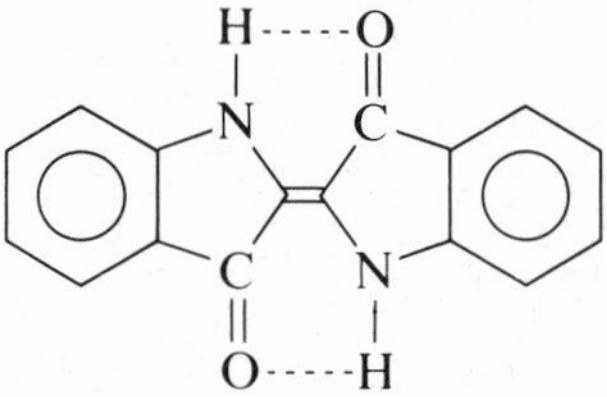

Hydrogen Bonding and Proton Magnetic Resonance

One of the most sensitive and informative techniques for detecting hydrogen bonding is nuclear magnetic resonance (Experiment 22). The condition under which resonance occurs depends upon the electron density surrounding the proton. As this increases, the surrounding electrons set up a magnetic field in opposition to the applied field partly cancelling out the latter which must then be increased in order to bring the nucleus back into resonance. It is found that hydrogen bonding causes a proton to resonate at a lower applied field and indicates that a reduction of electron density ("deshielding") (Figure 17–1b) must occur. This is in reasonable accordance with the fact that hydrogen bonding only occurs with highly electronegative atoms such as oxygen and fluorine.

The variation of the resonance condition for the hydroxyl proton in ethanol provides a striking illustration of the electronic consequences of hydrogen bonding.

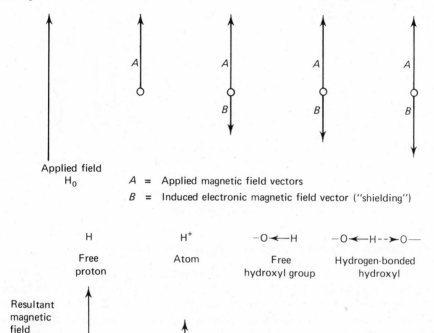

Applied field
H_0

A = Applied magnetic field vectors
B = Induced electronic magnetic field vector ("shielding")

H	H⁺	—O◄—H	—O◄—H--►O—
Free proton	Atom	Free hydroxyl group	Hydrogen-bonded hydroxyl

Resultant
magnetic
field
experienced
by proton

FIGURE 17–1

Experimental

Materials required

Ethanol, pure, and as 5% solutions in   Nuclear magnetic resonance
benzene, chloroform, cyclohexane, di-   spectrometer (Appendix B)
oxan, nitromethane[1]

Run the NMR spectra of ethanol and of its solutions in various solvents. Identify the signals due to the solvent, and those due to the methyl, methylene and hydroxyl protons of ethanol[2]. Record the chemical shifts of the latter, relative to the reference compound tetramethylsilane, and arrange the solvents in apparent order of increasing hydrogen bonding property.

[1] Other solvents may be added or substituted at the discretion of the instructor; diethyl ether is not recommended as the hydroxyl and methylene protons coincide.

[2] The hydroxyl signal is usually a singlet since splitting by the methylene group is not observed owing to rapid exchange and averaging of the environmental field. If a triplet is observed for the hydroxyl proton (such as when the ethanol is very pure and free of acid and base), the addition of a trace of acid or base will cause it to collapse to a singlet and facilitate identification.

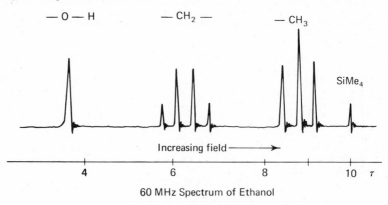

60 MHz Spectrum of Ethanol

FIGURE 17–2

Examination of Hydrogen Bonding by Infrared Spectroscopy

The participation of a proton in a hydrogen bond is accompanied by stretching and weakening the formal covalent bond with which the proton is bound to the rest of the molecule, X. The vibrational frequency of the X—H bond is thereby lowered and the corresponding infrared absorption band moves to a longer wavelength (lower wavenumber). Moreover the continual exchange of hydrogen-bonded partners and the fact that the hydrogen bond is not as rigidly uniform energetically speaking, as a normal covalent bond combine to make this infrared band much broader than that due to a nonhydrogen-bonded group. For less obvious reasons the intensity or extinction coefficient of the band increases markedly with hydrogen bonding, Figure 17–2. The bathychromic shift, band broadening and increase in intensity may be used as criteria to detect and estimate the presence and extent of hydrogen bonding. The influence of the following parameters will be examined:

Concentration [4].   An increase in concentration will cause an increase in the extent of intermolecular hydrogen bonding, because of the closer average proximity of the molecules, but will not greatly affect intramolecular hydrogen bonding. Increasing concentration will tend to drive the equilibrium to the right,

$$n\text{ROH} \quad \rightleftharpoons \quad (\text{ROH})_n \qquad (1)$$

Temperature.   An increase in temperature and hence of molecular motions will tend to break up the rather weak hydrogen bonds and drive the equilibrium in Eq. (1) to the left.

Solvent.   Solvents containing electronegative atoms (usually oxygen) will themselves form hydrogen bonds with suitable protons. Hydrogen bonding to solvents such as ethers, alcohols, ketones etc. will compete with both inter- and intramolecular hydrogen bonding.

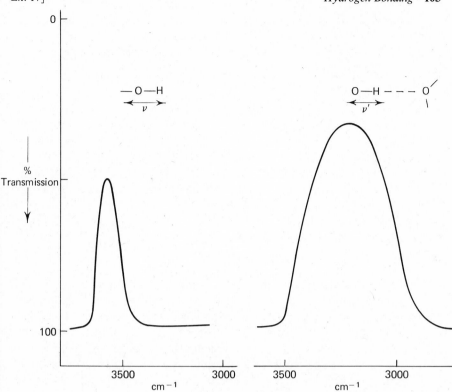

FIGURE 17–3 Effect of hydrogen-bonding on infrared spectra.

Substituents.   The formation of a hydrogen bond might conceivably take place with electron donation from the proton to the electronegative atom or in the reverse direction. The effects of adding electron-donating or -withdrawing substituents to one component of the hydrogen-bonded system should permit a distinction to be made between these two possibilities. The effect of a substituent on the hydrogen bond formed between two identical molecules however, should cancel:

Experimental

Materials Required

p-Chlorophenol	Carbon tetrachloride
p-Cresol	Infrared spectrophotometer of moderate or

p-Hydroxyanisole
o-Nitrophenol
Benzyl alcohol
Phenol[1]

good resolution. It is advantageous to expand the horizontal scale between 3000–5000 cm^{-1} (3.3–2.0 μ) to facilitate measurement.

CONCENTRATION EFFECTS

Measure the infrared spectrum between 3000–5000 cm^{-1} of solutions of benzyl alcohol in carbon tetrachloride at the following concentrations: 0.5 M, 0.25 M, 0.10 M, 0.05 M, 0.025 M, 0.01 M. Use a fixed-path cell[2] of thickness 1–2 mm and the same solvent as reference.

Interpret the spectra obtained in terms of intermolecular hydrogen bonding, of the benzyl alcohol. Identify the free OH and hydrogen-bonded OH bonds, and plot $\bar{v}_{max}$ for the latter against concentration.

Repeat this experiment using acetic acid in place of benzyl alcohol. Interpret the spectra in terms of the intramolecular hydrogen bonding.

TEMPERATURE EFFECTS

A variable temperature fixed-path cell (path length 0.1–0.5 mm) may be used for this experiment. If this is not available a suitable apparatus may be improvised by wrapping an ordinary fixed-path cell with an electric heating tape using a thermometer attached directly to the sides of the salt windows to read the temperature which is controlled manually by a "variac" transformer. The cell is placed in the spectrophotometer, and heated *in situ*. Fill the cell with 0.5 M benzyl alcohol solution in carbon tetrachloride and record the infrared spectrum between 3000–5000 cm^{-1} at room temperature. Raise the temperature slowly to prevent cracking the windows and allow about ten min for the liquid to reach equilibrium. Scan the spectrum at 10° intervals up to about 65°. Interpret the spectra in terms of intermolecular hydrogen bonding. Make a graph plotting $\bar{v}_{max}$ for the hydrogen-bonded OH bond against temperature.

SOLVENT EFFECTS

In a fixed-path cell (1-2 mm) measure the infrared spectra between 3000–5000 cm^{-1} of 0.01 M solutions of benzyl alcohol in the following solvents: carbon tetrachloride, benzene, acetonitrile, dioxane, and pyridine. Record the spectrum also of pure benzyl alcohol measured as a thin film between two salt plates.

Determine Δv the shift of the maximum of the hydrogen-bonded OH bond for each solvent relative to carbon tetrachloride. Δv may be considered to be an empirical parameter expressing the hydrogen-bonding ability of each solvent. Does any correlation exist between Δv and the corresponding Z value (Experiment 25)?

[1] Other *para*-substituted phenols, in which the substituent is not hydrogen bonding, may be added at the discretion of the instructor.

[2] If not already available, a fixed-path cell may be improvised by attaching a sodium chloride disk with epoxy cement to either side of a 1–2 mm steel washer with a slot cut into it. Fill and empty with a hypodermic syringe.

SUBSTITUENT EFFECTS

Make up solutions of the listed phenols, 0.125 M in carbon tetrachloride and measure the infrared spectra between 3000–5000 cm^{-1}. Locate the bands due to free OH and hydrogen-bonded OH and estimate their relative areas. Arrange the compounds in order of increasing hydrogen bonding and correlate this with the properties of the substituents in the *para* position of each. (Compare with σ-values, Experiment 2.)

Hydrogen Bonding and Electronic Spectra

The excitation energy of many chromophores is affected to a greater or lesser degree, by the solvent (compare Experiment 25), a phenomenon known as *solvatochromism.* It has been shown that absorption bands involving excitation (Figure 17–4) of unshared pairs of electrons on oxygen or nitrogen ($n \rightarrow \pi^*$ transitions) move progressively towards shorter wavelengths as the solvent is

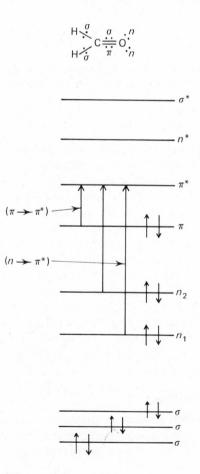

FIGURE 17–4

changed from hexane to alcohol to water ("blue shift"). On the other hand, bands due to excitation of π-electrons ($\pi \rightarrow \pi^*$ transitions) are less affected and may move towards longer wavelengths ("red shift") under the same conditions. The reason is probably due to the formation of a hydrogen bond between the hetero atom, using unshared electrons, and a hydroxylic solvent molecule. During an $n \rightarrow \pi^*$ transition, this hydrogen bond must be broken hence the energy of excitation is greater (shorter wavelength) than is needed in a non-hydrogen bonding solvent such as hexane. No such hydrogen bonds occur involving π-electrons hence the absence of a blue shift. The observed red shift may be due to the greater stabilization of the excited state (which might involve separation of charge) by the more polar solvent.

In this experiment, the solvatochromic effect on the two absorption bands in nitromethane and the one band of acetone are studied and assigned as either $\pi \rightarrow \pi^*$ or $n \rightarrow \pi^*$ transitions. The energy of the hydrogen bond is estimated spectroscopically.

Experimental

Materials Required

Ultraviolet-visible Spectrophotometer	Nitromethane
(Beckmann DU, DK, or equivalent.)	Hexane (spectrograde)
Acetone	Ethanol (spectrograde)

UV SPECTRA OF NITROMETHANE

Fill a 1 cm silica absorption cell with hexane and run its ultraviolet spectrum with another cell containing hexane as reference. Ensure that the solvent is sufficiently transparent down to at least 210 mμ. Now take a drawnout piece of glass rod, about 1 mm in diameter, dip it in a sample of pure nitromethane and then in the sample cell, stirring the solution at the same time. This method of addition gives a solution of approximately the correct concentration for observing qualitatively the high intensity band, and avoids using excessive quantities of the spectrograde solvent. Run the spectrum of the nitromethane solution between 200 and 300 mμ, and record the position of maximum intensity of the band located around 210 mμ. Add one small drop of nitromethane to the cell, mix and rerun the spectrum. Observe and record the position of the low intensity band which occurs around 270 mμ. (Figure 17–5).

Repeat these measurements using ethanol and water in turn as solvents. Tabulate the values of λ_{max} for each band in each solvent and decide whether a red shift or blue shift is present.

UV SPECTRA OF ACETONE

Using the same method detailed, examine the spectrum of acetone in hexane and ethanol, which exhibits one fairly intense maximum around 270 mμ (Figure 17–5) and assign the character of the transition.

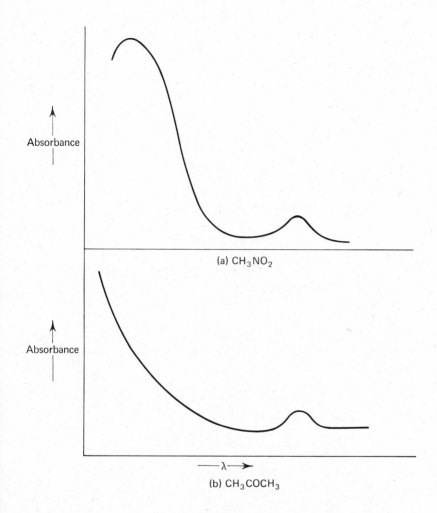

FIGURE 17–5 Ultraviolet spectra of (a) nitromethane and (b) acetone.

Questions

1. What effects on the listed physical properties would you predict to be caused by a) intramolecular and b) intermolecular hydrogen bonding?

   a. molecular weight
       (determined in solution)
   b. viscosity
   c. thermal conductivity
   d. molar volume

   e. vapor pressure
   f. melting point
   g. surface tension
   h. boiling point
   i. solvent properties

2. Explain why:

a. The melting points of 2- and 4-hydroxydiphenylsulfones both pure and in the presence of a little water are,

	pure	wet	change (Δ)
(2-isomer)	96	83	13
(4-isomer)	136	84	52

b. The two isomeric 1,3-cyclohexanediols in solution show infrared bands at 3620 cm^{-1} and $3619, 3544 \text{ cm}^{-1}$ respectively. Which is the *cis* and which the *trans* isomer?

c. The three isomeric hydroxybenzaldehydes melt at $-7°$, $106°$ and $116°$. What are their probable structures?

d. The rates of phenylhydrazone formation with some aromatic aldehydes and their hydroxy derivatives are,

e. Reduction in acid solution of *o*-nitrophenol is easily stopped at the *o*-hydroxyphenylhydroxylamine stage whereas the *p*-nitrophenol under similar conditions is reduced to *p*-aminophenol. In alkaline solution, reduction of *o*-nitrophenol gives only *o*-aminophenol.

f. The first and second ionization constants for some pairs of isomeric dibasic acids are,

	$10^5 k_1$	$10^5 k_2$
phthalic	121	0.36
terephthalic	31	1.52
maleic	1200	0.06
fumaric	96	4.13

g. 2,6-Dihydroxybenzoic acid is nearly a thousand times stronger as an acid than benzoic acid.

References

1. W. M. Latimer and W. H. Rodebush, *J. Amer. Chem. Soc.*, **42**, 1419 (1933).
2. L. K. Runnels, *Sci. Amer.*, Dec, 118 (1966).
3. G. C. Pimentel and A. L. McClellan, *The Hydrogen Bond*, Freeman, San Francisco, Calif., 1959.
4. N. D. Coggeshall, *J. Chem. Phys.*, **18**, 978 (1950).
5. N. D. Coggeshall and E. L. Saier, *J. Amer. Chem. Soc.*, **73**, 5414 (1951).
6. E. Greinacher, W. Luttke, and R. Mecke, *Z. Electrochem.*, **59**, 23 (1955).

Assignment of an
Infrared Spectral Band

EXPERIMENT 18

Absorption of infrared radiation by an organic compound occurs when the frequency of the incident light matches the natural frequency of vibration of a given mode in the molecule, which is thereby elevated to an excited vibrational state.

Covalent bonds joining atoms in a molecule behave like stiff springs in that they may be caused to stretch and bend elastically under the appropriate stress, the energy, however, is quantized. We may therefore apply a form of Hooke's Law to the vibrational excitation of the molecule:

$$v = \frac{c}{\lambda} = c\bar{v} = \frac{1}{2\pi c}\left(\frac{f}{\mu}\right)^{1/2} \qquad 1$$

where v = frequency of a given vibrational mode of the molecule; (= frequency of light which excites this mode;) λ = wavelength; $\bar{v}$ = wavenumber (cm^{-1}); c = velocity of light; f = force constant associated with the above mode; μ = reduced mass of the vibrating system, e.g., for the stretching vibration of X-Y, $\mu = m_X m_Y/(m_X + m_Y)$.

In general, a nonlinear molecule possessing n atoms exhibits $(3n - 6)$ modes of vibration of which $(n - 1)$ are stretching modes and the remainder are bending modes. This is illustrated for a tetraatomic molecule (Figure 18–1).

An infrared spectrum will consist of a number of regions of absorption (absorption bands) each corresponding to a mode of vibration or combinations

[1] Other such compounds may be added or substituted at the discretion of the instructor.

112

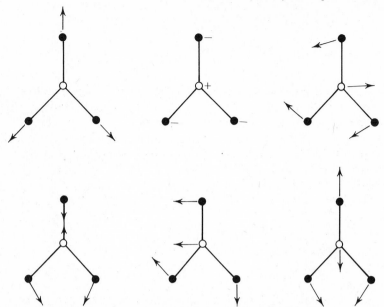

FIGURE 18–1 Normal vibrational modes for a planar AB₃ molecule.

of modes. The important feature from a practical point of view is that the position of each band is characteristic of a certain group of atoms in the molecule and is relatively unaffected by structural changes in the remainder of the molecule. Hence, once the assignment of a band has been made to a particular structural feature, this assignment can be used diagnostically for identification in unknown compounds. For instance, a strong band in the region 1700 ± 50 cm^{-1} ($5.9 \pm 0.2\ \mu$) indicates a carbonyl group (C=O stretch) and occurs in ketones, esters, lactones, amides, carboxylic acids, anhydrides, carbamates etc.

In the first instance the position in the spectrum of a given group absorption cannot be predicted from theory owing to our lack of information on the appropriate force constants and minor perturbing influences. The assignment of a band to a particular structural feature is usually inferred by observation of the spectra of a large number of compounds containing that structure taken together with some reasonable assumptions on the position and strength of the band.

Experiment 18 utilizes this principle to try to locate the position of the C—O single bond stretching frequency,

$$X-\overset{\leftarrow}{C}-\vec{O}-Y$$

Experimental

Materials Required

Diethyl ether	*m*-Cresol
Di-isopropyl ether	Ethyl acetate

Dibutyl ether	Tetrahydrofuran
Anisole	Hexane
Ethyl alcohol	Acetone
Propyl alcohol	Infrared spectrophotometer[2]

Run the infrared spectra of a selection of ethers, alcohols and esters as suggested above, using a thin film of sample held between sodium chloride plates. Avoid getting moisture on the surface of the plates since this will cause etching and loss of transparency. Examine the spectra and try to identify a band in each which can be ascribed to the stretching of the C—O bond using the following principles to guide your decision.

1. Single bond stretching frequencies occur at lower frequencies (wavenumbers) than the corresponding double bonds which are in turn lower than triple bonds (Table 18-1).

TABLE 18-1

	Variable	
C≡C	C≡N	
2120 ± 20 cm^{-1}	2250 ± 10	
C=C	C=N	C=O
1650 ± 30	1650 ± 40	1720 ± 20
C—C	C—N	C—O
~1000	1100 ± 100	?

The assignment you make should fit rationally into this scheme. Note also that the spread increases somewhat with single bonds compared to multiple bonds.

2. If we assume similar force constants exist for a series of bonds between carbon and the more electronegative elements we may use Eq. (1), plotting $\bar{v}$ against $(1/\mu)^{1/2}$ and obtain an approximately linear relationship from the slope of which a value for f may be deduced and $\bar{v}$ for the C—O system obtained by interpolation, thus,

	$\bar{v}$ (stretch)
C—N	1100 cm^{-1}
C—F	1000
C—Cl	750

For each bond, calculate the reduced mass μ assuming that it vibrates independently of the mass of the remainder of the molecule, that is,

$$\text{C—N } \mu = \frac{(12)(14)}{(12 + 14)} = 6.47$$

[2] A low-resolution instrument is quite adequate for this experiment.

Plot $\bar{v}$ against $(1/\mu)^{1/2}$ and draw the best straight line. Interpolate an expected value of $\bar{v}$ for the C—O bond. The above calculation is extremely crude but will help to place confidence in the location of the band which is sought.

3. The intensity of the C—O band should be high since there is a considerable difference in electronegativity between carbon and oxygen and there will be a large displacement of charge during a stretching vibration.

4. When you have tentatively assigned C—O stretching bands in the spectra measured, check that a similar band occurs in tetrahydrofuran. If you were observing a C—O bending vibration, the band would be expected to shift considerably when the ether oxygen is confined to a rigid five-membered ring. Ring formation should not affect a stretching mode to any great extent.

5. As a further check, run the spectrum of hexane and of acetone to ensure that they do not exhibit the C—O band.

Tabulate your results and determine a median value for $\bar{v}_{\text{C—O}}$ with the observed limits of variability. Do you think the C—O band is suitable for structural identification?

Question

1. Using the infrared assignments listed in Appendix C or the references interpret as much of the spectra a–g given on the following pages as possible.

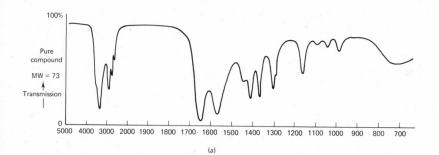

(a)

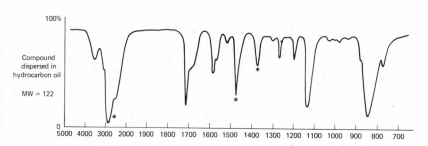

*bands, due to hydrocarbon oil

(b)

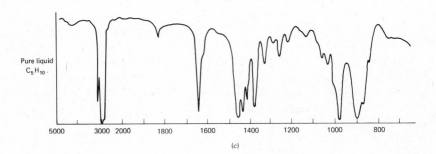

Pure liquid
C_5H_{10}

(c)

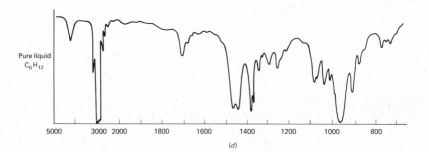

Pure liquid
C_6H_{12}

(d)

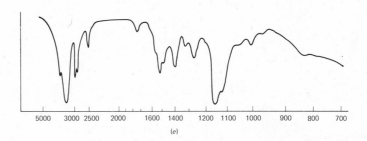

(e)

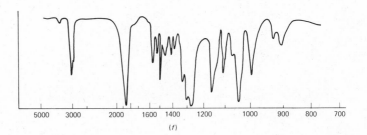

(f)

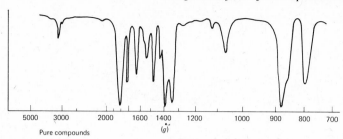

Pure compounds   (*g*)

References

1. A. D. Cross, *Introduction to Practical Infrared Spectroscopy*, 2nd Edition, Butterworth, London, 1964.
2. L. J. Bellamy, *The Infrared Spectra of Complex Molecules*, Methuen, London, 1958.

Charge-Transfer Complexes

It has long been known that picric acid and 1,3,5-trinitrobenzene form crystalline addition compounds with aromatic hydrocarbons and amines. It is also a familiar fact that solutions of iodine in certain solvents such as carbon tetrachloride are magenta while in benzene, ethanol and other liquids they are brown. These observations are related in that both phenomena are due to the formation of molecular or charge-transfer complexes [1, 2]. In the case of the iodine, the spectrum of a magenta solution of iodine, and also of iodine vapor, is due essentially to molecular iodine, I_2 and displays a maximum at about 500 mμ ($\varepsilon = 10^3$). This band is present in a brown solution of iodine but in addition a new and more intense band at approximately 300 mμ, ($\varepsilon = 10^4$) is present, the tail of which extends into the visible region and modifies the color. From the work of Benesi and Hildebrand [3], the 300 mμ band is now known to be caused by a third species present, a complex consisting of one molecule of iodine with one of solvent. An equilibrium exists in which the solvent, eg., benzene, acts as a Lewis base or electron donor and the iodine acts as a Lewis acid, or electron acceptor. The arrow used in the formula of the complex indicates the direction of movement of electron density:

π-complex or charge-transfer complex.

The addition compounds between aromatic hydrocarbons and polynitro compounds may be interpreted similarly, naphthalene picrate, e.g.:

Examples of typical donor and acceptor molecules are given below.

Donors:

$$R_3N: > R_2O$$

Acceptors:

$$\sim I_2 >$$

The heat of formation of such complexes, which may not be isolable, is quite low (2–20 kcal mole^{-1}). The bonding may be considered [4, 5] from a molecular orbital viewpoint to result from the overlapping of filled π- or n-orbitals of the donor with vacant or depleted orbitals of the correct symmetry in the acceptor.

Two new molecular orbitals, peculiar to the complex, are produced, the lower of the two being occupied in the ground state and of greater stability than the component orbitals:

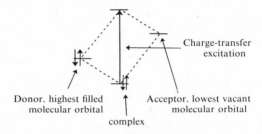

Donor, highest filled
molecular orbital

Charge-transfer
excitation

Acceptor, lowest vacant
molecular orbital

complex

Excitation of one electron to the higher molecular orbital of the complex is possible by absorption of the appropriate radiations. The transition is frequently of quite low energy and occurs in the visible region thus accounting for the production of colored complexes from colorless components. For example, aniline (λ_{max} 280 mμ) and tetracyanoethylene (λ_{max} 300 mμ) when mixed in chloroform solution produce a deep blue complex (λ_{max} 610 mμ).

The valence-bond picture of complex formation regards adducts as being resonance hybrids of an uncharged and a charged form interconvertible by the exchange of an electron, hence their designation as charge-transfer complexes:

$$\text{DA} \longleftrightarrow \text{D}^+\text{A}^-$$
$$\psi_1 \qquad\qquad \psi_2$$

The total wave function may be written:

$$\psi = a\psi_1 + b\psi_2$$

where, for the ground state of the complex, $a > b$, the amount of charge transfer is relatively small: in the excited state, $a < b$.

The complexes consist inevitably of one molecule each of donor and acceptor, oriented, as shown by x-ray studies on crystalline complexes, so as to permit maximum overlap of the appropriate orbitals. Donor molecules may be aromatic, in which case the π-electrons are used in bonding, or amines, ethers and alcohols in which unshared pairs of electrons are donated. The common acceptors include the halogens, silver ion, *p*-benzoquinone, polynitroaromatic compounds, maleic anhydride and tetracyanoethylene. The last named compounds possess π-systems which are somewhat depleted of electrons because of inductive withdrawal by powerful electronegative groups such as nitro, carbonyl and cyano.

The experiments which follow outline methods for the detection of charge-transfer complexes and the determination of their stoichiometry, and for the isolation of stable crystalline examples.

Experimental—Spectroscopic Properties of Charge-Transfer Complexes

COMPLEXES BETWEEN IODINE AND AROMATIC HYDROCARBONS [3]

Materials Required

Iodine	Toluene
Hexane	*p*-Xylene
Benzene	Chlorobenzene

Prepare a solution of iodine (0.25 g, 0.001 mole) in hexane, 100 ml. Transfer 0.1 ml of the solution to a 10 ml volumetric flask and make up to the mark with hexane. Measure the visible-ultraviolet spectrum of the solution in a suitable spectrophotometer between 250 and 600 mμ, with hexane as reference liquid, using 10 mm cells. Repeat using the aromatic liquids in turn to dilute the iodine solution and as reference liquids. Compare your spectra and interpret the bands observed. Measure the position of maximum absorption of the charge-transfer band. Discuss the reasons for differences observed using the various aromatic solvents.

COMPLEXES BETWEEN TETRACYANOETHYLENE AND AROMATIC AMINES [6]

Materials Required

Tetracyanoethylene	*m*-Toluidine
Dichloromethane	Aniline
N,N-Dimethylaniline	*p*-Bromoaniline
p-Toluidine	3,5-Dichloroaniline
N-Methylaniline	

Prepare a solution of 0.1 g tetracyanoethylene (TCNE) in 50 ml dichloromethane. Assemble eight clean test tubes and place 5 ml of this solution in each. To successive tubes add a small quantity of an aromatic amine dispensed on the end of a glass rod, using the list of amines suggested. Note the colors produced and measure the visible spectrum between 500 mμ and 800 mμ. The colors and absorption bands observed are due to charge-transfer complex formation between the amine and tetracyanoethylene:

colorless   blue

Plot the absorption maximum for each complex against the dissociation constant, pK_A of the amine. Interpret the meaning of the relationship found.

Allow the mixture of N,N-dimethylaniline and TCNE solution to stand for a few hours and examine the spectrum. Consult Reference 6 for the interpretation of any changes which are noted.

COMPLEXES BETWEEN TETRACYANOETHYLENE AND AROMATIC HYDROCARBONS [7]

Materials Required

Tetracyanoethylene (TCNE)	Chlorobenzene
Dichloromethane	Anisole
Benzene	Ethylbenzoate
o-Xylene	Hexamethylbenzene
p-Xylene	Biphenyl
Mesitylene	UV visible spectrophotometer

(The substituted benzenes suggested here are representative: any may be substituted by similar compounds.).

Method. Prepare 0.5 molar solutions of the aromatic compounds in dichloromethane and 10 ml of a 0.05 M solution of TCNE in the same solvent. Transfer by pipette 0.25 ml of TCNE solution to a 5 ml volumetric flask and make up to the mark with the benzene solution. Place the mixture in a 1 cm absorption cell and measure the visible spectrum between 330 and 500 mμ. Observe the charge-transfer band and measure the wavelength of maximum absorption (λ_{max}). Repeat using the solutions containing the substituted benzenes.

Treatment of results. Calculate the difference in wavelength, $\Delta\lambda$, between the value of λ_{max} for each compound and that of benzene which may be regarded as the parent compound. Plot $\Delta\lambda$ against the Hammett σ-value[1] for the appropriate substituent. Suggest an explanation for the correlation obtained. Repeat using frequency differences Δv [Eq. (1)] instead of wavelength differences and comment on the new shape of the curve obtained:

$$\Delta v(\text{sec}^{-1}) = \frac{3 \times 10^{10}(\text{cm sec}^{-1})}{\Delta\lambda(\text{cm})} \tag{1}$$

The Stoichiometry of a Charge-Transfer Complex [7]

Choose one of the solutions of substituted benzenes prepared in the first part of this experiment. In a 5 ml volumetric flask place 0.25 ml of 0.05 M tetracyanoethylene solution and make up to the mark with the solution of the

---

[1] The values of σ found in Experiment 2 may be used or obtained from standard physical-organic texts or as quoted by J. Clark and D. D. Perrin, *Quart. Rev.*, 303 (1964), a selection of which are included in Appendix D.

aromatic compound to be examined. Measure the absorbance, A, (optical density) of the charge-transfer band at the wavelength of maximum absorption. If the spectrophotometer used is calibrated with a per cent transmission (T) scale, the two are simply related by the expression:

$$A = \log \frac{1}{T} \tag{3}$$

Repeat the experiment using 0.5, 0.75 and 1.0 ml of TCNE solution. Tabulate values of A, concentrations of TCNE and aromatic compound, B.

Treatment of results.   For 1:1 complex formation

$$\text{TCNE} + B \underset{}{\overset{K}{\rightleftharpoons}} C \text{ (complex)}$$

$$\therefore K = \frac{[C]}{([\text{TCNE}] - [C])([B] - [C])} \tag{4}$$

where $[C]$ = Equilibrium concentration of complex (moles/liter)
$[\text{TCNE}]$ = Initial concentration of TCNE
$[B]$ = Initial concentration of aromatic compound
since $[B] \gg [C]$, $([B] - [C]) \approx [B]$

It is convenient at this point to define a slightly different equilibrium constant, using the mole fraction of B, N_B instead of molarity:

$$K' = \frac{[C]}{([\text{TCNE}] - [C])N_B} \tag{5}$$

Also, according to the Beer-Lambert Law:

$$[C] = \frac{A}{l\varepsilon} \tag{6}$$

ε = molar extinction coefficient of C
l = optical path length of the cell
Substituting Eq. (6) in Eq. (5) and rearranging

$$\frac{[\text{TCNE}]l}{A} = \frac{1}{N_B K' \varepsilon} + \frac{1}{\varepsilon}$$

which is of the form $y = mx + c$. Hence if the original assumption of a 1:1 complex is correct, a plot of $[\text{TCNE}]l/A$ against $1/N_B$ will be linear, with slope $= 1/K'\varepsilon$ and intercept $= 1/\varepsilon$.
Make such a plot and verify that the complex studied has the assumed stoichiometry. Estimate K' and ε from the graph. Show that the graph of $[\text{TCNE}]l/A$ against $1/N_B$ would not be linear for a 2:1 complex.

Preparation of Crystalline Charge-Transfer Complexes

DIOXANE-BROMINE

To 1 ml 1,4-dioxane in a test tube, add bromine dropwise using a fumehood in which to perform the experiment and cooling the tube in icewater. A pale orange crystalline solid soon separates out which may be filtered, dried in air for a few minutes and then sealed into a glass ampoule.

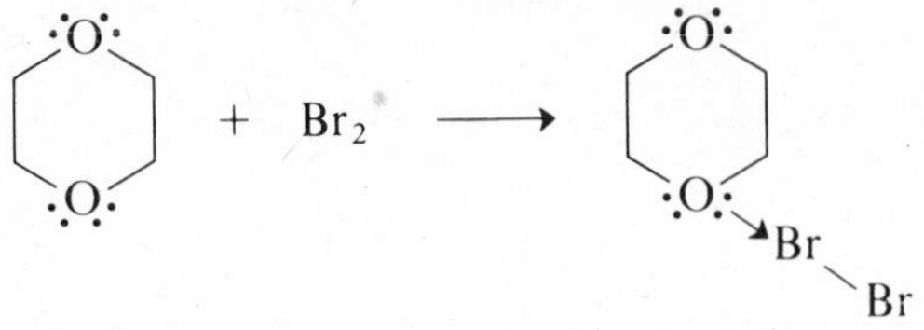

The structure of the solid has been shown to consist of bromine molecules linked to the oxygens of dioxane molecules in chains:

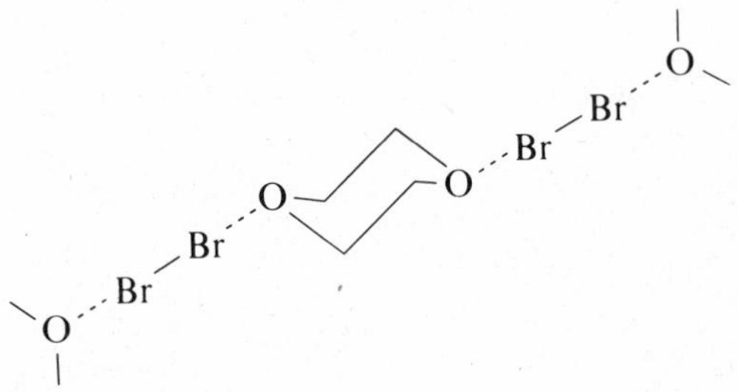

The compound is quite stable, though volatile, and behaves like free bromine in bromination reactions while easier to handle.

CYCLOOCTATETRAENE-SILVER NITRATE [8]

Dissolve 2 g silver nitrate in 5 ml water and add a mixture of 2 ml cyclo-octatetraene and 5 ml petroleum ether (bp 50–60°). Stopper and shake until a fine white precipitate is obtained. Warm the mixture to 50–60° until this just dissolves, then allow to cool slowly. Filter the colorless needles obtained.
The crystal structure [9] of the compound is:

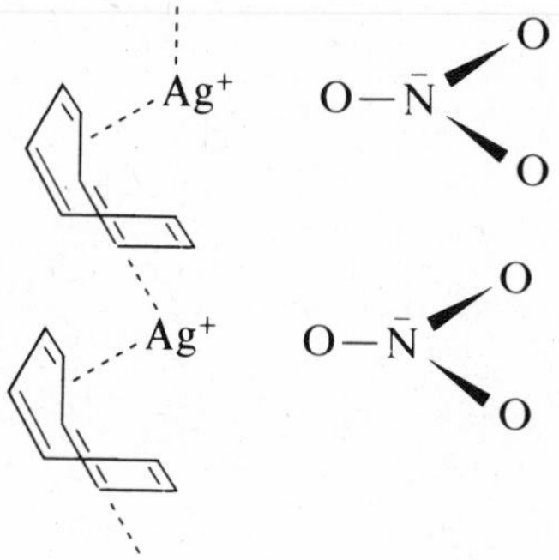

Questions

1. Derive an expression relating absorbance to donor (acceptor) concentration assuming a 2:1 complex.
2. Donor ability of an aromatic compound, ArH, should be manifested in many properties. By examination of the literature draw conclusions whether charge-transfer spectra are in fact a measure of donor ability by correlating these spectral measurements with ionization potential (e.g. J. Walkley, D. N. Glew and J. H. Hildebrand, *J. Chem. Phys.*, **33**, 621 (1960).), Hammett and other substituent constants (Appendix D), the energies of the highest occupied orbitals (M. J. Dewar, and H. Rogers, *J. Amer. Chem. Soc.*, **84**, 395 (1962).) and parallelisms between the complexes with different acceptors but a common series of donors (see R. M. Keefer, and L. J. Andrews, *J. Amer. Chem. Soc.*, **74**, 4500 (1952); ibid, **77**, 2164 (1955); M. Tamres, D. R. Virzi, and S. Searles, ibid, **75**, 4358 (1953); R. Foster, D. L. Hammick, and B. N. Parsons, *J. Chem. Soc.*, 555 (1956); R. E. Merrifield and W. D. Phillips, *J. Amer. Chem. Soc.*, **80**, 2778 (1958).).
3. Devise an experiment to test the significance of steric effects in the formation of charge-transfer complexes with substituted benzenes.

References

1. L. J. Andrews and R. M. Keefer, *Molecular Complexes in Organic Chemistry*, Holden-Day, San Francisco, 1964.
2. L. N. Ferguson, *The Modern Structural Theory of Organic Chemistry*, Prentice-Hall, 1963, pp. 103–125.
3. H. A. Benesi and J. H. Hildebrand, *J. Am. Chem. Soc.*, **71**, 2703 (1949).
4. R. S. Mullikan, *J. Am. Chem. Soc.*, **74**, 811 (1952).
5. M. J. S. Dewar and A. R. Lepley, *J. Am. Chem. Soc.*, **83**, 4560 (1961).
6. N. S. Isaacs, *J. Chem. Soc.* 1053 (1966).
7. R. E. Merrifield and W. D. Phillips, *J. Amer. Chem. Soc.*, **80**, 2778 (1958).
8. A. C. Cope and F. A. Hochstein, *J. Am. Chem. Soc.*, **72**, 2515 (1950).
9. F. S. Mathews and W. W. Lipscomb, *J. Phys. Chem.*, **63**, 845 (1959).

The Use of
Woodward's Rules

EXPERIMENT *20*

The energy of an electronic excitation, and thus the position of an absorption band in the ultraviolet-visible spectrum, is influenced by substituents attached directly to the chromophore [1]. This is because the substituents, by virtue of their electronic effects, perturb the energies of the orbitals of the chromophore which are concerned in excitation, normally the highest filled and the lowest unfilled (Figure 20–1) of the molecule concerned.

Moreover, the spectral shifts caused by substituents are sufficiently additive to be predictable by the application of simple rules. For example the substitution of methyl into benzene and acetone is associated with bathychromic (i.e., towards the red) shifts of about 5 and 3 mμ respectively on certain of their transitions (Table 20–1).

TABLE 20–1. Effect of methyl substitution on the short wavelength band of benzene and the $n \rightarrow \pi^*$ transition of acetone

	λ_{max} (mμ)	$\Delta\lambda/n^1$(mμ)
Benzene	184	
Toluene	189	5
p-Xylene	193	4.5
Mesitylene	198	5
CH_3COCH_3	274	
$CH_3COCH_2CH_3$	277	3
$CH_3COCH(CH_3)_2$	281	3.5
$CH_3COC(CH_3)_3$	285	3.6

[1] $\Delta\lambda/n$ = Shift relative to parent compound/number of methyl substituents

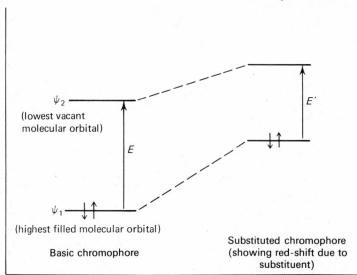

FIGURE 20–1 Substituent effect on electronic spectrum.

A number of extensive surveys of substituent effects on ultraviolet spectra have been made and sets of empirical rules drawn up for the prediction of the value of λ_{max} for a given structure [2]. The most useful of these rules covering aliphatic conjugated systems is due to R. B. Woodward [3], Table 20–2.

TABLE 20–2. U.V. Spectral Assignments

Isolated Chromophores	λ_{max} (mμ)	(ε_{max})
$H_2C{=}CH_2$	175	(10^4) (add $+5$ for each R substituent)
$RCH{=}CHR$	175	(10^4)
$R_1R_2C{=}O$	270–285	(10–20)
RCHO	280–300	(10–15)
RCOOH	200–210	(50)
$RN{=}NR$	350	(5)
$RN{=}OH$	190	(10^{3-4})
RCN	150	
	300	(100)
$R{-}N{=}O$	665	(20)
R_2S	210 (10^3) 229	(150)

Aromatic Compounds

Benzene 185, (10^4); 203 (7,400);		254 (200)—6–7 characteristic
($+$ simple derivatives including pyridines)		fine structure peaks
Add for nonconjugating substituents		$+5$–10
Add for conjugating substituents		20–25
Naphthalene 220, 270, 310		

TABLE 20–2. (Continued)

Conjugated Systems—Woodward's Rules

a. *Dienes*

Butadiene–basic system  ⟋⟍⟋	217 (2×10^4)
Add: for each R^1 substituent	+5
for each exocyclic double bond	+5
for each halogen substituent	+17
for each extra double bonds extending conjugated systems	+50, 40, 30, 25, 20 successively
homoannular diene	+36

b. *α–β Unsaturated Ketones, Acids, Esters* (enones)

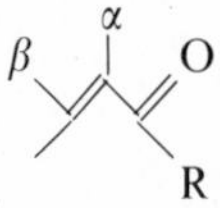

215 (10^4)

R = R, COOH, COOEt

Add for each extra R α, or β	+10
OH α, or β	+35
an additional double bond extending the conjugation	+30
exocyclic double bond	+5

c. *Dienones*

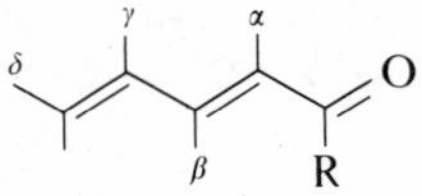

(Also show the *enone* bond at shorter wavelengths)   245

Add for each R		
	α	+10
	β	+12
	γ or δ (including those on extra double bonds)	+18
	OH, α	+35
	Cl α	+15
	Br α	+23
	exocyclic double bond	+5
	homoannular diene component	+39
	extra double bond extending conjugation	+30

Auxochromic Groups Add—

Substituent	System 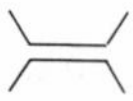	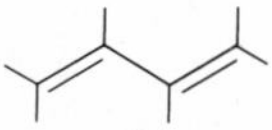	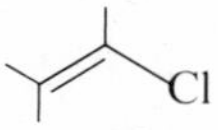	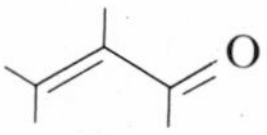	−Ph (Aromatic band)
R_2N-	+40	+65	+58	+95	+43
$RO-$	+30			+50	+17
$RS-$	+45	+28		+85	+23
$Cl-$	+5	+6		+20	+2
$Br-$		+10	+14	+30	+6

^{1} R = saturated carbon

TABLE 20–2. (Continued)

Solvent corrections to α,β-Unsaturated Ketone Absorption

Ethanol, methanol	0–reference
Chloroform	+1
Ether	+7
Hexane	+11
Water	−8
Dioxane	+5

THE USE OF TABLE [20–2]

Each feature set out in the table contributes to the absorption maximum of the parent system independently. The following examples will illustrate this principle: the calculated and experimental values of λ_{max} can be expected to agree within about 2–3 mμ depending on the complexity of the calculations.

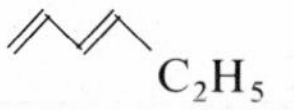

Hexa-1,3,-diene

Butadiene	217
add 1 R group	+ 5

222 mμ (observed 222)

cyclohexa-1,3-diene

Butadiene	217
add 2 R groups	+10
homoannular diene	+36

263 mμ (observed 262)

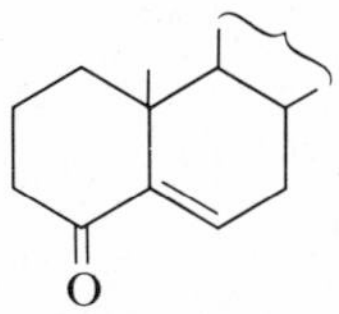

enone	215
2R (α, β)	20
exocyclic double bond	5

240 mμ (observed 241)

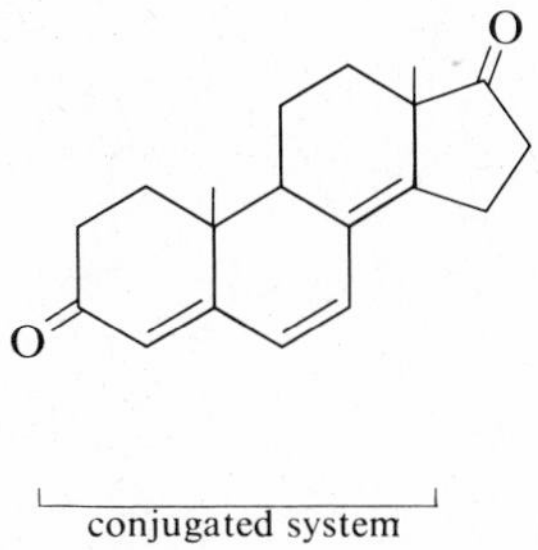

conjugated system

dienone	245
extra double bond	
conjugated	30
3 exocyclic double bonds	15
R substituents 1α	10
3δ	54

344 mμ (observed 348)

Experimental

Materials Required

Solutions of the following compounds[1] at 10^{-3} to 10^{-4} molar concentration in 100% ethanol[2] are provided, in unlabelled bottles.

Piperylene, I	3,5-Cholestadiene-7-one, V
Ergosterol, II	4-Androstene-3,17-dione, VI
16-Dehydroprogesterone, III	Vitamin D_3, VII
Toluene, IV	Hexa-2,4-dienal, VIII

Record the ultraviolet spectrum of each solution between 200 and 350 mμ using quartz absorption cells of 1 cm pathlength, and ethanol as reference. Match the spectra obtained to the values of λ_{max} calculated from the structures of the compounds using Woodward's Rules and hence identify the contents of each flask.

[1] A chemical supply company, e.g. Aldrich Chemicals, Milwaukee, Wis., will provide a small sample of each of these at quite low cost on request.

[2] Use a sample of ethanol with reasonably good transparency at least to 210 mμ.

Questions

1. Predict the position of the absorption maximum for the following compounds:

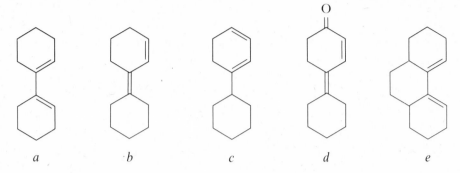

| *a* | *b* | *c* | *d* | *e* |

Check your results with experimental values taken from the literature (search *Chemical Abstracts* and spectral indexes such as *Organic Electronic Spectral Data*, Ed. J. P. Phillips and F. C. Nachod, Interscience, New York, 4 vols up to 1959.).

2. How could spectroscopy be used to follow the kinetics of the reaction between butadiene and ethyl crotonate ($CH_3CH = CHCOOEt$)?

3. Compound A, (no absorption > 200 mμ)$C_{10}H_{16}$, is converted by OsO_4 to a saturated compound B (no absorption > 200) periodate oxidation of which yields a diketone, C, $C_{10}H_{16}O_2$ ($\lambda_{max} = 280$, $\varepsilon = 20$). In 20% sulfuric acid, B is converted to D, ($\lambda_{max} = 280$, $\varepsilon = 20$), $C_{10}H_{16}$ D reacts with bromine in acetic acid to give E ($\lambda_{max} = 300$, $\varepsilon = 25$), $C_{10}H_{15}OBr$ which in boiling pyridine is transformed to F, $C_{10}H_{14}O$ ($\lambda_{max} = 225$, $\varepsilon = 10^4$). F reacts with N-bromosuccinimide to give G, $C_{10}H_{13}OBr$ ($\lambda_{max} = 228$, $\varepsilon = 10^4$) which in boiling pyridine is converted to H, $C_{10}H_{12}O$ ($\lambda_{max} = 302$, $\varepsilon = 3 \times 10^4$).

  H yields no formaldehyde on ozonolysis but may be oxidized to I, $C_7H_{10}O_4$ on treatment with chromic acid and readily decarboxylates to cyclopentane carboxylic acid.

  Deduce formulae for the compounds A–I.

References

1. H. H. Jaffé and M. Orchin, *Theory and Applications of Ultraviolet Spectroscopy*, Wiley, New York, 1962.

2. L. F. Fieser and M. Fieser, *Steroids*, Reinhold, New York, 1959; R. C. Cookson and S. H. Dandegaonker, *J. Chem. Soc.*, 165 (1955); H. Booker, L. K. Evans, and A. E. Gillam, *J. Chem. Soc.*, 1453 (1940); L. Dorfman, *Chem. Revs.*, **53**, 47 (1953).

3. R. B. Woodward, *J. Amer. Chem. Soc.*, **63**, 1123 (1942); **64**, 72 (1943).

Measurement of a Keto–Enol Ratio

Carbonyl compounds possessing at least one α-hydrogen atom may enolize by a proton shift from carbon to oxygen:

$$\underset{\text{keto}}{\overset{\overset{\displaystyle O}{\|}\ \overset{\displaystyle H}{|}}{-C-C-}} \rightleftharpoons \underset{\text{enol}}{-C=C}$$

In saturated aliphatic aldehydes and ketones the keto form is considerably more stable than the enol which, at equilibrium is found only in a minute proportion. Enolization is, nevertheless, of great importance since many reactions at the α-carbon atom take place only via the enol. For instance, bromination and deuterium exchange occur at the same rate indicating that the rate determining or slow step in the reaction is the same in either case, namely enolization:

$$-C-C-H \rightleftharpoons -C=C \overset{Br_2,\ fast}{\underset{D^+,\ fast}{\Huge<}} \begin{array}{c} -C-C-Br + HBr \\[2mm] -C-C-D + H^+ \end{array}$$

The equilibrium enol content of β-dicarbonyl compounds is very much higher since an internal hydrogen bond can provide additional stabilization of this form both on account of the energy of the hydrogen bond and also because of resonance between two canonical structures:

keto, 20 %   enol, 80%

The classical method for estimating enol content is by a rapid bromine titration carried out before the equilibrium shifts appreciably. Infrared spectroscopy provides an alternative method. The carbonyl-stretching frequency in the keto form will be almost normal and occur at about $1720 \, \text{cm}^{-1}$ (5.8 μ) while that in the enol (when $R_1 = R_2$, both oxygens are identical through resonance) has less double bond character and hence vibrates at a lower frequency (longer wavelength), Figure 21–1.

Assuming that the extinction coefficients for each band are equal, the proportion of keto to enol is given by the ratio of their intensities.[1]

The same experiment may be adapted to examine the effects of temperature and of solvent on the keto-enol equilibrium. An internally hydrogen-bonded enol is not able to form any other hydrogen bonds to solvent molecules whereas the open keto form is able to bond to two hydroxylic molecules thus lowering its energy. Hydroxylic solvents therefore should favor an increase in the proportion of keto form and the converse in nonpolar, nonhydrogen bonding solvents, Figure 21–2.

Experimental

Materials Required

Ethyl acetoacetate	Infrared spectrophotometer
Solvents: carbon tetrachloride	capable of resolution
hexane	$5 \, \text{cm}^{-1}$ or better
ether	
chloroform	
methanol	
ethanol	

[1] As has been mentioned, the determination of absolute percentage compositions of the carbonyl compounds rests on the assumption that the extinction coefficients for each carbonyl frequency are the same, an assumption which may not be true since hydrogen bond formation is known (Experiment 2) to be accompanied by an increase in intensity in some cases. Furthermore while the low-frequency band has been interpreted as due to the enolic C—O group by Bernstein [3], the same band has been assigned to the enolic C=C group by LeFevre [4]. In either case it is due to the enolic form but if the latter interpretation is correct there is even less grounds for assuming equal extinction coefficients. These considerations will not affect the principle of the experiment nor arguments depending on changes in the relative proportions of the two forms.

0
100
% Transmission
A_e
A_k
1600
1700
1800
cm^{-1}

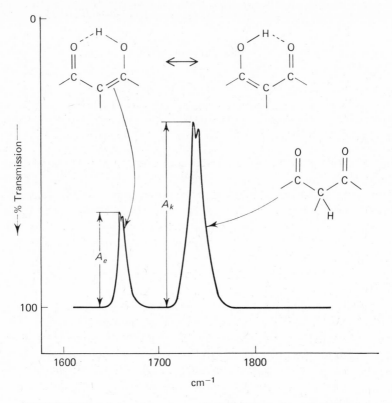

FIGURE 21–1 Infrared spectrum of a β diketone in the carbonyl region.

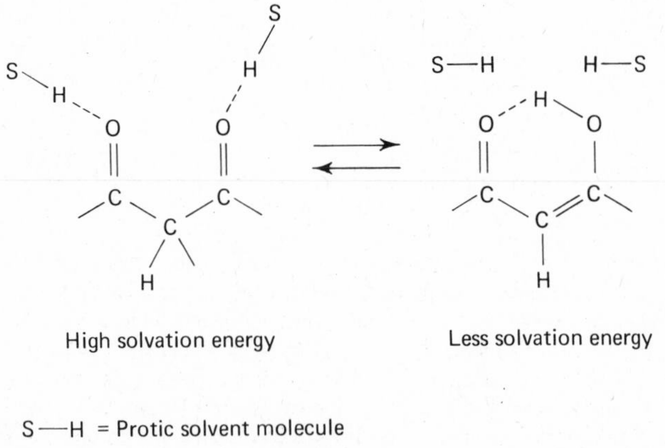

High solvation energy
Less solvation energy
S—H = Protic solvent molecule

FIGURE 21–2

Prepare solutions of pure ethyl acetoacetate in carbon tetrachloride at the following concentrations: 5, 4, 3, 2, 1% by weight. Set up the infrared spectrometer to give the best resolution by cutting down the slit width and scanning time and increasing the gain and damping period. Record the spectrum of each solution between 1540 and 1800 cm^{-1}, (6.5–5.5 μ) using 0.1 mm fixed-path cells with solvent as reference. Identify the bands due to the enol and keto forms of ethyl acetoacetate[1] and measure their relative intensities, A_e and A_k. Plot A_e and A_k separately against concentration and draw the best straight lines. The ratio of slopes gives the ratios of the two forms in dilute carbon tetrachloride solution.

SOLVENT EFFECTS

Choose a concentration which gives a conveniently sized spectrum and make up solutions of ethyl acetoacetate at that concentration in a series of solvents such as hexane (or other paraffin), ether, methanol, ethanol, chloroform or any other that does not itself absorb in the carbonyl region. Measure the keto-enol ratio, A_k/A_e and tabulate the solvents in increasing order of stabilization of the enol.

How does this order compare with the solvent polarity order found in Experiment 25?

TEMPERATURE EFFECTS

Using one of the solutions prepared for solvent effects determine the keto-enol ratio at different temperatures heating the cell by the technique used in Experiment 17. By applying Le Chatelier's Principle, determine which tautomer is the more stable.

STRUCTURAL EFFECTS

Make up 3% w/w solutions in carbon tetrachloride of acetylacetone I, and diethyl malonate II, and measure their keto-enol ratios as above. Account for any differences you observe in the series acetylacetone, ethyl acetoacetate III, diethyl malonate:

$$
\begin{array}{ccc}
\text{CH}_3 & \text{EtO}_2\text{C} & \text{EtO}_2\text{C} \\
\quad\diagdown\ \text{C=O} & \quad\diagdown\ \text{C=O} & \quad\diagdown\ \text{C=O} \\
\diagup & \diagup & \diagup \\
\text{CH}_2 & \text{CH}_2 & \text{CH}_2 \\
\quad\diagdown\ \text{C=O} & \quad\diagdown\ \text{C=O} & \quad\diagdown\ \text{C=O} \\
\diagup & \diagup & \diagup \\
\text{CH}_3 & \text{CH}_3 & \text{EtO}_2\text{C} \\
\text{I} & \text{III} & \text{II}
\end{array}
$$

[1] Each band is split into a doublet, probably due to Fermi resonance coupling between the two carbonyl groups.

Questions

1. Interpret the above spectrum of acetylacetone (proton resonance at 40 Mc/sec, pure compound).

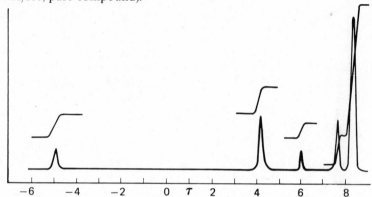

2. Suggest mechanisms for the following carbonyl reactions:

a. $2\,PhCHO \xrightarrow{OH^-} PhCH(OH)COPh$

b. $PhCOCH_3 + ClCH_2COOEt \longrightarrow$ PhC—CHCOOEt with CH$_3$ group and O

c.

d. $Me_2CO + H_2^{18}O \xrightarrow{AcOH} Me_2C^{18}O$

e. $3\,Me_2CO \longrightarrow$ benzene ring with Me, Me, Me

f.

References

1. E. S. Gould, *Mechanism and Structure in Organic Chemistry*, Holt, Rinehart, and Winston, New York, 1959, p. 376.
2. J. Hine, *Physical-Organic Chemistry*, McGraw-Hill, New York, 1962, Chapter 10.
3. J. Powling and H. J. Bernstein, *J. Amer. Chem. Soc.*, **73**, 4353 (1951).
4. R. J. W. LeFevre and H. Welsh, *J. Chem. Soc.*, 2230 (1949).

Inductive and
Steric Effects on
Proton Resonance Spectra

EXPERIMENT 22

Nuclear magnetic resonance, introduced into chemical usage around 1950, has already become one of the most widespread, versatile and powerful techniques available for a variety of chemical problems. The principles of NMR are only briefly outlined in this experiment; the reader is referred to the many excellent texts [1] on the subject for further information.

Any nucleus possesses magnetic properties (which may be seen as the consequence of a *spinning*, charged particle) described by its *nuclear spin number, I*, such that in an externally applied magnetic field, $(2I + 1)$ orientations of the nucleus with respect to the direction of the field, are permitted, each being associated with a definite energy. Values of I may be zero, integral or half-integral depending on the particular nuclide. Those with zero spin have no preferred orientation and are of no interest in NMR. Some values of I for common nuclei are given in Table 22–1 and a representation of the permitted states for nuclei of $I = \frac{1}{2}$ and $I = 1$ in Figure 22–1.

Transitions between spin states are permitted as indicated by the arrows in Figure 22–1, energy being absorbed or released in the process. The condition for resonance absorption of electromagnetic radiation is given by:

$$\Delta E = h v = \frac{\mu \beta H}{I} \qquad (1)$$

where ΔE represents the difference in energy between the spin levels, $h v$ (Planck's constant × frequency) is the energy of the quantum absorbed, $\mu =$ magnetic

TABLE 22–1. Nuclear Spin Numbers

	Spin No, I
^1H	$\frac{1}{2}$
^2H	1
^3H	$\frac{1}{2}$
^{12}C	0
^{13}C	$\frac{1}{2}$
^{14}N	1
^{16}O	0
^{19}F	$\frac{1}{2}$
^{31}P	$\frac{1}{2}$
^{32}S	0
^{35}Cl	$\frac{3}{2}$
^{127}I	$\frac{5}{2}$

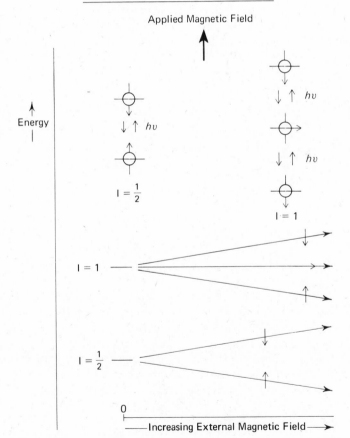

FIGURE 22–1 Splitting of nuclear spin states in a magnetic field.

moment of the nucleus and β is a constant (the nuclear magneton). H is the applied magnetic field strength.

From this equation it is seen that splitting of the spin states only occurs in an applied magnetic field and the energy gap is proportional to the field strength. This then is an example of the Zeeman Effect more familiar in atomic spectra. The NMR spectrum is a result of transitions between spin states. Proton resonance is by far the commonest form of NMR (Nuclei of spin $\frac{1}{2}$ give spectra which are sharper and easier to interpret than those of higher spin.). Typical resonance conditions for the proton are $H = 9365$ gauss at 40 MHz[1] or 13,446 gauss at 60 MHz. Most modern instruments now operate at 60 MHz which is in the radiofrequency part of the electromagnetic spectrum. Nuclear resonance would be of no interest to chemistry were it not for another effect. While the resonance condition is a property of the proton, the actual magnetic field experienced by a proton in a molecule is invariably less than that of the applied field since electronic motions in the bonds and the filled orbitals set up secondary fields, h, in opposition to the applied field. Moreover this effect depends upon the precise chemical nature of the proton in question. We find in practice that the applied field at a fixed radiofrequency required for resonance differs with different types of protons as shown in Figure 22–2.

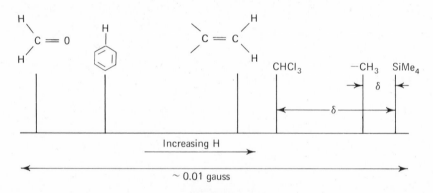

FIGURE 22–2

The NMR spectrum then consists of a series of lines each of which represents a chemically different proton. The position in the spectrum, relative to a *standard* proton—usually that of tetramethylsilane, a highly shielded proton–is characteristic and typical assignments are set out in Appendix C. The *chemical shift*, δ, is the difference between the resonance position for a given proton and that of tetramethylsilane expressed in cycles per second (Hz) or the dimensionless parameter, τ:

$$\tau = 10 - \frac{\delta \times 10^6}{\text{radiofrequency c/sec}}$$

[1] MHz = megahertz = 10^6 cycles per second, a unit of frequency.

One of the factors which affects the chemical shift is the inductive effect of neighboring substituents. Withdrawal of electron density from a proton *deshields* it and hence lowers τ, Figure 22–3.

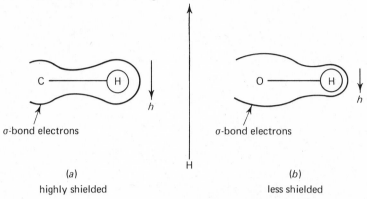

(a)   (b)

highly shielded   less shielded

Proton resonates at lower applied field

FIGURE 22–3 Correlation of shielding with electronegativity.

The first part of the experiment explores the inductive effects of substituents on the resonances of the methyl and methylene protons of the ethyl group. These normally occur in different parts of the spectrum, the methyl protons being the more highly shielded. An electron-attracting group will deshield the methylene protons to a greater extent than the methyl protons which are one bond further removed. Hence, the separation of the methyl and methylene protons, Δ gives an index of the electron attracting power (inductive effect) of the substituent [2]. Under high resolution (60 Mc/sec spectra), the resonances of the methyl and methylene protons are split into a triplet and a quartet by mutual coupling (see Experiments 23, 24) but this does not affect the measurement which is made from the centers of each band system (Figure 22–4).

The second part of the experiment is concerned with stereochemical factors. The cyclohexane system is known to exist in two strain free, rapidly interchanging conformations (chair forms) in either of which there are two sets of chemically distinct protons, six equatorial (*e*) and six axial (*a*):

At room temperature, a single resonance is obtained which is the weighted time average of the two conformations but as the rate of interchange is reduced by lowering the temperature, this splits into two components [3], one due to the axial and one due to the equatorial protons yielding information on the activation barrier for the conformational interchange.

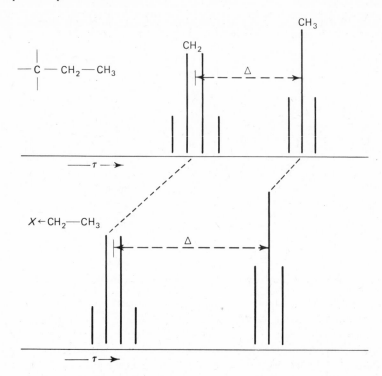

FIGURE 22–4 Effects of electron-withdrawal on the proton resonance of the ethyl group.

Experimental

MEASUREMENT OF INDUCTIVE EFFECTS BY NMR

Materials Required

A selection of compounds of formula X-Et such as ethyl bromide, ethyl iodide, diethyl ether, *n*-butane, ethyl-benzene, ethyl cyanide, nitroethane, ethanol, phenetole, NMR spectrometer (preferably 60 Mc/sec)

Run the proton resonance spectra of the ethyl compounds selected using approximately 10% solutions in carbon tetrachloride with tetramethylsilane as an internal reference. Measure the separation of the midpoints of the methyl and methylene resonances, Δ, and list these values in increasing order.

Assuming the values of Δ are linearly dependent on the electronegativity of the groups X, prepare a scale of electronegativities. Make a comparison of your values of Δ with the various linear free energy parameters listed in Appendix D (or calculated in Experiment 2).

MEASUREMENT OF CONFORMATIONAL EQUILIBRIA BY NMR

Materials Required

Cyclohexane

NMR spectrometer (60 Mc/sec)

Variable temperature probe

Measure the proton resonance spectrum of pure cyclohexane at temperatures from $+30°C$ down to about $-80°C$. At the lower temperatures, the single resonance splits into two complex resonances. Treat these as two bands and measure their separation, Δ, as a function of temperature. The units of Δ should be c/sec.

Treatment of Results.   The plot of Δ against T is sigmoid (why?) in shape, Figure 22–5. Select several points along the curve in the steepest region (shaded) (where the rate of interchange is neither too fast nor too slow for the method to be applicable.

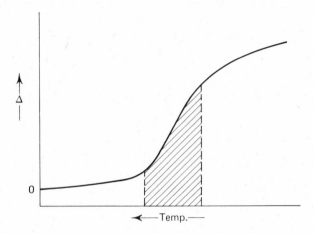

FIGURE 22–5

At each point calculate the rate constant k for the conformational interchange from the expression,

$$k = \frac{2\pi\Delta}{\sqrt{2}} \text{ sec}^{-1}$$

Plot $\log k$ against $1/T$ K in the usual Arrhenius plot (Appendix A) and calculate the activation energy for this process from the slope.

Extension of this Experiment.   Similar results are obtained from the temperature dependent NMR spectra of the methyl resonances of N,N-dimethylformamide or N,N-dimethylacetamide [4]. In this case the equilibrium is the restricted rotation about the C—N bond on account of partial double bond character:

$$
\underset{\|}{\overset{O}{-C}}-N\overset{/}{\underset{\backslash}{}} \quad \longleftrightarrow \quad \overset{O^-}{\underset{\backslash}{C}}=\underset{+}{N}\overset{/}{\underset{\backslash}{}}
$$

At sufficiently low temperatures (just below room temperature in this case), the N-methyl resonance splits into two distinct bands owing to freezing of the configurational equilibrium, the two methyl groups being chemically distinct.

Question

1. Interpret the following 60 MHz ^{1}H-NMR spectra on the following page.

References

1. General texts on NMR theory and practice include: L. M. Jackman, *Nuclear Magnetic Resonance Spectroscopy*, Pergamon, New York, 1959; J. A. Pople, W. G. Schneider, and H. J. Bernstein, *High Resolution Nuclear Magnetic Resonance*, McGraw-Hill, New York, 1959; J. W. Emsley, J. Feeney, and L. H. Sutcliffe, *High Resolution Nuclear Magnetic Resonance Spectroscopy*, 2 Vols, Pergamon, New York, 1966.
2. H. Spiesicke and W. G. Schneider, *J. Chem. Phys.*, **35**, 722 (1961).
3. F. R. Jensen, D. S. Noyce, C. H. Sederholm, and A. J. Berlin, *J. Amer. Chem. Soc.*, **84**, 386 (1962).
4. H. S. Gutowsky and C. H. Holm, *J. Chem. Phys.*, **25**, 1228 (1956).

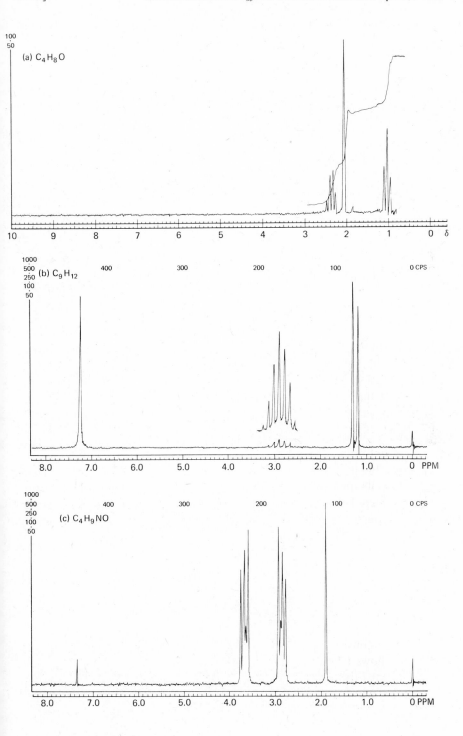

Geometrical Isomerism
and Proton Resonance

The nature of the nuclear resonance condition is such that, at a constant radio-frequency, the magnetic field which is applied to bring a given proton into resonance is a direct measure of the magnetic field in its vicinity due to the structure of the remainder of the molecule. In addition to the variation of the position of the resonance on a suitable horizontal scale (chemical shift), τ, fine structure within the individual resonance lines provides valuable information. For instance, a proton, H_α, will give a doublet when it is adjacent to a second and nonequivalent proton, H_β, due to the fact that in half the molecules H_β has its spin moment oriented with the applied field (thereby augmenting the apparent field at H_α) and half have spin moments opposed to the applied field (weakening the field at H_α):

$$
\begin{array}{cc}
\alpha & \beta \\
C\!\!-\!\!C \\
| & | \\
H & H \\
| & | \\
J_{\alpha\beta} & J_{\alpha\beta}
\end{array}
$$

The same consideration applies to the resonance of H_β and the resulting spectrum shows two doublets whose components are each separated by the same amount—the coupling constant of H_α and H_β, usually referred to as $J_{\alpha\beta}$ and expressed in frequency units (cycles per second).

146

This example is the simplest one possible. In general, the line due to a given proton or group of equivalent protons is split into ($2NI + 1$) lines by a group of N equivalent protons located on a neighboring atom. Some examples of splitting patterns are given in Figure 23–1.

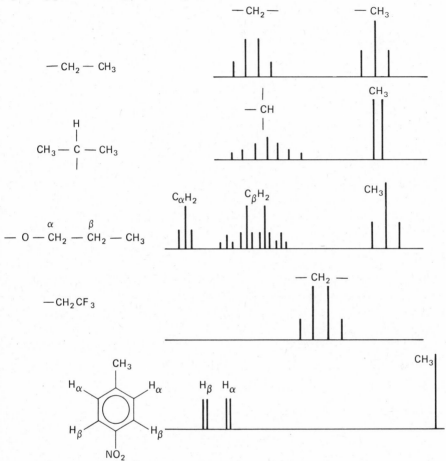

FIGURE 23–1 Some schematic splitting patterns.

The magnitude of the coupling constant is often characteristic of the nature of the two protons coupled (see Appendix C) and depends both on their chemical and spatial environment. Thus the measurement of J can be used not only for chemical identification but will also give information on conformational and geometrical isomerism.

In the experiment which follows, the *cis* and *trans* forms of but-2-enoic acid are prepared and distinguished by the magnitudes of $J_{\alpha\beta}$. It is known from other examples that the coupling constant between *trans* protons is greater than that between *cis* protons (Appendix C).

$$H_\beta \diagdown \diagup H_\alpha$$
$$C = C$$
$$\diagup \diagdown$$
$$CH_3 \quad COOH$$

Isocrotonic acid
(*cis* but-2-enoic acid)

$$H_\beta \diagdown \diagup COOH$$
$$C = C$$
$$\diagup \diagdown$$
$$CH_3 \quad H_\alpha$$

Crotonic acid
(*trans* but-2-enoic acid)

Experimental

Materials Required

Ethyl acetoacetate	Sodium amalgam, (1%)
Phosphorus pentachloride	Benzene, dry

PREPARATION OF *Cis* AND *Trans*-BUT-2-ENOIC ACIDS

In a 250 ml Erlenmeyer flask fitted with a standard taper neck place phosphorus pentachloride (250 g). Add 100 ml dry benzene and stir the slurry magnetically maintaining the temperature at 0° by immersing the flask in an ice bath. Add ethyl acetoacetate (80 g) in portions over a period of 4–6 hours and then allow the mixture to stand at ice temperature overnight. Add ice water, over 4–6 hours, stirring and cooling all the time. This part of the experiment is best conducted under a hood. Separate the benzene layer, extract the aqueous layer with several portions of ether and combine these extracts with the benzene solution. Extract the products into sodium bicarbonate solution, then acidify and extract with ether. Dry over anhydrous sodium sulfate and remove the solvents to obtain a crude mixture of *cis* and *trans* 3-chlorobut-2-enoic acids (3-chloro*iso*crotonic I and 3-chlorocrotonic acids II):

$$CH_3\overset{\overset{\displaystyle O}{\|}}{C}CH_2COOEt \xrightarrow{PCl_5}$$

$$\begin{matrix} Cl & & H \\ \diagdown & & \diagup \\ & C = C & \\ \diagup & & \diagdown \\ H_3C & & COOH \end{matrix} \quad + \quad \begin{matrix} Cl & & COOH \\ \diagdown & & \diagup \\ & C = C & \\ \diagup & & \diagdown \\ H_3C & & H \end{matrix}$$

I   II

Separate the isomers by steam distillation. One isomer crystallizes in the distillate, mp 61° while the other remains in the flask and crystallizes on cooling, mp 94°.

Prepare 200 g of a 1% sodium amalgam (see Experiment 31). Reduce each chlorobutenoic acid separately by shaking vigorously in a strong bottle 100 g of amalgam, 2 g of the acid and 30 ml of ethanol. Release the pressure from time to time and continue shaking until the formation of sodium chloride is complete. Filter and remove the ethanol on the rotary evaporator to obtain the isomeric butenoic acids. These may be purefied in the usual way according to their properties, one being crystalline, mp 72° and the other an oil bp 169°, 70–75°/15 mm.

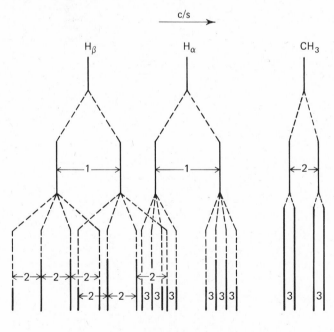

PROTON RESONANCE SPECTRA OF THE BUT-2-ENOIC ACIDS

Measure the proton resonance spectrum of each product in approximately 5–10% solution in benzene. In addition to the resonances due to solvent (very strong, 2.6τ) and the hydroxyl group (at -2τ), the spectrum contains lines due to H_α, H_β, and CH_3, mutually coupled. The spectrum is analyzed in Figure 23–2 and is of the ABX_3 type (two single but distinct protons of similar τ and a group of three identical protons of very different τ all coupled together). Note that each proton splits the methyl line into a doublet but the methyl splits each proton into a quartet, the splittings being the same.

Analyze the spectra and measure the coupling constants. On the basis of your measurements identify the *cis* and *trans* acids.

FIGURE 23–2 Analysis of an ABX_3 spectrum

Questions

1. Interpret the 60 MHz NMR Spectrum, of compound *A* formed by the action of hydrogen peroxide and formic acid on styrene.

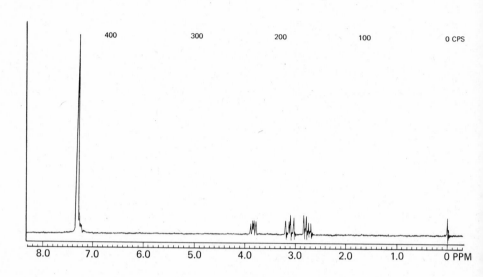

References

1. L. M. Jackman, *Applications of Nuclear Magnetic Resonance Spectroscopy in Organic Chemistry*, Pergamon, New York, 1959.
2. D. E. Jones, R. O. Morris, C. A. Vernon, and R. F. M. White, *J. Chem. Soc.*, 2351 (1960).

Hydrocarbon Radical Ions and Related Compounds

EXPERIMENT 24

Many polycyclic aromatic hydrocarbons, such as naphthalene, anthracene etc. react with alkali metals in ethereal solvents to yield ionic compounds in which the metal atom has transferred one electron to the aromatic system [1, 2].

$$Na\cdot + C_{10}H_8 \longrightarrow Na^+ + C_{10}H_8^-\cdot$$

naphthalene
(colorless)

naphthalene
anion-radical
(green)

The resulting species are anion-radicals of the hydrocarbons and bear one extra π-electron in an *anti* bonding orbital (Figure 24–1). Despite the reduction in delocalization energy (Experiment 12) of the system, the anion-radicals are stable though highly reactive compounds and show many of the reactions of carbanions:

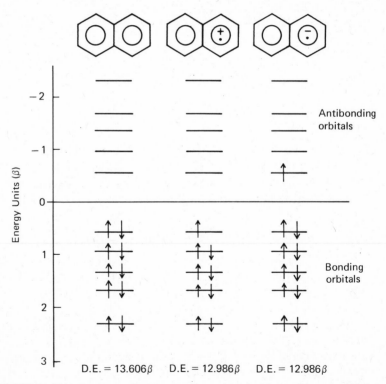

The formation of the anion-radical of naphthalene is a one electron reduction process and the reactivity of the compound is a reflection of the fact that a rather powerful reducing agent—sodium—was needed to prepare it from the parent

D.E. = 13.606β D.E. = 12.986β D.E. = 12.986β

FIGURE 24–1 Energy levels of naphthalene and its radical-anion and radical-cation.

hydrocarbon. Tetracyanoethylene however is reduced to its anion-radical by such mild reagents as iodide or cyanide ion [3] and as a consequence is found to be so stable that it can be isolated as its sodium salt and handled without special precautions. The stability is accounted for since the central double bond of this conjugated system is heavily depleted of electrons by the four electron-withdrawing cyano groups:

The interest in these radical ions lies in the fact that much information concerning the energy levels in the molecules may be obtained by examination of their electron-spin resonance spectra (esr).

Removal of a π-electron from these hydrocarbons, (one-electron oxidation) is also possible and occurs when they are dissolved in conc sulfuric acid [4]. The radical-cation possesses the same amount of delocalization energy as the anion-radical, as shown in Figure 24–1.

$$\underset{\text{anthracene}}{C_{14}H_{10}} \xrightarrow{H_2SO_4} C_{14}H_{11}^{+} + HSO_4^{-}$$

$$C_{14}H_{11}^{+} + C_{14}H_{10} \rightleftharpoons C_{14}H_{11} + C_{14}H_{10}\overset{+}{\cdot}$$

$$C_{14}H_{11} + 2H_2SO_4 \rightleftharpoons C_{14}H_{10}\overset{+}{\cdot} + 2H_2O + SO_2 + HSO_4^{-}$$

Electron-Spin Resonance [5, 6]

The electron, like certain nuclei (see Experiment 22) behaves as a small magnet since it possesses the properties of charge and motion (spin) about an axis. In the presence of an external magnetic field it will achieve a minimum energy state with its magnetic axis pointing in the direction of the applied field. Unlike a macroscopic magnet, however, other orientations in the magnetic field are subject to quantum restrictions and, like the proton, one other only is permitted, namely with the magnetic axis in opposition (antiparallel) to the field. In general the number of permitted states is given by $(2I + 1)$ where I is the spin number, $= \frac{1}{2}$ for the electron. Values for some nuclei are given in Table 22–1. The energy of an electron in an external magnetic field is, then, split into two possible values, the difference ΔE being given by:

$$\Delta E = g\frac{ehH}{4\pi mc} = g\beta H \qquad (1)$$

(compare Equation (1), p. 138) where g is a constant ≈ 2, $e =$ the electronic charge, $h =$ Planck's constant, $m =$ mass of the electron, $c =$ velocity of light, $H =$ applied magnetic field strength and β is the Bohr magneton. At a field strength of 3.6 kilogauss, this energy spacing is only of the order of 1 cal/mole hence at room temperature both levels are almost equally populated, a very slight excess of electrons in the lower state being predictable from the Boltzmann Distribution Law (Experiment 15). Excitation from the lower to the upper state, described as spin inversion, may be achieved by absorption of a quantum of electromagnetic radiation of the correct energy, ΔE (Figure 24–1). Thus, the resonance condition requires that:

$$\Delta E = h\nu = \frac{hc}{\lambda} = g\beta H \tag{2}$$

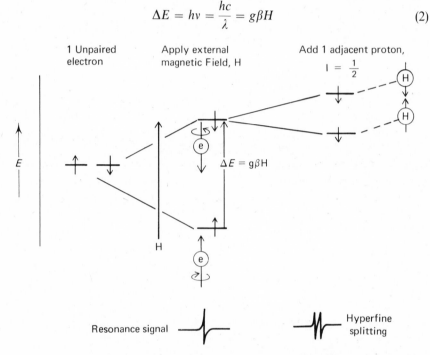

FIGURE 24–2 Origin of electron-spin resonance signals.

Quanta of energy 1 cal/mole are associated with a wavelength of about 3 cm hence this form of spectroscopy falls in the microwave (radar) region and uses its appropriate techniques. In practice, the sample is placed in the resonance cavity of a microwave generator and a transverse magnetic field applied with gradually increasing strength until a sudden loss of energy from the cavity indicates absorption by the sample. It should be noted that resonance absorption is only displayed by compounds possessing *unpaired* electrons, such as free radicals, since spin inversion of one electron which is paired with another would be a violation of the Pauli Exclusion Principle.

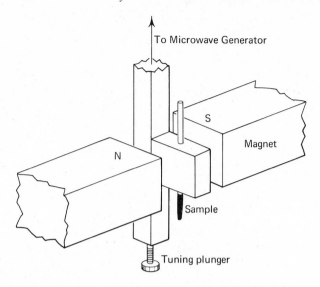

In addition to the detection of unpaired electrons, electron-spin resonance (also known as electron paramagnetic resonance) can also yield information about their environment. If an unpaired electron may reside close to a nucleus which possesses a non-zero spin moment (e.g. a proton, $^1H, I = \frac{1}{2}$), the resonance line will be split into $(2I + 1)$ lines since the nuclear magnet will either add to or detract from the value of the external magnetic field experienced by the unpaired electron, (Figure 24–2). In general, the resonance signal is split into N hyperfine lines by interaction with n_1 nuclei of spin number I_1, n_2 nuclei of spin number I_2 etc. where

$$N = (2n_1I_1 + 1)(2n_2I_2 + 1)(\dots \text{etc}) \tag{3}$$

where n_1, n_2 may refer to different nuclei or to groups of similar nuclei in different chemical environments. The intensities of the hyperfine lines may be calculated by considering all possible permutations of the nuclear magnet orientations (Figure 24–3), while the separation between the hyperfine lines (the coupling constant, a), will be the same for the lines of a given group but may be different for each group of identical interacting nuclei (*see* the naphthalene radical spectrum, Figure 24–4).

Experimental

Materials Required

Naphthalene	Sodium
Anthracene	Electron spin resonance
Tetrahydrofuran	spectrometer (Appendix B)

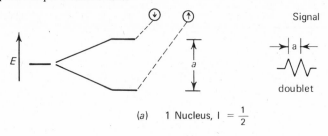

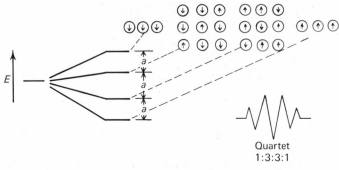

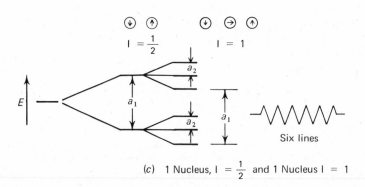

FIGURE 24–3 Examples of hyperfine splitting.

PREPARATION OF SODIUM NAPHTHALENIDE

Dissolve 6.4 g (0.05 mole) of pure naphthalene in 50 ml tetrahydrofuran dried over sodium or molecular sieve. Place the solution in a stoppered flask and sweep out air with a stream of inert gas. Add 1.25 g (0.055 moles) of clean sodium in the form of thin wire or slices, stopper and stir or shake the solution until the sodium has dissolved leaving a green solution of sodium naphthalenide. Use the solution for the following experiments immediately.

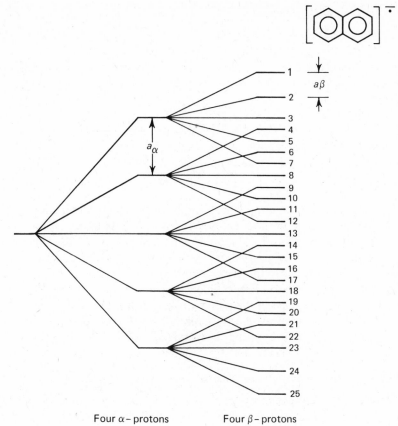

Four α-protons   Four β-protons

$$N = \left[(2 \times 4 \times \tfrac{1}{2}) + 1\right]\left[(2 \times 4 \times \tfrac{1}{4}) + 1\right] = 25$$

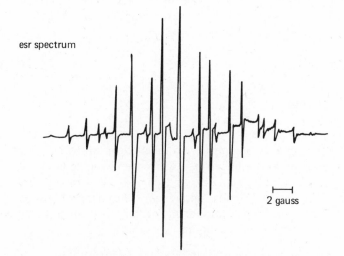

esr spectrum

2 gauss

FIGURE 24–4 *d*-Naphthalene anion radical.

Electron-Spin Resonance of Sodium Naphthalenide.   Place a specimen of the solution in a dry sample tube which should be stoppered. Run the esr spectrum of the solution and confirm the presence of unpaired electrons. Analyze the spectrum as set out in Figure 24–4 and measure the values of the two coupling constants, a_α and a_β.

PREPARATION OF 1,2-DIPHENYLETHANE

Place 6.0 g (0.045 mole) pure benzyl chloride in a two-necked flask equipped with dropping funnel and calcium chloride tube

$$2PhCH_2Cl + 2C_{10}H_8^- Na^+ \longrightarrow PhCH_2CH_2Ph + 2C_{10}H_8 + 2NaCl$$

(or single-necked flask and pressure-equilibrating funnel), all apparatus having been thoroughly dried in the oven. Add 25 ml of sodium-dried tetrahydrofuran and place the remainder of the sodium naphthalenide in the dropping funnel. Cool the flask in a bath of acetone-dry ice to about $-40°C$ and add the naphthalenide solution dropwise to the benzyl chloride, over a period of 15–20 min. The color of the naphthalenide is immediately discharged. When all the solution has been added, remove most of the tetrahydrofuran on the rotary evaporator and steam distill the residue to remove naphthalene. The residue contains an oil which solidifies on cooling and may be recrystallized from a little light petroleum to yield 1,2-diphenylethane, mp 50–51°. Yield, about 3 g 65%.

PREPARATION OF POTASSIUM TETRACYANOETHYLENE $K^+(C_6N_4)^{\bar{\cdot}}$

Dissolve 1.0 g tetracyanoethylene[1] in 30 ml of methyl cyanide and add 1.8 g finely crushed, dry potassium iodide. Stopper and stir or shake until the potassium iodide has dissolved. A deep yellow color of the radical-anion develops. Allow the mixture to stand in ice when a crystalline precipitate of potassium tetracyanoethylene forms. Filter the bronze-colored crystals and dry in the air. Recrystallization may be achieved from methyl cyanide if desired. The compound is stable in air for periods of weeks.

$$2 \quad \overset{NC}{\underset{NC}{>}} C=C \overset{CN}{\underset{CN}{<}} + 2K\overset{+}{I}^- \longrightarrow 2 \left[\overset{NC}{\underset{NC}{>}} C=C \overset{CN}{\underset{CN}{<}} \right]^{\bar{\cdot}} K^+ + I_2$$

Electron-Spin Resonance of Potassium Tetracyanoethylene.   Dissolve approximately 0.1 g potassium tetracyanoethylene in 2 ml of methyl cyanide and measure the electron spin resonance spectrum of the solution.

Interpret the spectrum obtained and compare it with the one you would expect on theoretical grounds, taking into consideration the fact that the unpaired electron is coupled to four nitrogen atoms which are all equivalent and have $I = 1$. Measure the coupling constant, a.

[1] If the material is dark-colored, it may be purefied by sublimation at 100°/15 mm.

The Electronic Spectrum of Potassium Tetracyanoethylene. Make up an approximately 10^{-4} *M* solution of the radical in methyl cyanide and run the ultraviolet spectrum from 300–500 mμ. Compare the spectrum with that of tetracyanoethylene obtained under the same conditions, and also with that of tetracyanoethylene in chloroform. Interpret these spectra in the light of the discussion in this experiment and also Experiment 22.

Electron-Spin Resonance of the Triphenylmethyl Radical. Measure the esr spectrum of the trityl radical using the benzene solution prepared in Experiment 32. Compare the number of lines obtained with that calculated from Eq. (3) on the basis of coupling with six *ortho*, six *meta* and three *para* protons.

Electron-Spin Resonance of the Anthracene Radical-Cation. Make up a 0.02 *M* solution of pure anthracene in 98% sulfuric acid and measure the esr spectrum of the solution immediately.

Equation (3) predicts that the spectrum should show 75 lines (verify this) but it is in practise much simpler since the coupling constants for the three groups of protons which couple with the odd electron are in the ratio *meso* : α : β as 4 : 2 : 1 and many lines coincide, thus.

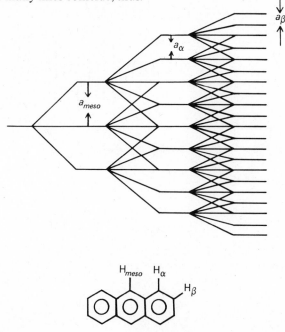

FIGURE 24–5

ELECTRON DENSITIES OF THE HYDROCARBONS

It may be shown that the coupling constant with a given proton is proportional to the electron density at the carbon to which it is attached. The latter may be calculated from molecular orbital theory but esr measurements provide a convenient experimental approach in good agreement with theory.

Calculate the relative electron densities on the α- and β-positions of naphthalene and on the *meso*, α- and β-positions of anthracene.

Do these values agree with the observed properties of the hydrocarbons, for example, the preferred position of nitration?

Questions

1. The esr spectrum of the tetracyanoethylene anion-radical contains nine equally spaced lines. Show how these are derived and calculate their intensity pattern. How does this compare with the cyclooctatetraene radical-anion. Check your results by reference to *J. Org. Chem.*, **25**, 1470 (1960) and *J. Chem. Phys.*, **32**, 1873 (1960).
2. Calculate the expected esr spectrum of the perinaphthene radical-ion assuming zero electron density at the β carbon atoms (as well as at the angular positions). The observed spectrum is as shown below. To what extent is the assumption justified?

6 canonical structures

References

1. D. E. Paul, D. Lipkin, and S. I. Weissman, *J. Amer. Chem. Soc.*, **78**, 116 (1956); D. Lipkin, F. R. Galiano, and R. W. Jordan, *Chem. and Ind.*, 1657 (1963).
2. H. Gusten and L. Horner, *Angew. Chem.* (Internat. Ed.) 455 (1962); *Annalen*, **652**, 99 (1962).
3. O. W. Webster, W. Mahler, and R. E. Benson, *J. Org. Chem.*, **25**, 1470 (1960); *J. Amer. Chem. Soc.*, **84**, 3678 (1962).
4. S. I. Weissman, E. de Boer, and J. J. Conradi, *J. Chem. Phys.*, **26**, 963 (1957); A. Carrington, F. Dravnieks, and M. C. R. Symons, *J. Chem. Soc.*, 947 (1959).
5. D. J. E. Ingram, *Free Radicals as Studied by Electron-Spin Resonance*, Butterworth, London, 1958: K. Higasi, H. Baba, and A. Rembaum, *Quantum Organic Chemistry*, Interscience, New York, 1965, Chapter 10.

Measurement of
Solvent Polarity

EXPERIMENT 25

The organic chemist tends to apply the term *polar* to solvents in a somewhat intuitive manner based on their ability to dissolve, and hence their resemblance to, polar materials—ionic or dipolar substances. Thus, an order of 'polarity' may be established qualitatively, eg.,

water > alcohols ≈ carboxylic acids > ketones > ethers > aromatic

hydrocarbons > paraffins

In order to investigate the interactions between solvent and solute molecules and the role which the solvent plays in reactions, many empirical scales of polarity [1] have been devised in order to give a semiquantitative meaning to this term. These include simple physical measurements such as dielectric constant [2] (Experiment 14) and a variety of solvent-dependent chemical and physical properties, a number of which are summarized in Table 25–1. Needless to say, it is desirable that all the scales should be consistent with each other. Discrepancies are often noted between two scales however, since the basis of the physical effects which they measure may be quite different, which illustrates the fact that solvent polarity is a complex term containing a number of properties each of which may be more or less accentuated by the method of measurement (Figure 25–1), such as ability to solvate ions and dipoles (Experiment 5), hydrogen-bonding properties (Experiment 17) or electron donor properties (Experiment 19).

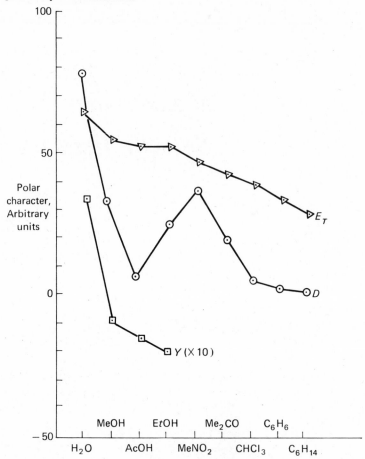

FIGURE 25–1 Comparison of polarity scales for a series of solvents.

Physically, ion or dipole solvation may be described by the free energy of interaction (attractive) between a given electric charge or pair of charges and neighboring solvent molecules. Schematically, the effect of introducing a charged species into a dipolar solvent may be shown as in Figure 25–2. Rearrangement of solvent molecules to form a sphere of charge of the opposite

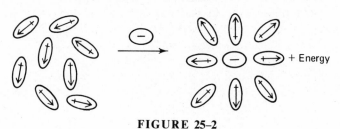

FIGURE 25–2

sign surrounding the ion lowers the energy of the system and also its entropy (disorder). A solvent effect upon a reaction is observed when these interactions differ between the ground and excited states (initial and transition states) and, moreover, this difference changes from solvent to solvent.

TABLE 25–1 Some Solvent Polarity Scales

Dielectric Constant, D	Ratio of capacitances of capacitor with solvent and with air as dielectric. Measures work required to align molecules in an electric field (Experiment 14).
Y (Reference 3)	Ratio of solvolysis rates of *tert*-butyl chloride in solvent to that in 80% ethanol at 25°C. Measures ability to stabilize a polar transition state.
Z, E_T (Reference 4, 5)	Position of maximum absorption of solvatochromic dyes such as I, II.

I

II

	Measures ability of solvent to lower the relative energies of excited- to ground-states.
Ω (Reference 6)	Ratio of *endo* to *exo*-product in Diels-Alder reaction between cyclopentadiene and methyl acrylate (Experiment 42). Measures ability to stabilize the *endo* transition state which has greater dipole moment than the *exo*.
X (Reference 7)	Ratio of rate of bromination of tetramethyltin in solvent to that in glacial acetic acid.

$$Me_4Sn + Br_2 \rightarrow Me_3Sn^+Br^- + MeBr$$

Ability to stabilize polar transition state.

S (Reference 8)	Adaptation of the above scales to linear free-energy form, such that $\log f(S)/\log f(E) = SR$ where the functions f may be any of the solvent-dependent parameters for the given solvent (S), referred to the standard, ethanol (E). R is a measure of the susceptibility of the given parameter to solvent effects (cf. Hammett ρ-value, page 25).

Solvatochromic Effects [9]

A compound is said to exhibit solvatochromism when its electronic spectrum is influenced by the medium in which it is dissolved (excluding chemical reaction), and especially when the absorption maximum of a given transition varies in a regular and sensible fashion with solvent polarity. A great many compounds are solvatochromic to some degree, the most useful as polarity indicators being those which show the effect to the greatest degree. Two solvatochromic dyes have been used to define polarity scales, 1-ethyl-4-carbomethoxy-pyridinium iodide (I) [4], and 1-(p-hydroxyphenyl)-2,4,6-triphenylpyridinium betaine (II) [5]. The pyridinium iodide possesses a low intensity absorption band in the visible and near-ultraviolet regions of the spectrum which is due to a charge transfer type of excitation (see Experiment 19):

ground state (greater charge separation)   excited state (less charge separation)

Since the excited state is less polar than the ground state, the latter is relatively stabilized in a polar solvent, hence more energy will be needed for excitation in this medium than in a nonpolar one since greater attractive interactions will have to be overcome. The compound absorbs at progressively shorter wavelengths as the solvent polarity increases. The pyridinium betaine (II) (Table 25–1), shows even greater shifts of λ_{max} which occurs in the visible region. The color in methanol is red, isopropanol, blue, acetone, green etc.

Experimental

Materials Required

Isonicotinic acid[1]	acetonitrile
HCl gas	nitromethane
Ethyl iodide	benzonitrile
Solvents:[2]	nitrobenzene
water	acetone
ethanol	acetophenone
methanol	dichloromethane
n-propanol	chloroform
isopropanol	U.V.—visible Spectrophotometer
acetic acid	(preferably recording)

[1] Isonicotinic acid may readily be prepared from γ-picoline by oxidation with neutral permanganate [10] or by nitric acid oxidation of the methylene derivative [11].

[2] Any of the solvents may be omitted or others included at the discretion of the instructor.

Methyl isonicotinate. Esterify isonicotinic acid (5 g) by suspending in 150 ml dry methanol, refluxing gently, and passing in a steady stream of dry HCl gas until all the solid goes into solution. Remove the solvent on the rotary evaporator.

Yield 5.3 g, quantitative

COOH   COOMe

$+$ MeOH $\xrightarrow{\text{HCl}}$ $+$ H$_2$O

4-Carboxymethylpyridinium iodide, I. To 5.3 g methyl isonicotinate, add 6.5 g ethyl iodide, stopper and allow the mixture to stand for $\frac{1}{2}$–1 hour at room temperature. Stir with ether and filter the orange crystalline solid. Dry in the air.

COOMe   COOMe

$+$ EtI $\longrightarrow$ I$^-$

N$_+$
|
Et
I

MEASUREMENT OF SOLVENT POLARITIES

Take 5 ml of each of the solvents in turn, which should be pure and dry, and add a little of the 1-ethyl-4-carboxymethylpyridinium iodide. Warm and stir if necessary to effect solution. The required concentration must be found by trial, but the solution should possess some visible color. Measure the ultraviolet spectra of each solution using the appropriate solvent as reference in each case, and 1 cm quartz absorption cells. Locate the charge-transfer band which is on the long wavelength side of the intense aromatic absorption and may be rather broad (Figure 25–3). Measure λ_{max} ($\bar{\nu}_{max}$) for each solvent.

Treatment of results. Kosower defined his polarity parameter, Z, as the molar excitation energy expressed in kcal mole^{-1} for the charge-transfer band of 1-ethyl-4-carboxymethylpyridinium iodide in the appropriate solvent:

$$E_T \text{ (ergs)} = hv$$

$$= \frac{hc}{\lambda_{max}}$$

$$= hc\bar{\nu}_{max}$$

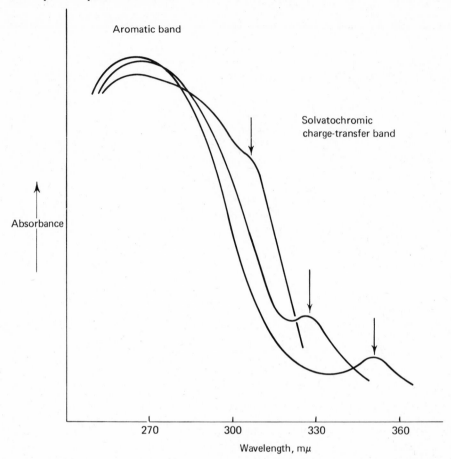

FIGURE 25–3 Spectra of 1-ethyl-4-carboxymethylpyridinium iodide in different solvents.

where

$$h = \text{Planck's Constant} = 6.624 \times 10^{-27} \text{ erg sec}$$

$$c = \text{velocity of light} = 3 \times 10^{10} \text{ cm sec}^{-1}$$

$$v = \text{frequency}$$

$$\lambda = \text{wavelength}$$

$$\bar{v}_{max} = \text{wave-number of the radiation}$$

Now 1 kcal $= 4.184 \times 10^{10}$ erg and Avogadro's number, $N_0 = 6.023 \times 10^{23}$

$$E_T \text{ (kcal/mole)} = \left(\frac{6.624 \times 10^{-27}}{4.184 \times 10^{10}} \right)(3 \times 10^{10})(6.023 \times 10^{23})\bar{v} = Z$$

$$Z = 2.86 \times 10^{-3}\bar{v}_{max}$$

a. Calculate Z for each solvent examined and arrange the solvents in order of their polarity.

b. Measure Z values for ethanol-water mixtures starting with 10% w/w water and increasing the amount by increments of 10%. Plot these values of Z against the Y values for the same mixture obtained from Reference 3a and examine the correlation with this other solvent polarity parameter.

c. Choose a solvent not listed above and one whose solvent properties you know nothing about. Measure Z and place the solvent on the polarity scale.

Questions

1. Using the polarity scales shown in Figure 25–1 and a source of data such as the *Handbook of Chemistry and Physics* Chemical Rubber Publishing Co., Cleveland, Ohio (annual), examine the postulate that the following properties might be used as indexes of solvent character:
   Refractive index
   Viscosity
   Solubility of a standard solute
   Dipole moment
   Boiling point relative to straight-chain paraffin of equal molecular weight
2. *No one polarity scale is adequate to describe the properties of solvents in all systems.* Discuss this statement.
3. Design a reaction whose rate could be used as a polarity index when carried out in various solvents (in the same way as the Y scale) but which could be extended to the solvents of low polarity.

References

1. C. Reichardt, *Angewandte Chemie* (Internat. Ed.), **4**, 29 (1965).
2. K. J. Laidler, *Reaction Kinetics* Vol. II, Commonwealth and International Library, Macmillan, New York, 1963.
3. (a) E. Grunwald and S. Winstein, *J. Amer. Chem. Soc.*, **70**, 846 (1948);
   (b) S. Winstein and E. Grunwald, *J. Amer. Chem. Soc.*, **73**, 2700 (1951);
   (c) A. H. Fainberg and S. Winstein, *J. Amer. Chem. Soc.*, **78**, 2770 (1956).
4. E. M. Kosower, *J. Amer. Chem. Soc.*, **80**, 3253, 3261 (1958).
5. K. Dimroth, C. Reichardt, T. Siepmann, and E. Bohlmann, *Ann.*, **661**, (1963).
6. J. Berson, Z. Hamlet, and W. A. Mueller, *J. Amer. Chem. Soc.*, **297** (1962).
7. M. Gielen and J. Nasielski, *Rec. Trav. Chim.*, **82**, 228 (1963); *J. Organomet. Chem.*, **1**, 173 (1964).
8. S. Brownstein, *Can. J. Chem.*, **38**, 1590 (1960).
9. H. H. Jaffé and M. Orchin, *Theory and Applications of Ultraviolet Spectroscopy*, Wiley, New York, 1962.
10. G. Block, E. Depp, and B. B. Carson, *J. Org. Chem.*, **14**, 14 (1949).
11. H. Bartz, *Bull. Acad. Polansk. Sci.*, **2**, 395 (1954).

Chemical Preparations

PART **III**

Kinetic and Thermodynamic Control of a Reaction

In certain cases, a reaction system may give rise to two different products, P_1 and P_2, via different reaction pathways, 1 and 2, the products being interconvertible, directly, 3, or by the reversibility of the first reaction:

$$A + B \; \underset{2}{\overset{1}{\rightleftarrows}} \; \left. \begin{matrix} P_1 \\ P_2 \end{matrix} \right\} 3 \quad \text{or} \quad A + B \; \underset{2}{\overset{1}{\rightleftarrows}} \; \begin{matrix} P_1 \\ 3 \\ P_2 \end{matrix}$$

If the energetics of the system are as shown in Figure 26–1, we may infer the conditions under which each product will be formed. Three separate reactions are involved, each with their own activation energy. E_1 is considerably less than E_2 hence reaction 1 will be faster than reaction 2 although the disparity between the rates will decrease at higher temperatures. The most rapidly formed product will be P_1 and the system is said to be under kinetic control when this product is isolated. The kinetic product P_1 however, may now be converted to P_2 if sufficient time is allowed for this reaction to occur. When P_2 is obtained, the reaction is under thermodynamic control. The kinetic product in general will be obtained at relatively low temperatures and short reaction times while the thermodynamic product will be formed at higher temperatures and after prolonged reaction times. The same result is obtained if the kinetic product is formed reversibly and the thermodynamic product irreversibly as in 1b.

171

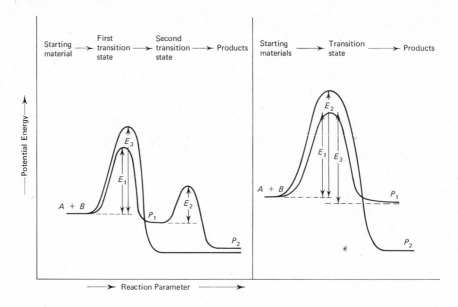

FIGURE 26–1 Energy schemes for reactions producing kinetic and thermodynamic products.

Two examples of this type of system are, the addition of hydrogen chloride to a conjugated diene and the bromination of 3-keto-5-α-substituted steroids. In the first example, the kinetic product is the 1,2-adduct (I) which reverts to the more stable 1,4-adduct (II) on warming in the presence of acid [1, 2]:

$$CH_2{=}\overset{\overset{\displaystyle CH_3}{|}}{C}{-}CH{=}CH_2 \xrightarrow{\text{HCl}} CH_3{-}\overset{\overset{\displaystyle CH_3}{|}}{\underset{\underset{\displaystyle Cl}{|}}{C}}{-}CH{=}CH_2$$

I

$$\downarrow$$

$$CH_3{-}\overset{\overset{\displaystyle CH_3}{|}}{C}{=}CH{-}CH_2Cl$$

II

In the second example, substitution occurs initially from the less hindered β-side giving the 4-β (axial) bromo compound (III) as the kinetic product. On prolonged treatment with HBr this rearranges to the 3-α (equatorial) isomer (IV) in which 1,3 interactions are minimized [3]:

5α-bromocholestan-3-one   4β,5α-dibromocholestan-3-one III

4α,5α-dibromocholestan-3-one IV

Experimental

Materials Required

Isoprene (2-methylbuta-1,3-diene)
Hydrogen chloride gas

THE HYDROCHLORINATION OF ISOPRENE

Dissolve 10.0 g pure redistilled isoprene in an equal volume of dry ether in a flask fitted with a gas inlet reaching under the surface of the liquid, and calcium chloride guard tube. Weigh the flask and contents and immerse in a bath of petroleum ether, cooled and maintained at -10 to $-20°$ by the addition of dry ice. Pass in dry hydrogen chloride until about $\frac{2}{3}$ molar proportion of the gas is absorbed, as determined by periodic weighing. Transfer half the contents of the flask to a clean container, stopper and store at $-10°$ for one to two hours. Add solid potassium carbonate and calcium chloride and allow the mixture to warm to room temperature. Finally distill the liquid collecting the kinetic product, 2-chloro-2-methylbut-3-ene at $80°/760$ mm, $n_D^{20} = 1.4191$.

To the remainder of the liquid in the flask, continue to pass HCl until saturated, keeping the temperature at around $-10°$ to prevent the formation of dichloro compounds. Allow the mixture to stand overnight at a low temperature, then neutralize, dry, and distill as before collecting 1-chloro-3-methylbut-2-ene, the thermodynamic product, at $110°/760$ mm, $n_D^{20} = 1.4450$.

Measure the infrared spectra of the two products examining, in particular, the olefinic out-of-plane bending vibrations between 700–1000 cm^{-1} which enable a distinction to be made between terminal and nonterminal olefins.

$$\begin{array}{c} R \\ \diagdown \\ \diagup \\ H \end{array} C{=}CH_2$$

out-of-plane bending mode, (cm^{-1})

905–915 (strong); 985–995 (medium)

$$\begin{array}{cc} R \quad & H \\ \diagdown & \diagup \\ & C{=}C \\ \diagup & \diagdown \\ R \quad & R \end{array}$$

790–850

Questions

1. The formation of a semicarbazone is reversible,

$$H_2NCONHNH_2 + R_2CO \underset{k_{-1}}{\overset{k_1}{\rightleftharpoons}} H_2NCONHN{=}CR_2 + H_2O$$

The equilibrium constant for this system may be expressed by

$$K = \frac{k_1}{k_{-1}} = \frac{[H_2NCONHN{=}CR_2][H_2O]}{[H_2NCONHNH_2][R_2CO]}$$

and the rate of formation of the semicarbazone by k_1. Values of K and k_1 for cyclohexanone and furfural are given below;

	K (relative)	k_1
	0.005	36
	1.4	0.73

Discuss methods whereby this reaction could be used to separate a mixture of cyclohexanone and furfural.

2. Naphthalene reacts in conc sulfuric acid at 80° to give naphthalene-1-sulfonic acid but at 160° the product is naphthalene-2-sulfonic acid. Discuss various interpretations of this observation and suggest experiments which would allow a distinction to be made between the possibilities.

3. Suggest a detailed mechanism for the Jacobsen rearrangement, an example of which is,

4. Why is II thermodynamically more stable than I?

References

1. W. J. Jones and H. W. T. Chorley, *J. Chem. Soc.*, 832 (1946).
2. A. J. Ultee, *J. Chem. Soc.*, 530 (1946).
3. J-C. Jaquesey and J. Levisalles, *Bull. Soc. Chim. (France)*, **189**, 1866 (1962).

Asymmetric Induction

It is well known that reactions between symmetrical compounds (compounds possessing a plane or center of symmetry) cannot produce an asymmetric product even though it is potentially resolvable. For example, the reaction between phenyl magnesium bromide and methyl ethyl ketone gives the *dl*-pair of enantiometric carbinols (I) with no excess of either *l*- or *d*-form. This means that there is an equal chance of the reagent attacking from either side of the carbonyl group:

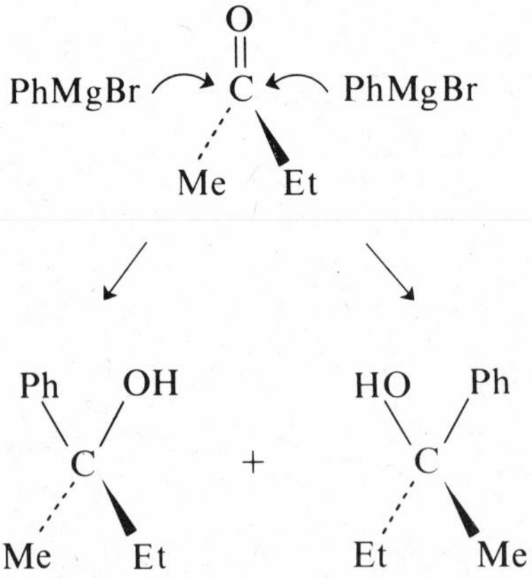

$$
\begin{array}{c}
\text{O} \\
\| \\
\text{PhMgBr} \longrightarrow \text{C} \longleftarrow \text{PhMgBr} \\
\diagup \ \diagdown \\
\text{Me} \quad \text{Et}
\end{array}
$$

Ph OH   HO Ph

C   +   C

Me   Et   Et   Me

50%   I   50%

dl mixture

If now an asymmetric substituent is placed in one of the reagent molecules, even in a position remote from the reaction center, it may tip the balance in favor of attack preferentially from one side and the product will possess an excess of one enantiomer and consequently a certain amount of optical activity *due to the new asymmetric center*. Asymmetry has been induced in the reaction by the asymmetric substituent. For example, attaching a (+) bornyl group to benzoylformic acid (II) and reacting with methyl magnesium bromide gives, after hydrolysis, an atrolactic acid (III) which possesses an 11% excess of the (+) form over the (−).

PhCOCOOH $\xrightarrow{\text{(+) Borneol}}$ PhCOCOO—(+) bornyl

(II)

$\downarrow$ MeMgBr

$$\underset{\text{(III)}}{\underset{\text{Me}}{\overset{\text{OH}}{\text{Ph—C—COOH}}}} \xleftarrow{\text{hydrolysis}} \underset{\text{Me}}{\overset{\text{OH}}{\text{Ph—C—CO—O—(+) bornyl}}}$$

(III)

$[\alpha_D] = +4.2°$

(+) Borneol has the structure

An even more dramatic example of asymmetric induction is the formation of mannononitrile (V) to the virtual exclusion of gluconitrile (VI) from the reaction between (+) arabinose (IV) and hydrogen cyanide.

$$\underset{\substack{\text{(V)} \\ \text{(95%)}}}{\underset{\text{CH}_2\text{OH}}{\overset{\text{CN}}{\begin{array}{c}\text{H—C—OH} \\ \text{H—C—OH} \\ \text{HO—C—H} \\ \text{HO—C—H}\end{array}}}} \qquad \underset{\text{(IV)}}{\underset{\text{CH}_2\text{OH}}{\begin{array}{c}\text{HCN} \nearrow \quad \overset{\text{H} \quad \text{O}}{\text{C}} \quad \nwarrow \text{HCN} \\ \text{H—C—OH} \\ \text{HO—C—H} \\ \text{HO—C—H}\end{array}}} \qquad \underset{\substack{\text{(VI)} \\ \text{(5%)}}}{\underset{\text{CH}_2\text{OH}}{\overset{\text{CN}}{\begin{array}{c}\text{HO—C—H} \\ \text{H—C—OH} \\ \text{HO—C—H} \\ \text{HO—C—H}\end{array}}}}$$

The origin of this preferred attack is mainly steric: an asymmetric environment of the carbonyl group is presented to the reagent which then attacks its least hindered side the more rapidly. After study of a number of cases of asymmetric induction, D. J. Cram [1] has rationalized the orientation of attack on the carbonyl group in a simple rule. It appears that the preferred conformation of the compound (VII) has the largest group, L, remote from the carbonyl oxygen.

Cram's Rule

The reagent then attacks preferentially from the side between the large (L) and small (S) groups rather than between large and medium (M) so that the product contains an excess of VIII over IX.

A related rule formulated by Prelog [2] is applicable to the esters of α-ketoacids with asymmetric alcohols which react with the Grignard reagent or aluminohydride ion to give an optically active α-hydroxy acid. The geometry of the ester is assumed to be such that the two carbonyl groups are antiparallel, the reagent then attacks preferentially between the medium and small groups.

Prelog's Rule

The percentage of asymmetry induced depends markedly on the location and the efficiency of the asymmetric group at shielding one side of the reaction site from attack; in favorable instances it may reach 20–30% and, rarely, higher. The following examples exploit two principles. In the first, the substrate, pyruvic acid (X) is made asymmetric by esterification with menthol and is then converted to optically active atrolactic acid (XI) by reaction with phenyl magnesium bromide [3];

$$\underset{X}{CH_3\overset{\overset{\displaystyle O}{\|}}{C}COOH} + (-)\,menthol \longrightarrow CH_3\overset{\overset{\displaystyle O}{\|}}{C}-CO-(-)\,menthyl$$

$$CH_3\overset{\overset{\displaystyle O}{\|}}{C}CO-(-)\,menthyl + PhMgBr \longrightarrow \underset{\underset{Ph}{|}}{\overset{\overset{\displaystyle OH}{|}}{CH_3C}}-CO-(-)\,menthyl \quad Xa$$

$$\underset{\underset{Ph}{|}}{\overset{\overset{\displaystyle OH}{|}}{CH_3C}}-CO-(-)\,menthyl \xrightarrow{\ OH^-\ } \underset{\underset{Ph}{|}}{\overset{\overset{\displaystyle OH}{|}}{CH_3C}}-COOH + (-)\,menthol \quad XI$$

$$(-)\,menthol = \qquad\qquad\qquad levorotatory$$

In the second, an asymmetric reagent is prepared by reaction of lithium aluminum hydride with a sugar derivative, cyclohexylidine glucofuranose (XII), which then reduces acetophenone to the optically active phenethyl alcohol (XIII) [4].

XIV   XV

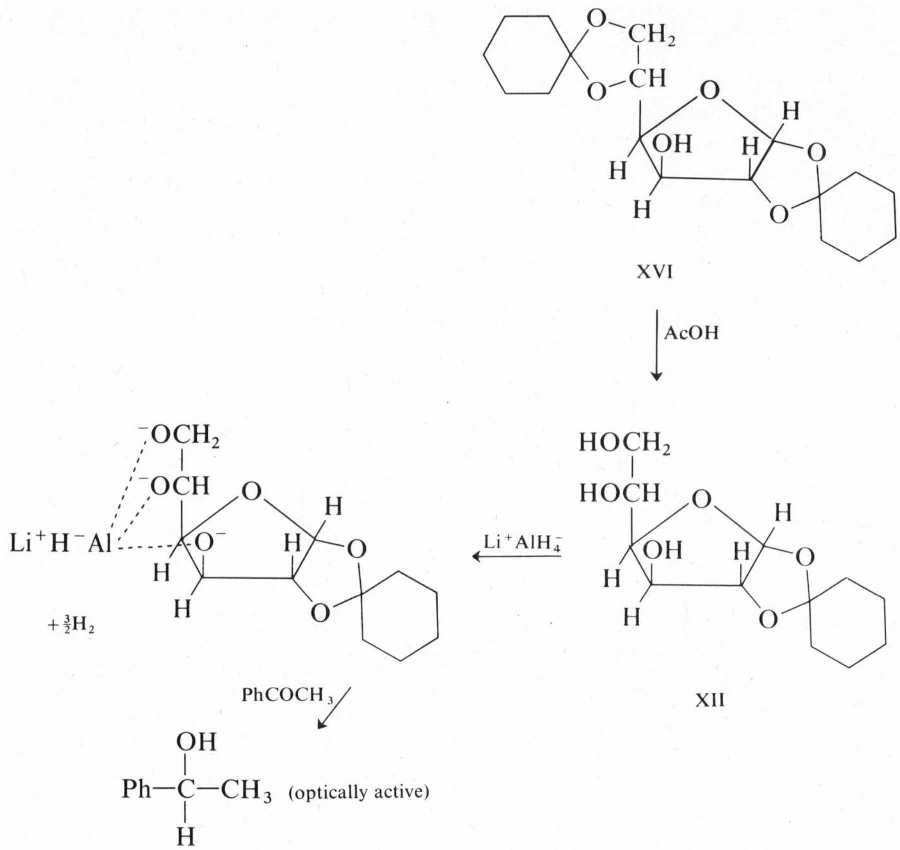

XVI

AcOH

XII

$Ph-\overset{\underset{\displaystyle H}{|}}{\underset{}{\overset{\displaystyle OH}{|}}}C-CH_3$ (optically active)

XIII

Glucopyranose, (ordinary glucose) (XIV) may be considered to exist in equilibrium with the furanose form (XV) which forms a diacetal (XVI) with excess cyclohexanone as it possesses two *cis*-diol groups. The sidechain acetal group is preferentially hydrolyzed off to give the required reagent (XII). Its three hydroxyl functions react with three hydrides of the AlH_4^- ion leaving a reagent with only one hydride function, now in an asymmetric environment (XVII). The compound still has five asymmetric centers, and reduction of a ketone such as acetophenone occurs preferentially from one side.

Experimental

Materials Required

Pyruvic acid (50% aqueous)	D-Glucose (anhydrous)
(−) Menthol (natural menthol)	Cyclohexanone
Toluene	Lithium aluminum hydride
Bromobenzene	Acetophenone
Magnesium turnings	Polarimeter

SYNTHESIS OF OPTICALLY ACTIVE ATROLACTIC ACID

Menthyl pyruvate.   Place 5.0 g (0.032 mole) (−) menthol in a 100 ml round-bottom flask and add 10 g (ca 0.05 mole) pyruvic acid (50% aqueous solution), 50 ml toluene and two drops conc sulfuric acid. Fit a Dean and Stark trap and reflux condenser to the flask (Figure 27–1) and allow the mixture to boil rapidly so that the toluene refluxes freely up to the condenser while water present initially and formed in the esterification reaction is carried up in the vapor and retained in the trap. Continue heating until no more water comes over and then for a further 30 min. Cool the flask and wash the liquid with a little sodium bicarbonate solution and dry the toluene layer over anhydrous sodium sulfate.

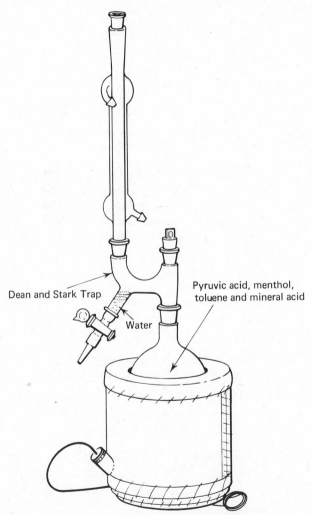

Dean and Stark Trap

Water

Pyruvic acid, menthol, toluene and mineral acid

FIGURE 27–1 Apparatus for the esterification of pyruvic acid.

Remove the toluene on the rotary evaporator to obtain crude (−) menthyl pyruvate as a pleasant smelling oil. This may be used in the next part of the experiment or may be purified by distillation collecting the ester at 150–160°/15 mm.

Yield, 6.5 g, 85%

(−) *Menthyl atrolactate, Xa.* Prepare a solution of phenyl magnesium bromide by placing in a dry flask fitted with reflux condenser, 3.14 g (0.02 mole) bromobenzene, 0.55 g (0.022 mole) magnesium turnings and 20 ml sodium-dried ether. Reflux the mixture until the magnesium goes into solution, adding a small crystal of iodine if the reaction is reluctant to start. Meanwhile, fit a dry two-necked 50 ml flask with dropping funnel and reflux condenser. Place the phenyl magnesium bromide solution in the funnel and protect it from the atmosphere with a calcium chloride tube. Place in the flask 5.0 g (−) menthyl pyruvate in 15 ml dry ether. Add the Grignard reagent from the funnel slowly, swirling the flask to ensure good mixing. When all the reagent has been added, reflux the mixture for 15 min and then pour into cold water. Extract the organic material with several portions of ether, separate, combine the ethereal layers and dry over anhydrous sodium sulfate. Remove the solvent on the evaporator to obtain (−) menthyl atrolactate as a pale yellow oil.

Yield, ca 6.0 g 90%

Atrolactic Acid, XI. Dissolve the crude (−) menthyl atrolactate in a solution of 1.5 g sodium hydroxide in 25 ml aqueous methanol (90% methanol, 10% water). Boil the solution rapidly under reflux for 1–1½ hours then remove the methanol on the rotary evaporator. Add 10 ml water and ensure the solution is strongly basic. Extract repeatedly with 10 ml portions of ether until no more menthol remains. Separate off the aqueous layer, cool in ice and cautiously acidify by the addition of a little conc hydrochloric acid. Extract the atrolactic acid which separates out with three 10 ml portions of ether, combine the ethereal extracts, dry over anhydrous sodium sulfate and remove the ether on the rotary evaporator, to obtain atrolactic acid, XI as a dark oil which crystallizes on standing and may be recrystallized from benzene, mp 70°C.

Yield, 2 g 60%

Optical Activity of the Product. Dissolve the atrolactic acid (which should not smell of menthol) in a little methanol and measure the rotation of the solution, α, expressing the optical activity as the specific rotation, $[\alpha]$:

$$[\alpha]_t^D = \frac{100\alpha}{lc}$$

where l = length of the polarimeter tube in cm and c, the weight of atrolactic acid per 100 ml solvent. Express the percentage optical purity of the product as:

$$\frac{(\text{measured specific rotation}) \, 100}{(\text{specific rotation for pure } (+) \text{ or } (-) \text{ acid})}$$

$$= + \text{ or } -37.7° \text{ (at 16°C)}.$$

SYNTHESIS OF OPTICALLY ACTIVE PHENETHYL ALCOHOL

Materials Required

D-Glucose	Acetic acid
Cyclohexanone	Lithium aluminum hydride
Sulfuric acid	Acetophenone

Dicyclohexylidineglucofuranose, XVI. Place cyclohexanone (98 g, 1 mole) in a 250 ml flask in an ice-bath. Stir vigorously while cooling and add slowly conc. sulfuric acid (6.5 ml). No darkening of the liquid should be apparent. Add powdered anhydrous D-glucose (45 g, 0.25 mole) and allow the mixture to shake overnight until it almost solidifies. Add 40–60° petroleum ether (250 ml), stir and warm until the solid dissolves and two liquid layers are formed. Separate the top (petroleum) layer and cool so that the di-cyclohexylidine compound crystallizes. This is pure enough to be used in the next stage but may be recrystallized from petroleum ether when the mp is 130–132°, $[\alpha]_D^{30} = -2.2°$ (EtOH).

Yield, 50 g, 55%

Monocyclohexylidineglucofuranose, XII. Dissolve dicyclohexylidineglucofuranose (20 g) in a mixture of glacial acetic acid, (60 ml) and water (20 ml). Allow it to stand on a hotplate or waterbath for one hour, the temperature of the solution being about 60°. Evaporate the solution to dryness on the rotary evaporator at around 50°. Recrystallize the solid material from ethanol-ether (4:1) to obtain monocyclohexylidineglucofuranose, mp 150°.

Yield 10 g, 66%

(−)Phenethyl Alcohol, PhCH(OH)CH₃. Assemble a carefully dried apparatus consisting of a two-necked 500 ml round bottomed flask fitted with a dropping funnel and a condenser topped by a calcium chloride drying tube. Arrange facilities for stirring, preferably magnetic.

Place 250 ml of sodium-dried ether in the flask and, carefully and in small portions, add lithium aluminum hydride (2.1 g, 0.026 mole); (CAUTION: eye protection should be worn all the time and flames removed from the vicinity of the apparatus). Stir the slurry and add in portions dry monocyclohexylidineglucofuranose (6.5 g, 0.025 mole); allow the solid to go into solution and the effervescence of hydrogen to cease. Add dropwise over 30–60 min, acetophenone (6.0 g, 0.025 mole) and finally reflux the mixture gently for a further 30 minutes. Cool the flask and cautiously add[1] moist ether until no more effervescence is evident. Add water (25 ml), dropwise at first stirring continuously and finally filter the solution. Separate the water layer and discard. Dry the ethereal layer over anhydrous sodium sulfate and remove the ether on the rotary evaporator. Distill the residue at 205° or preferably at reduced pressure (105–110/15 mm).

Yield 5.5 g, 90%

[1] During this part of the workup it is good practice to place a transparent screen between the worker and the apparatus.

Measure the specific rotation of the product as before and determine the percentage optical purity. $[\alpha]_D^{20} = -13°$ for pure $(-)$ phenethyl alcohol.

Questions

1. Using the Cram-Prelog rules, draw the absolute configuration of the major product expected from each of the following reactions, labelling it with the Cahn–Ingold–Prelog (R-S) symbol:

a.

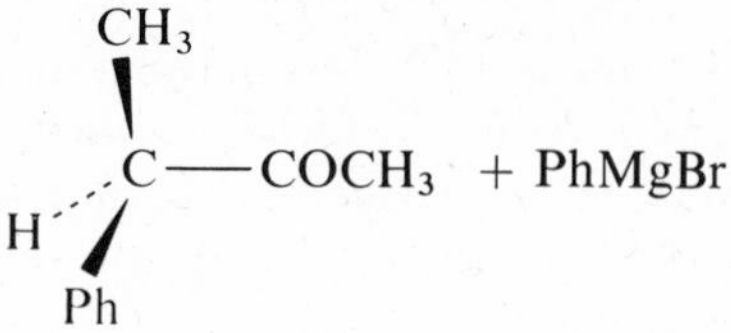

$$CH_3$$
$$C\!-\!COCH_3 + PhMgBr$$
$$H\diagdown Ph$$

b.

CH_3 ... $+ \ LiAlH_4$

c. R$-$PhCOCOOCHPh + MeMgI (with $\overset{CH_3}{|}$ on the CHPh)

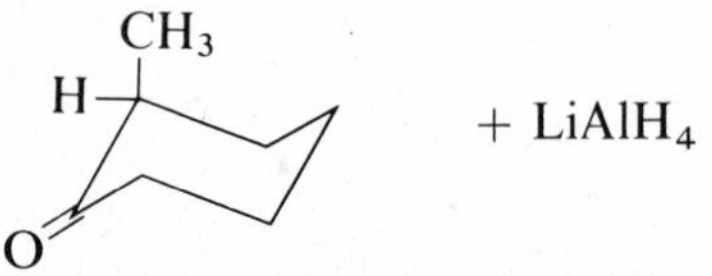

2. Suggest methods of preparation of optically active forms of the following compounds:

a. HOOCCH(OH)CH(OH)COOH
b. PhCH(NH_2)CH_3
c. PhCH(OH)CH_3
d. PhCHCH$_3$COCH$_3$
e. CH_3CH(NH_2)COOH
f. PhCHCH$_3$
   $\overset{|}{C_4H_9}$
g. PhNCH$_2$CH=CH$_2$
   $\overset{Me}{|}$ ... $\overset{|}{Et}$

h. 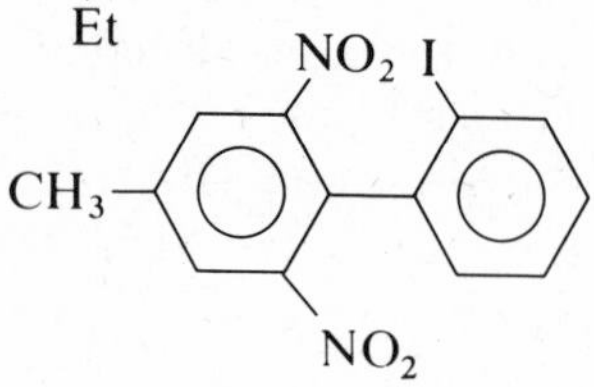 CH$_3$—

with NO$_2$, I, NO$_2$ substituents

i.

$$\underset{Br}{\overset{H}{>}}C=C=C\underset{Br}{\overset{H}{<}}$$

References

1. D. J. Cram and F. A. Abt Elhafez, *J. Amer. Chem. Soc.*, **74**, 5828 (1952).
2. V. Prelog, *Helv. Chim. Act.*, **36**, 308 (1953).
3. A. McKensie, *J. Chem. Soc.*, **85**, 1249 (1904).
4. S. R. Landor, B. J. Miller, and A. R. Tatchell, *J. Chem. Soc.*, 1822 (1966).

Mechanism of a Molecular Rearrangement

Molecular rearrangements involving the migration of an atom or group from one part of a molecule to another are known to occur by both intramolecular and intermolecular mechanisms [1]. In the first case, the migrating group never becomes detached from the parent molecule but proceeds to the migration terminus *within* the same species. An intermolecular mechanism involves fission of the migrating group and recombination at the migration terminus either on the same or another residue. These are illustrated, in the field of aromatic *side-chain to nucleus* rearrangements by the Claisen Rearrangement of allyl aryl ethers (I) [2]:

I

An Intramolecular Rearrangement

and the rearrangement of N-chloroacetanilide (II) [3], respectively:

$$CH_3-\overset{\overset{O}{\|}}{C}\diagdown_{\underset{\underset{C_6H_5}{|}}{N}}\diagdown Cl \quad \xrightarrow{HCl} \quad \underset{C_6H_5}{HN^+ \diagup COCH_3}\;Cl^-\; Cl^- \quad \longrightarrow \quad \underset{C_6H_5}{NH \diagup COCH_3}+Cl_2 \longrightarrow \underset{C_6H_4Cl}{NH \diagup COCH_3}+HCl$$

II   separate

An Intermolecular Rearrangement

A method for distinguishing between the two mechanistic types, makes use of the principle that the two fragments intermediate in the intermolecular reaction may be trapped by the addition of suitable reagents with the formation of distinctive products (see Experiment 30) whereas this will not be possible with the intramolecular mechanism.

The reaction to be examined is the rearrangement of diazoaminobenzene (III) to *p*-aminoazobenzene (IV), under acidic conditions:

$$\underset{III}{C_6H_5NH-N=NPh} \quad \xrightarrow{H^+} \quad \underset{IV}{p\text{-}PhN=N-C_6H_4-NH_2}$$

An intramolecular mechanism could be postulated, thus:

(structures III → V → VI → bracketed resonance intermediates $\longleftrightarrow$ etc. $\xrightarrow{-H^+}$ IV) with the two fragments held together by charge-transfer interactions (see Experiment 19), after fission of the N—N bond. An intermolecular mechanism could proceed as follows:

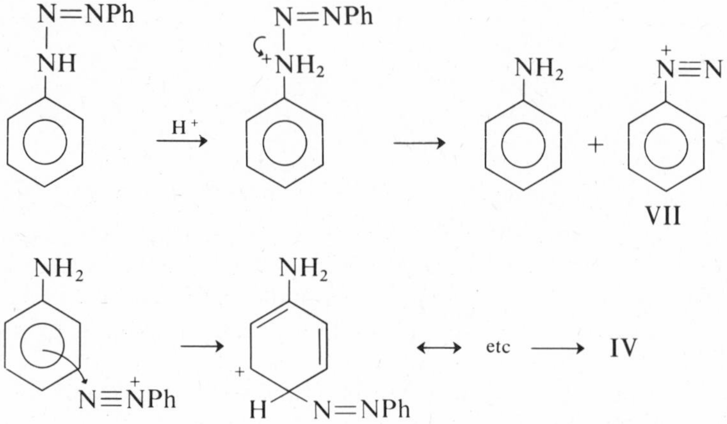

In the latter case, the free diazonium ion (VII) should be capable of being trapped by the addition of 2-naphthol which will compete with aniline for it to form a stable red dye: benzeneazo-2-naphthol (VIII):

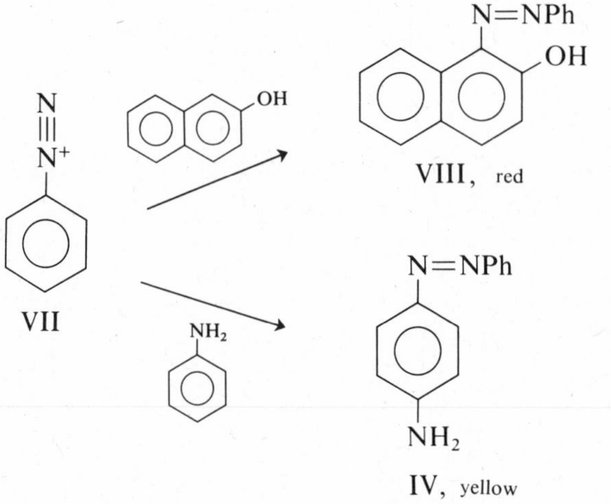

If this compound is formed, free aniline will remain to be isolated. If the mechanism is intramolecular, no red dye or free aniline should be capable of being isolated, unless the addition of 2-naphthol itself interferes with the rearrangement under study, by displacing the aniline group from diazoaminobenzene. The assumption of the absence of this reaction is a limitation of the usefulness of the method.

Experimental

Materials Required

| Aniline | Hydrochloric acid |
| Sodium nitrite | β-Naphthol |

PREPARATION OF DIAZOAMINOBENZENE, III

III

Dissolve 14 g aniline in a solution of 20 ml conc hydrochloric acid and 75 ml water. Cool in an ice-bath and add gradually a solution of 5.2 g sodium nitrite in 10 ml water, stirring vigorously meanwhile and maintaining the temperature at 5–10°. Allow the solution to stand for a few minutes when some precipitate may form. Raise the pH of the solution by adding a solution of 20 g sodium acetate in 40–50 ml water. Stir until the yellow precipitate coagulates then filter the diazoaminobenzene under suction, wash with water and dry in the air or vacuum desiccator. The product may be recrystallized from petroleum ether, and should be purified until the literature mp of 96°–98° is reached or difficulties will arise in later stages.

Yield 12 g, 85%

Rearrangement of Diazoaminobenzene [4].   Dissolve 6.8 g pure diazoamino-benzene in 22.5 ml aniline and add 4.5 g aniline hydrochloride as the acid. Warm the mixture at 40–50° for one hour, stirring or shaking to dissolve the solid. Add 45 ml of 1:1 aqueous acetic acid and stir to coagulate the precipitate of crude *p*-aminoazobenzene, cooling and adding a little more water if necessary. Decant off the supernatant liquid and purify the product by recrystallization from aqueous ethanol containing a few drops of concentrated ammonia solution and using decolorizing charcoal to remove the tarry material present. The final product is yellow, mp 122–123°.

Mechanism of the Rearrangement.   Add gradually 2 g of *p*-aminoazobenzene to 50 ml conc hydrochloric acid at 0°. Shake or stir vigorously to dissolve the solid. Allow to stand for 5–10 minutes then pour the mixture into a solution containing 1.5 g 2-naphthol, 2 g sodium hydroxide, 100 g water and, when cooled to 0°, 50 g ice. Stir and cool the solution, acidify slightly with hydro-chloric acid and filter the red precipitate. Compare its properties with those of benzeneazo-2-naphthol. Basify the filtrate, extract with ether and dry the ethereal extract over sodium sulfate. Examine the solution for the presence of aniline by standard tests.

Draw your conclusions as to the mechanism of the rearrangement on the basis of your findings.

Questions

1. Describe experiments which you could perform to determine whether the following rearrangements are inter- or intramolecular:

a.

b.

c.
$$\text{PhCH}_2\overset{+}{\underset{\underset{\text{CH}_2\text{Ph}}{|}}{\text{NMe}}_2}\text{Cl}^- \xrightarrow[\Delta]{\text{NaNH}_2} \text{Ph}\underset{\underset{\text{CH}_2\text{Ph}}{|}}{\text{CH}}{-}\text{NMe}_2$$

d.

e.
$$\underset{\underset{\text{PhC}=\text{CH}_2}{|}}{\overset{\text{OEt}}{|}} \xrightarrow[140°]{\text{Bu}^t_2\text{O}_2} \text{PhCOCH}_2\text{Et}$$

f.

2. Write intermolecular and intramolecular mechanisms for the following rearrangements and comment on the plausibility of each:

a.
$$Ph_2C{-}CPh_2 \xrightarrow{\;H^+\;} Ph_3CCOPh$$
$$\;\;\;|\;\;\;\;|$$
$$OH\;OH$$

b.

$$
\begin{array}{c}
CH_3CO \\
| \\
NCl
\end{array}
\quad \xrightarrow{\;H^+\;} \quad
\begin{array}{c}
CH_3CO \\
| \\
NH
\end{array}
\;Cl
\quad + \quad
\begin{array}{c}
CH_3CO \\
| \\
NH
\end{array}
\;Cl
$$

c.
$$Ph_2CH\overset{+}{N}Me_3 \xrightarrow{\;OH^-\;} Ph_2CCH_3$$
$$|$$
$$NMe_2$$

d.
$$PhCCH_3 \xrightarrow{\;H^+\;} PhNHCOCH_3$$
$$\|$$
$$NOH$$

References

1. P. De Mayo (Ed.), *Molecular Rearrangements*, Vol. 1, Academic Press, 1963.
2. D. S. Tarbell, *Org. Reactions*, Vol. II, Wiley, New York, 1944, p. 1.
3. K. J. P. Orton, F. G. Soper, and G. Williams, *J. Chem. Soc.* (1928), 998.
4. H. V. Kidd, *J. Org. Chem.*, 198 (1937).

Examination of the Auwers-Skita Rule

Table 29–1 lists some physical constants for a number of pairs of *cis-trans* isomers. The boiling points, densities and refractive indices of the *cis* isomers are seen to be higher than the values for the corresponding *trans* compounds. This fact was first noticed by v. Auwers and Skita [1] who proposed, on the assumption that this order of values holds generally, that the relationship be used to assign the configurations of pairs of isomers from physical measurements conducted in the liquid state. Some exceptions to the rule as stated above have been noted [2], however, particularly in certain cases where, contrary to the usual order, the *cis* isomer is thermodynamically the more stable of the two such as is the case with 1,3-dimethyl-cyclohexane (Table 29–1). A more fundamental version of the original rule ascribes the higher boiling point, density and refractive index to the *less stable* isomer.

TABLE 29-1 Physical Properties of Some Pairs of Stereoisomers

	n_D^{20}	d_4^{20}	bp^{760}
1,2-dimethylcyclohexane			
cis		0.7962	130
trans		0.7760	124
menthane			
cis	1.4414	0.8080	
trans	1.4366	0.7964	
ethyl 4-methylcyclohexanecarboxylate			
cis	1.4429	0.9448	
trans	1.4392	0.9361	
8-hydroxymenthane			
cis		0.9025	
trans		0.8962	

TABLE 29–1 (Continued)

	n_D^{20}	d_4^{20}	bp^{760}
1,2-dimethylcyclopropane			
cis	1.3822	0.6928	37
trans	1.3713	0.6769	29
diethyl cyclohexane-1,4-dicarboxylate			
cis	1.436	1.015	
trans	1.434	1.011	
diethyl cyclohexane-1,2-dicarboxylate			
cis	1.453	1.054	
trans	1.450	1.040	
(−)isocarvomenthone			
cis	1.4558	0.9102	
(−) carvomenthone			
trans	1.4536	0.9033	

TABLE 29–1 (Continued)

		n_D^{20}	d_4^{20}	bp^{760}
1,3-dimethylcyclohexane				
	cis	1.4254	0.7663	120
	trans	1.4269	0.7835	125

Experiment 29 outlines stereospecific syntheses of the *cis* and *trans* cyclohexane-1,2-diols whose configurations are known from their methods of preparation. The diols are converted to the liquid diacetates on which the Auwers-Skita Rule may be tested.

In the cyclohexane series, the stabilities of isomeric compounds are largely determined by the number of substituents which may reside in equatorial positions (*e*) which, compared to axial positions (*a*) are remote from repulsive 1,3-interactions (dotted lines):

Cis 1,2 and 1,4-disubstituted cyclohexanes are necessarily axial-equatorial whereas the *trans* isomers may adopt a diequatorial conformation and are thereby the more stable:

In 1,3 disubstituted cyclohexanes, however, it is the trans isomer which is axial-equatorial and the cis which can adopt the stable diequatorial conformation.

The basis of the Auwers-Skita rule is probably as follows. The molecule of the less stable isomer contains substituent groups packed more closely together and therefore occupying less space. This leads to a higher density in the liquid and, at the same time results in a generally closer approach of the molecules. The intermolecular attractive forces are thus somewhat higher and consequently also the boiling point, a measure of the energy required to separate the molecules. The higher density results in greater interactions between the molecules and a light beam traversing them and thus a reduced velocity of the light which is equivalent to an increased refractive index.

The *cis* isomer is formed when the olefin is treated with permanganate (the Baeyer test for unsaturation) with which it forms a cyclic manganate ester, necessarily in the *cis* configuration:

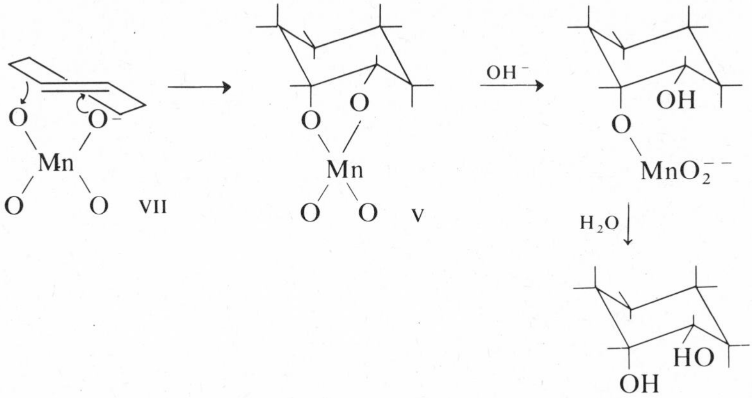

Unfortunately the yield in this reaction tends to be very poor [3] since the diol may be degraded further by permanganate. A better procedure utilizes iodine and silver acetate [4] and probably proceeds through an iodonium ion intermediate (V):

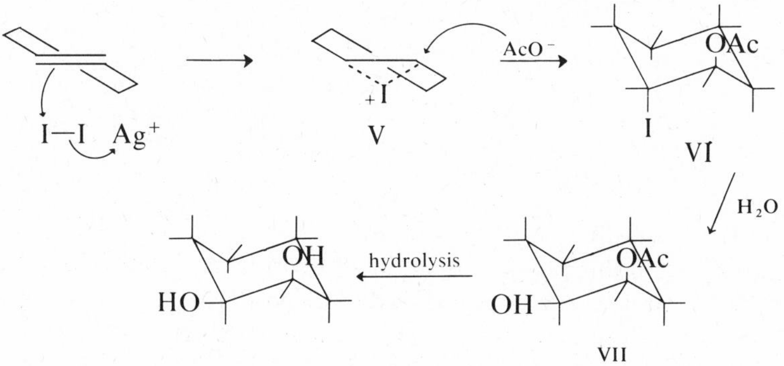

The latter would be expected to solvolyze in acetic acid to form a *trans* iodo-acetate (VI) which on hydrolysis suffers a Walden inversion to give the *cis* diol monoacetate (VII) and *cis* diol in good yield.

Trans cyclohexanediol is prepared [5] by first treating the olefin with perform-ic acid (prepared from hydrogen peroxide and formic acid), to give cyclohexene oxide (VIII). This epoxide ring for steric reasons can only be fused *cis* to the cyclohexane ring. The epoxide undergoes ring-opening on treatment with base by means of nucleophilic attack on carbon with a Walden inversion to give the *trans* diol:

VIII

Experimental

Cis CYCLOHEXANE-1,2-DIOL

Materials Required

Cyclohexene	Abbé refractometer (reading to ±0.0001)
Iodine	Formic acid
Silver acetate	Hydrogen peroxide, 30%
Acetic acid	Acetic anhydride

Set up a 250 ml three-necked flask fitted with reflux condenser, mechanical stirrer and thermometer reaching towards the bottom of the flask. Place 16 g (0.096 mole) silver acetate, 150 ml glacial acetic acid and 3.4 g (0.0416 mole) cyclohexene in the flask and stir vigorously. Add 11.7 g (0.046 mole) of iodine in portions over a period of 30 min followed by 0.7 g water. Continue stirring and raise the temperature of the liquid to 90–95° for a further 2–3 hours. Cool the mixture and filter off the precipitated silver iodide which should be recovered and placed in a bottle for silver residues. Evaporate the filtrate on the rotary evaporator until a darkish oil remains consisting of the *cis* diol diacetate. Distill the oil under vacuum and collect *cis* cyclohexanediol diacetate, bp 120°/15 mm. Retain a drop of the product taken from the middle fraction for refractive index measurements.

Dissolve the remainder of the diacetate in 25 ml of 18% potassium hydroxide in ethanol and reflux for 1 hour. Evaporate the solution to dryness and extract the residue with several portions of ether. Combine the ethereal extracts, remove the ether on the evaporator to obtain *cis* cyclohexane-1,2-diol which may be recrystallized from a little carbon tetrachloride to a solid product, mp 97–98°.

Yield, 3.2 g, 65%

Trans 1,2-CYCLOHEXANEDIOL

Using the same apparatus as described for the *cis* diol, place 14 ml of 30% hydrogen peroxide and 60 ml 100% formic acid in the flask and add with stirring over a period of 10 min, 10 ml of cyclohexene keeping the temperature of the mixture at 40–45° with a cooling bath if necessary. After addition of the cyclohexene, maintain the temperature of the mixture at 40° for a further 45 min then remove the water and most of the formic acid on the rotary evaporator keeping the temperature below 50°. The residue contains cyclohexene oxide which need not be isolated. Cool the flask and make alkaline by the slow addition of a solution of 8 g sodium hydroxide in 15 ml water. Warm the mixture to 45° for 10 min to ensure complete reaction then cool and extract three times with 25 ml portions of ethyl acetate. Combine the ethyl acetate extracts and evaporate the solvent until the product solidifies. Cool the solution and filter at the pump to obtain colorless crystals of *trans* cyclohexane-1,2-diol, mp 101°.

Yield, 6.6 g, 55%

Trans 1,2-CYCLOHEXANEDIOL DIACETATE

Dissolve 2 g of the diol in 5 ml of acetic anhydride and warm the mixture on a steam bath for 15 minutes. Remove excess acetic anhydride and acetic acid on the rotary evaporator and distill the oily residue in a semimicro distillation apparatus collecting *trans* 1,2-cyclohexanediol diacetate bp 120°/15 mm. Retain a drop of the product from the middle fraction for measurement of refractive index.

EXAMINATION OF THE AUWERS-SKITA RULE

Refractive Index.   Measure the refractive indices of the *cis* and *trans* diacetates under the same conditions, using an Abbé refractometer.

Density.   Carefully weigh at room temperature a micro-pyknometer or a lambda syringe of capacity 1–5λ (μl). Fill as exactly as possible to the mark with each of the liquid esters in turn and weigh each time, preferably to 0.00001 g. Determine the densities of the two liquids.

Determine whether the Auwers-Skita rule is applicable in the present case.

Questions

1. By the use of space-filling (Fischer–Hirschfelder–Taylor) models, rationalize the stabilities predicted for the *cis* and *trans* isomeric pairs in Table 29–1.
2. It has been shown (*Angewandte Chemie*, **75**, 793 (1963)) that the *cis* forms of some fluorinated olefins are more stable than the *trans*:

| *cis, cis* | *cis, trans* | *trans, trans* |

Give an explanation.

References

1. K. v. Auwers, *Liebig's Annalen*, **410**, 287 (1915). A. Skita, *ibid*, **420**, 91 (1920).
2. I. N. Nazarov and A. A. Akhrem, *Zhur. Obshchei Khim.*, **28**, 1791 (1958).
3. M. F. Clarke and L. N. Owen, *J. Chem. Soc.*, 315 (1949).
4. R. B. Woodward and F. V. Brutcher, *J. Amer. Chem. Soc.*, **80**, 209 (1958).
5. A. Roebuck and H. Adkins, *Org. Syn.*, Vol. 28, 35 (1948).

Trapping Unstable Intermediates

Organic reactions frequently proceed by way of intermediate species of high reactivity whose presence can only be inferred from the reaction products after addition of suitable reagents to trap them in a recognizable form.

A familiar example of this principle is found in the unimolecular decomposition of a tertiary halide to give a solvated carbonium ion which is rapidly trapped by any nucleophilic species present such as water, hydroxide ion, chloride ion or azide ion:

$$
\begin{array}{c}
\text{Me} \\
| \\
\text{RC}-\text{Cl} \\
| \\
\text{Me}
\end{array}
\xrightarrow{\text{H}_2\text{O}}
\left(
\begin{array}{c}
\text{Me} \\
| \\
\text{RC}^+ \\
| \\
\text{Me}
\end{array}
\right)_{\text{solv}}
+ \text{Cl}^-
$$

$$
\begin{array}{cccc}
\text{Me} & \text{Me} & \text{Me} & \text{Me} \\
| & | & | & | \\
\text{RC}-\text{OH} + \text{H}^+ & \text{RC}-\text{OH} & \text{RC}-\text{Cl} & \text{RC}-\text{N}_3 \\
| & | & | & | \\
\text{Me} & \text{Me} & \text{Me} & \text{Me}
\end{array}
$$

Additional evidence for the carbonium ion mechanism is furnished by the observation that the rate of formation of the products is independent of the concentrations of the nucleophiles.

In Experiment 30, three intermediates are chosen for discussion, carbenes, arynes and reactive quinones.

Carbenes and Related Species

Carbene (or methylene) is the name given to the species $:CH_2$. It is electron-deficient (six electrons in the valence orbitals) and clearly would be expected to be highly reactive towards nucleophiles. While carbene itself is probably not formed in solution, several of its more stable derivatives have been implicated in organic reactions.

The earliest proposal of carbene intermediate was probably that of Geuther [1] who in 1862 suggested that the basic hydrolysis of chloroform was initiated by the removal of HCl. In modern terms the mechanism envisaged the formation of dichlorocarbene:

$$CHCl_3 + OH^- \longrightarrow [:CCl_2] + Cl^- + H_2O$$

$$\downarrow H_2O$$

$$CO, HCO_2^-$$

With the tetracovalency of carbon established later in the nineteenth century, however, this proposal was abandoned as being unreasonable and it was not until 1950 that prejudice against the carbene mechanism was broken down and Geuther's guess shown to be essentially correct by Hine [2]. The most telling evidence for this α-elimination in aqueous media, comes from the anomalously high rates of hydrolysis of the haloforms, CHX_3 compared to the di- and tetra-halomethanes, CH_2X_2 and CX_4. In nonaqueous media, the carbene may be trapped by cycloaddition to an olefin leading to a cyclopropane derivative:

[CCl₃]
7,7-dichlorobicyclo-(4.1.0)-heptane
(dichloronorcarane)

A considerable variety of carbenes have now been generated and trapped [3]; some examples are given below:

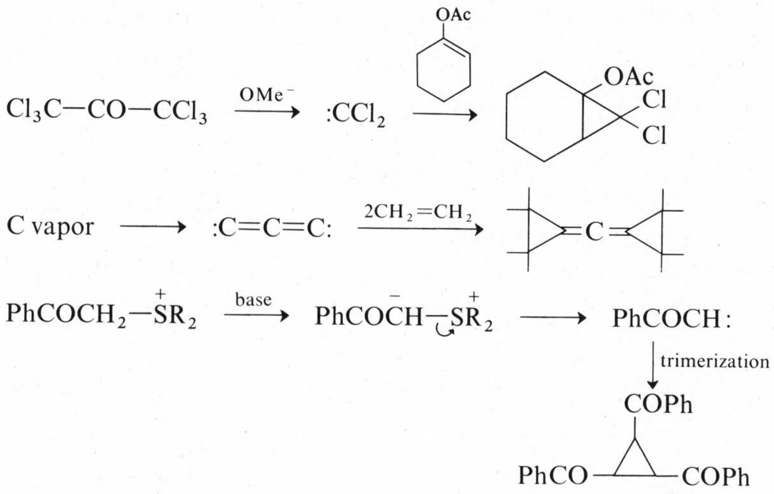

$$Cl_3C-CO-CCl_3 \xrightarrow{\text{OMe}^-} :CCl_2 \longrightarrow$$

$$\text{C vapor} \longrightarrow :C=C=C: \xrightarrow{2CH_2=CH_2} \qquad \qquad$$

$$PhCOCH_2-\overset{+}{S}R_2 \xrightarrow{\text{base}} PhCO\overset{-}{C}H-\overset{+}{S}R_2 \longrightarrow PhCOCH:$$

$$\downarrow \text{trimerization}$$

Nitrogen analogs of the carbenes, nitrenes are also known. They will add to a double bond or insert in a single bond. They are used commercially in the cross-linking of polypropylene.

$$PhSO_2N_3 \xrightarrow[120°]{\Delta} PhSO_2-N: \xrightarrow{PhCH_3} PhSO_2NHCH_2Ph \text{ etc}$$

Benzenesulfonylazide $+N_2$ Benzenesulfonbenzylamide

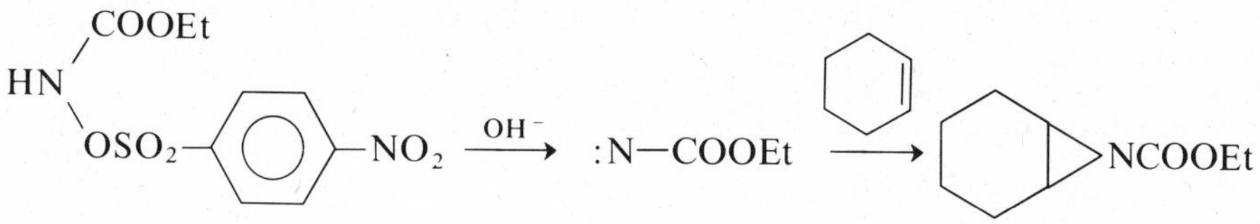

$$\xrightarrow{\text{OH}^-} :N-COOEt \longrightarrow \qquad NCOOEt$$

Experimental

PREPARATION OF 7,7-DICHLOROBICYCLO-(4,1,0)-HEPTANE, I, (DICHLORONOR-CARANE)

Materials Required

Trichloracetic acid
Ethylene glycol dimethyl ether
Cyclohexene

$$Cl_3C\overset{-}{C}OO \xrightarrow{\Delta} :CCl_2 + CO_2 + Cl^-$$

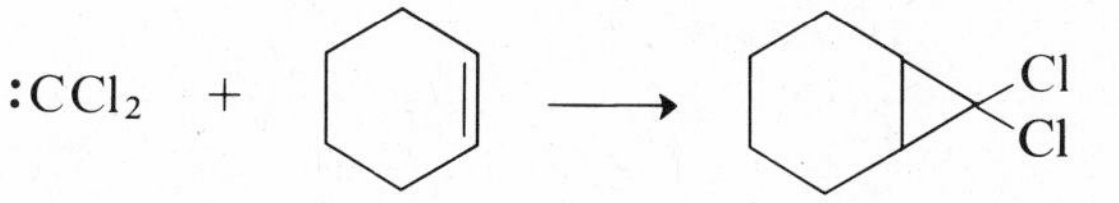

$$:CCl_2 + \qquad \longrightarrow \qquad$$

I

Dissolve 8 g trichloracetic acid in water and neutralize the solution by addition of sodium hydroxide (approximately 2 g is required). Remove the water on the rotary evaporator and dry the crystalline sodium trichloracetate in the oven.

Place the dry sodium trichloracetate in a round bottomed flask and add 20 ml ethylene glycol dimethyl ether and 25 ml cyclohexene. Heat gently for an hour and then boil rapidly for a further hour or until no further evolution of CO_2 is evident. Cool, add ether and wash several times with water to remove inorganic products and the glycol ether. Dry the ethereal solution over anhydrous sodium sulfate and distill the product collecting finally dichloronorcarane at 75–80°/15 mm as a colorless liquid with a characteristic odor.

Yield, 4 g, 40%

PREPARATION OF THE DICHLOROCARBENE-CYCLO-OCTA-1,5-DIENE ADDUCT, II

II

Mix in a flask 14.5 g sodium trichloroacetate (prepared as above) 20 ml trichloroethylene, 5 ml of ethylene glycol dimethyl ether and 5 ml 1,5-cyclooctadiene. Heat under reflux until the evolution of CO_2 ceases (about $1\frac{1}{2}$ hours) then add 75 ml water and heat to distill off the trichloroethylene. The product separates as an oil which crystallizes on cooling. It may be extracted into methylene chloride, the solution dried with anydrous sodium sulfate and the solvent removed. Recrystallization from ethyl acetate gives white crystals mp 175°C.

Yield, 2–4 g, (10–20%)

ARYNES

The term aryne signifies an aromatic system which lacks a pair of hydrogen atoms. This additional unsaturation may be represented as a triple bond in the ring or as a diradical or dipole. Thus, benzyne, the most commonly met example, may be written:

The true structure may be represented as a hybrid of these forms since none are alone completely satisfactory.

Benzyne was first implicated to explain the distribution of products of the amination of the chlorotoluenes with sodamide in liquid ammonia [4]. For example, *m*-chlorotoluene gives all three toluidines:

+ NH$_3$ + Cl$^-$

Benzyne is too reactive to possess independent existence although its spectrum in the gas phase has been recorded. It rapidly adds active hydrogen compounds or a conjugated diene system in the Diels–Alder reaction or will dimerize to diphenylene. Some methods of generation of benzyne and some reactions follow [5].

Experimental

Materials Required

Anthracene	Anthranilic acid
Isoamyl nitrite	Maleic anhydride
Ethylene glycol dimethyl ether	Triethylene glycol dimethyl ether

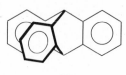

III

PREPARATION OF TRYPTYCENE (III)

Set up a round bottomed flask fitted with a reflux condenser and surmounted by a dropping funnel arranged so that liquid added through the funnel falls directly into the flask.

Place a mixture of anthracene (2 g) isoamyl nitrite[1] (3 g) and ethylene glycol dimethyl ether in the flask. Dissolve the anthranilic acid (5 g) in 20 ml of the glycol dimethyl ether and place the solution in the dropping funnel. Heat the contents of the flask to boiling over a microburner and allow half the anthranilic acid solution to drip in over a period of not less than 20 minutes. Add a further 3 g of isoamyl nitrite to the flask, continue boiling and add the remainder of the anthranilic acid solution over a further 20 minutes. After an additional period of refluxing for 10 minutes, add 10 ml ethanol and a solution of sodium hydroxide (3 g) in water (40 ml). A solid separates immediately which after cooling becomes crystalline. Filter the solid, a mixture of triptycene and unreacted anthracene, wash with water and ice cold methanol-water (1:4) and dry at 100° in the oven.

To remove anthracene, mix 2 g maleic anhydride with the product and 10 ml triethylene glycol dimethyl ether. Boil the mixture under reflux for five min adding a little more solvent if any solid remains. Cool, add 10 ml ethanol and 50 ml 2 *M* sodium hydroxide solution and stir to dissolve the acidic components. Cool the solution and filter off the triptycene. Recrystallize by dissolving the product in 10 ml of methylene chloride and filtering the solution if turbid. Add 20 ml of methanol and boil on a steam bath allowing the methylene chloride to evaporate until crystals begin to form. Cool and filter, mp 255°C.

Yield, 1 g, 15%

[1] Caution, alkyl nitrites are powerful heart stimulants; do not inhale the vapor. If not already available, isoamyl nitrite may be prepared by the addition over one hour of a mixture of *iso*amyl alcohol (55 g) and conc sulfuric acid (17 ml) to a solution of sodium nitrite (48 g) in 185 ml of water, keeping the temperature at 0° ± 1. After standing, the upper oily layer of isoamyl nitrite is removed, washed, dried and distilled, bp 99°C.

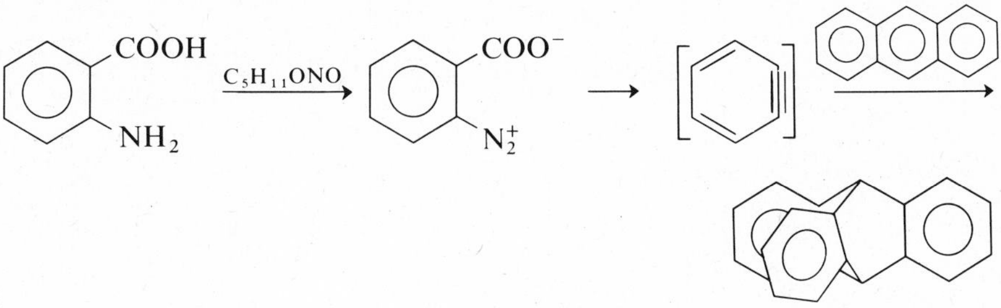

Triptycene III

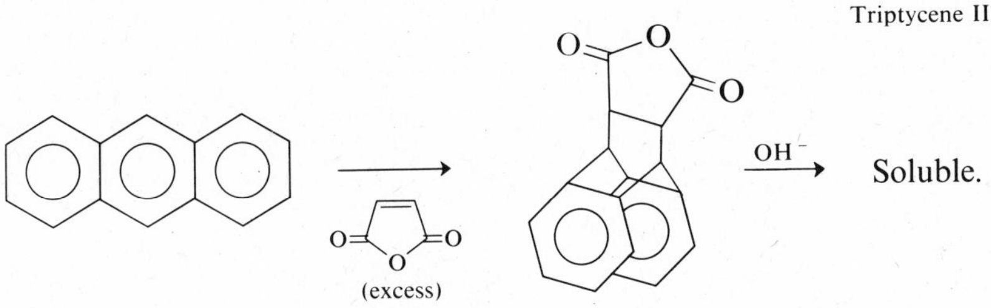

(excess)

$\xrightarrow{\text{OH}^-}$ Soluble.

QUINONOID INTERMEDIATES

Substitution into the aromatic ring of a 1,2- or 1,4-diphenol will occur readily with nucleophiles in the presence of an oxidizing agent. The aromatic compound, normally resistant to nucleophilic attack, is oxidized to a quinone (IV) which readily adds by a Michael reaction [6] such species as arylsulfinate ion, thiourea, nitrite and dimedone (5,5-dimethylcyclohexane-1,3-dione), thus:

PREPARATION OF S-(3,4-DIHYDROXYPHENYL)ISOTHIOUREA, V

Materials Required

Catechol (*o*-dihydroxybenzene)	Thiourea
Potassium hexacyanoferrate-(III)	Dimedone
(ferricyanide)	

Dissolve 13 g potassium hexacyanoferrate-(III) and 20 g sodium acetate hydrate in 50 ml water and add the mixture over 5 minutes with stirring to a solution of 2.6 g (0.023 mole) catechol and 2 g (0.026 mole) thiourea in 20 ml of water. The product begins to separate immediately. Add a further 20 g of sodium acetate, stir and, after allowing the precipitate to coagulate, filter, wash with cold water and dry.

Yield, 3.5 g, 80 %

PREPARATION OF A COUMARONE DERIVATIVE, VI

Add to a solution containing 1 g (0.009 mole) catechol, 2 g (0.015 mole) dimedone and 12 g sodium bicarbonate dissolved in 150 ml of water, a solution of 3 g (0.009 mole) potassium hexacyanoferrate-(III) in water over a period of 5 minutes. Note the transient blue color of the solution which may be due to a quinonoid intermediate. Cool the resulting mixture and filter the crystalline precipitate of VI.

Yield, 1.5 g, 80 %

Questions

1. Suggest mechanisms for the following reactions:

a.

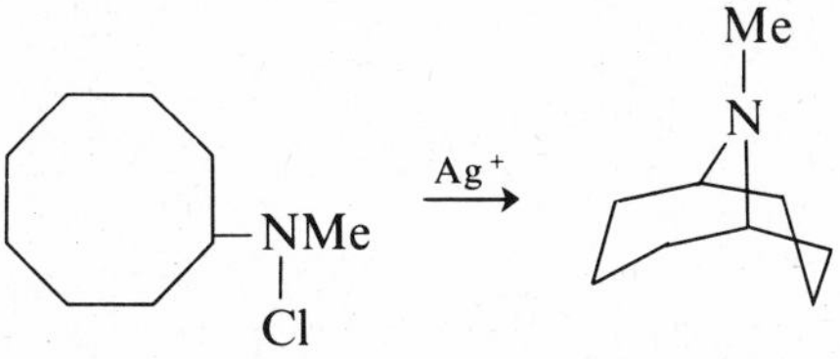

b. PhCOCH$_2$SR$_2$ $\xrightarrow{\text{CH}_2\text{N}_2}$ PhCO⟶△⟶COPh (with COPh at top)

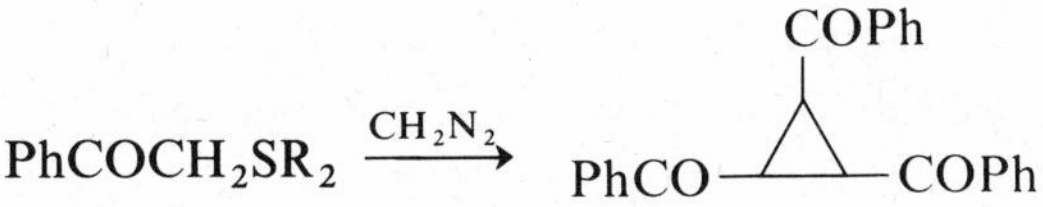

c. Carbon vapor evaporated in vacuum on to a paraffin surface, treated with ethylene gives $\triangleright\!=\!C\!=\!\triangleleft$

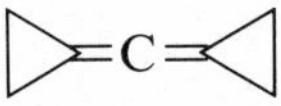

d.

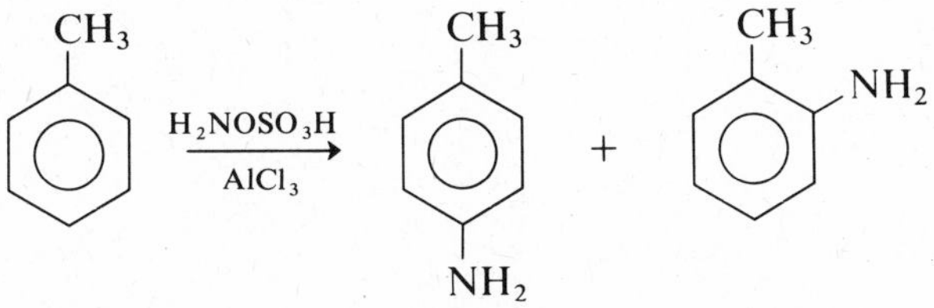

e.

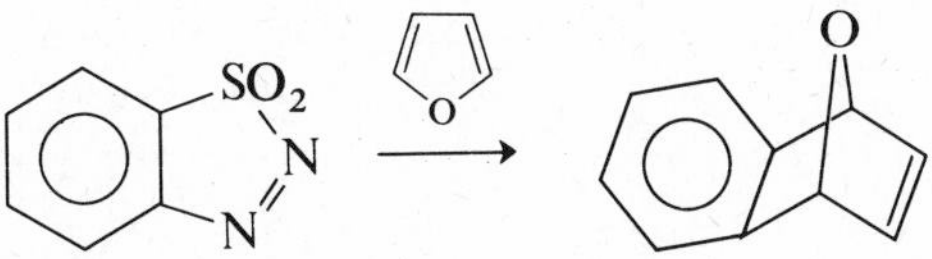

f.

g.

h.

References

1. A. Geuther, *Liebig's Annalen*, **123**, 121 (1862).
2. J. Hine, *J. Amer. Chem. Soc.*, **72**, 2438 (1950).
3. For reviews on the subject see, for example, W. Kirmse, *Carbene Chemistry*, Academic Press, New York, 1964; J. Hine, *Divalent Carbon*, Ronald Press, New York, 1964; W. Kirmse, *Prog. Org. Chem.*, **6**, 164 (1964).
4. E. S. Gould, *Mechanism and Structure in Organic Chemistry*, Holt, Rinehart and Winston, New York, 1959, p. 461.
5. H. Heaney, *Chem. Revs.*, **62**, 81 (1962).
6. H. W. Wanzlick, *Angew. Chem.* (Internatl. Ed.), **3**, 401 (1964).

Stable Carbon Ions and Radicals

EXPERIMENT 31

Many organic reactions are believed to take place via the trivalent carbon intermediates described as carbonium ions (*a*), carbon radicals, (*b*), or carbanions (*c*) which in addition to three covalent bonds bear, respectively, a vacant *p*-orbital, a half-filled orbital and a filled (unshared) sp^3-hybrid orbital.

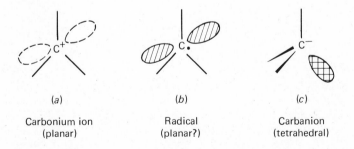

(a)	(b)	(c)
Carbonium ion (planar)	Radical (planar?)	Carbanion (tetrahedral)

These species are usually too reactive to be isolated and their intermediacy in a reaction has to be inferred indirectly. In all three cases the stability is increased by attachment of an extended conjugating system to the central carbon such that the charge or odd electron may be delocalized over as large a structure as possible. Such an arrangement is found in triphenylmethyl (trityl), Ph_3C which may readily be obtained as a carbonium ion, radical or carbanion

211

and in which the central carbon atom is conjugated with three phenyl groups involving ten canonical structures of significance:

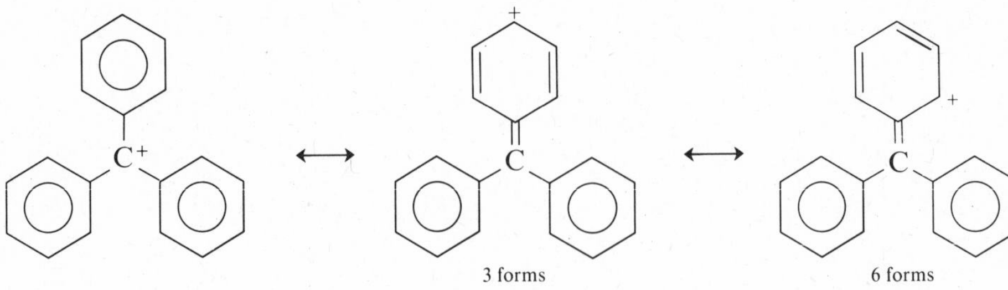

Carbonium ions are formed by ionization of a suitable group from carbon either in very polar solvents or with the aid of electrophilic catalysis (eg., by silver ion):

$$Ph_3C-Cl \underset{}{\overset{\text{liquid } SO_2}{\rightleftharpoons}} Ph_3C^+Cl^-$$

$$Ph_3C-Cl + Ag^+ \longrightarrow Ph_3C^+ + Ag^+Cl^-$$

Carbonium carbon is isoelectronic with trivalent boron and likewise is a powerful Lewis acid (electron-pair acceptor). Consequently even simple aliphatic carbonium ions can exist in highly acidic media such as conc sulfuric acid or antimony pentafluoride-HF [5] (see Experiment 7, 24):

$$Ph_3C-OH \overset{H_2SO_4}{\underset{SO_3}{\longrightarrow}} Ph_3C\overset{+}{-}OH_2 \longrightarrow Ph_3C^+ + (H_2O)$$

They will not be stable in the presence of nucleophiles including water with which the trityl cation gives triphenylcarbinol:

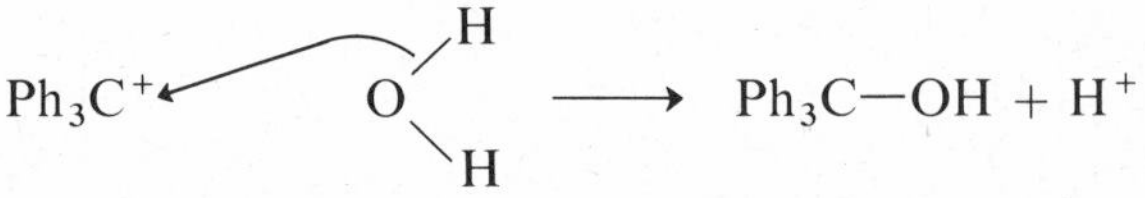

$$Ph_3C^+ \longleftarrow O\overset{H}{\underset{H}{\big\langle}} \longrightarrow Ph_3C-OH + H^+$$

For the same reason, it will only be possible to isolate a truly ionic carbonium ion salt if the anion has negligible nucleophilic character, such as perchlorate or fluoborate.

Carbanions possess an unshared electron pair which is available for bonding and so are isoelectronic with nitrogen in the trivalent state and are powerful Lewis bases. Carbanions may be regarded as the conjugate bases of carbon acids and, since the latter are normally extremely weak acids, they exist only in highly basic media:

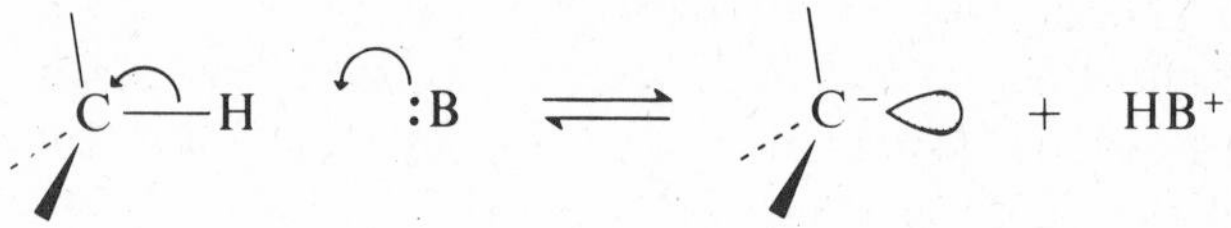

$$\overset{|}{\underset{}{C}}-H \quad :B \rightleftharpoons \overset{|}{\underset{}{C}}^- + HB^+$$

Anions of β-dicarbonyl compounds (experiment 44) and enamines (experiment 43) possess carbanionic character, but most of the charge is resident on a hetero atom, oxygen or nitrogen.

In order to obtain a stable carbanion, the cation with which it is associated must have negligible electrophilic character, such as the alkali metal cations. The trityl carbanion is capable of displacing chloride from dichloromethane and hydroxide ion from water:

$$Ph_3C^- \quad \overset{H}{\underset{\underset{Cl}{H}}{C}}\!\!-\!\!Cl \quad \xrightarrow{S_N2} \quad Ph_3C\!-\!\overset{H}{\underset{\underset{Cl}{\diagdown H}}{C}} \quad + \; Cl^-$$

$$Ph_3C^- \!\frown\! H\!-\!\underset{H}{O} \quad \longrightarrow \quad Ph_3CH \; + \; OH^-$$

Free radicals are formed as a result of thermal fission of rather weak homonuclear bonds, such as peroxides,

$$RO\!-\!OR \; \rightleftharpoons \; 2\,RO\cdot$$

Carbon-carbon bonds normally possess a bond-strength (enthalpy of homolytic fission $\Delta H^{\ddagger}$) of about 80 kcal/mole. Due to steric crowding of the substituent groups and high stability of the trityl radical, the central bond in hexaphenylethane is weakened, $\Delta H^{\ddagger}$ being only 11 kcal/mole so that this compound exists in equilibrium with the trityl radical in solution at ordinary temperatures:

$$Ph_3C\!-\!CPh_3 \; \rightleftharpoons \; 2\,Ph_3C\cdot$$

As a radical it couples with unpaired electrons in other molecules including molecular oxygen:

$$2\,Ph_3C\cdot + O_2 \; \longrightarrow \; Ph_3C\!-\!O\!-\!O\!-\!CPh_3$$

The Electronic Spectra of the Trityl System

Molecular orbital theory may be used to explain and even predict certain aspects of the electronic spectra of the trityl cation, anion and radical. Absorption of light is accompanied by the promotion of an electron from a high lying molecular orbital of the π-system in the ground state to an empty orbital of higher energy, the energy of the photon being equal to the difference in energy of the orbitals concerned (Figure 31–1).

The relative energies of the orbitals may be calculated to a fair degree of approximation from first principles and are indicated for the trityl system in Figure 31–1. While a considerable amount of calculation is necessary to produce these figures it is possible to make a comparison of the spectra of the cation, radical and anion with that of, say, benzene, by inspection.

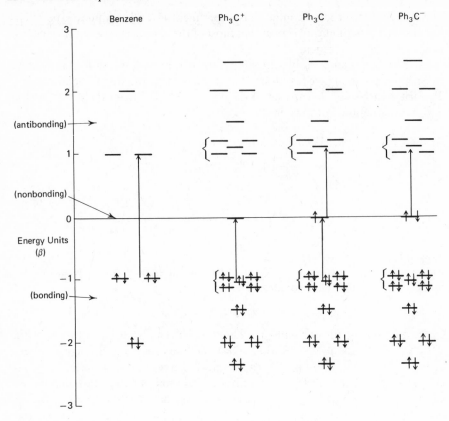

FIGURE 31–1 Molecular orbitals of benzene and trityl. Arrows between orbitals show lowest energy transitions.

Trityl belongs to the class of *odd-alternant* hydrocarbons[1] which are characterized by having the molecular orbitals (of which there are as many as there are carbon atoms conjugated) arranged in symmetrical pairs of bonding and antibonding types, with energies equal in magnitude but opposite in sign, and the remaining orbital (or other odd number) nonbonding (zero energy). The

---

[1] In a conjugated system of carbon atoms, designate one atom as *starred* and the adjacent ones as *unstarred* and so on. If no two adjacent atoms then bear the same designation the system is *alternant*; otherwise it is *non-alternant*. *Odd* and *even* refer to the number of carbon atoms.

even   odd

alternant   non-alternant

energy scale here is a relative one, that of an isolated carbon-$2p$ orbital being taken as zero. The trityl cation has eighteen π-electrons and hence all the bonding orbitals are filled in the ground state. The radical and anion have in addition one and two electrons respectively in the nonbonding orbital. It will be seen from Figure 31–1 that the energy gap separating the highest filled and lowest unfilled orbitals is the same in each case. Therefore to a first degree of approximation we may expect the longest wavelength absorption of all three species to be in the same part of the spectrum. Furthermore we see that whereas the lowest energy transition in benzene, corresponding to absorption at the longest wavelength namely 260 mμ, is 2β that in the trityl system is β.

$$\frac{E(\text{trityl})}{E(\text{benzene})} = \frac{hc/\lambda(\text{trityl})}{hc/\lambda(\text{benzene})}$$

$$\frac{1}{2} = \frac{260}{\lambda(\text{trityl})}$$

$$\lambda(\text{trityl}) = 520 \text{ m}\mu.$$

Therefore we would expect the long wavelength band of all three trityl systems to be found in the vicinity of 520 mμ. The above treatment is highly approximate; how good this approximation is may be examined experimentally.

It should be noted that the spectrum of a covalent trityl compound such as triphenylcarbinol or triphenylmethane is very similar to that of benzene since the three phenyl groups are now isolated. Ultraviolet-visible spectroscopy provides a criterion for distinguishing ionic and radical character in trityl compounds.

Experimental

Materials Required

Triphenylcarbinol	Sodium
Acetyl chloride	Mercury
Silver carbonate	Zinc dust
Hydrofluoric acid, 40%	Dichloromethane
Boron trifluoride etherate	

PREPARATION OF TRIPHENYLMETHYL FLUOBORATE

Dissolve 5 g triphenylcarbinol in 10 ml acetic anhydride and add 1.5 ml 40% tetrafluoboric acid. Stopper the mixture and allow to stand for a few minutes when the precipitate becomes granular. Filter the white, crystalline triphenylmethyl fluoborate, wash quickly with ether, and immediately store in a desiccator.

Properties of the Triphenylmethyl Carbonium Ion. Measure the ultraviolet-visible spectrum of the product in acetone solution between 300 and 600 mμ.

Treat some of the product with water. Note the instant discharge of the yellow color and formation of a precipitate of triphenylcarbinol.

Sᴏᴅɪᴜᴍ Tʀɪᴘʜᴇɴʏʟᴍᴇᴛʜʏʟ, $Na^+Ph_3C^-$

Preparation of Triphenylmethyl Chloride.   Place 13.0 g (0.05 mole) triphenyl-carbinol and 10 ml benzene in a 100 ml round bottomed flask fitted with reflux condenser and calcium chloride moisture trap.

$$Ph_3COH + AcCl \longrightarrow Ph_3CCl + AcOH$$

Add 8.0 ml (0.1 mole) of acetyl chloride in portions down the condenser and reflux for 15–30 minutes. Cool the mixture and add 60–70 ml of petroleum ether (bp 20–40°) and filter from the excess acetyl chloride the white precipitate of triphenylmethyl chloride. Wash with a little petroleum ether and transfer quickly to a desiccator. Trityl chloride is a covalent compound and rapidly hydrolyzed by moisture, mp 112°.

Yield, 12 g, 90 %

Dissolve 2.0 g sodium cut into pea-sized pieces in 200 g mercury in a mortar by pressing the pieces under the surface of the mercury and exposing a fresh surface with a knife. This operation is rather vigorous and must be performed under a fumehood, the operator wearing eye-protection. Place the resulting 1% sodium amalgam, which should be liquid, in a strong 500 ml bottle, add 150 ml sodium-dried ether and 12 g trityl chloride and sweep out the air with nitrogen or natural gas. Stopper well, cool in ice for 10 min and shake vigorously, preferably with a mechanical shaker, for about 45–60 min, occasionally return-ing the bottle to the ice bath. The ether layer develops a deep red color due to the triphenylmethyl carbanion which is stable in the absence of air and water.

$$Ph_3CCl + 2Na \longrightarrow Na^+Ph_3C^- + NaCl$$

Properties of Sodium Triphenylmethyl.   Using very carefully dried apparatus, fill a 1 cm spectrophotometer cell two-thirds full of sodium-dried benzene and add the red solution dropwise from a pipet until the color remains permanently in the cell. Stopper and measure the ultraviolet-visible spectrum between 300 and 600 mμ.

Remove about 25 ml of the red solution keeping nitrogen or gas passing through the bottle and drop into a damp beaker. Note the instantaneous dis-charge of the color and formation of crystals of triphenylmethane. Since the starting material was triphenylcarbinol, a reduction has been achieved.

$$Ph_3C^-Na^+ + H_2O \longrightarrow Ph_3CH + NaOH$$

To the remaining product in the bottle add 10 ml of dichloromethane [2]. The instant decolorization is indicative of the powerful nucleophilic properties of the anion. Filter the ether layer and remove the solvent to obtain crystals of 2,2,2-triphenylchloroethane, mp 97°.

$$Ph_3C^- \quad \overset{\frown}{} \overset{\bullet}{C}H_2 \overset{\frown}{-} Cl \longrightarrow Ph_3C-CH_2Cl + Cl^-$$
$$\underset{Cl}{|}$$

THE TRIPHENYLMETHYL RADICAL $Ph_3C\cdot$

Place 2.7 g (0.01 mole) of triphenylmethyl chloride in a 500 ml bottle, add 20 ml dry benzene and 1.0 g zinc dust. Sweep out the air with nitrogen or natural gas, stopper tightly and shake for one hour. Allow the solid matter to settle and observe the yellow color due to the presence of the radical.

$$2Ph_3CCl + Zn^{++} \longrightarrow \underset{\text{yellow}}{2Ph_3C\cdot} \rightleftharpoons \underset{\text{colorless}}{Ph_3C-CPh_3}$$
$$+ ZnCl_2$$

Properties of the Triphenylmethyl Radical. Withdraw a little solution, diluting if necessary with benzene and record the ultraviolet-visible spectrum between 300 and 600 mμ. Compare this with the spectra of the triphenylmethyl carbonium ion and carbanion.

Measure the electron-spin resonance spectrum of the yellow solution and confirm the presence of unpaired electrons. Twenty-one peaks may be resolved but detailed analysis of the spectrum is very complicated [4] (Experiment 24).

Shake a little of the yellow solution with air and note the disappearance of the yellow color and formation of colorless peroxides.

Warm the bottle containing the radical solution by standing in hot water. Note and explain any change of colour.

Without admitting any air, add to the remainder of the radical solution 0.5 g isoprene and allow the mixture to stand for a few hours. Filter the solution and remove the solvent on a rotary evaporator to obtain crystals of 3-methyl-1,1,1,6,6,6-hexaphenylhex-3-ene.

$$2Ph_3C\cdot + \overset{}{\diagup\!\!\!\diagup\diagdown} \longrightarrow Ph_3C \overset{}{\diagup\!\!\diagdown\!\!\!\diagup\!\!\diagdown} -CPh_3$$

ELECTRONIC SPECTRA

Measure the electronic spectra of the following compounds:

a. Benzene, approx $10^{-4}M$ solution in hexane between 200–400 mμ
b. Triphenylmethane or triphenylcarbinol, approx $10^{-4}M$ solution in hexane between 200–400 mμ
c. Triphenylcarbinol in conc. sulfuric acid, (300–500 mμ).
d. Trityl fluoborate in acetone ⎫
e. Sodium trityl in ether   ⎬ as set out in the Experiment 32.
f. Trityl radical in benzene   ⎭

Compare the spectra obtained in the light of the above discussion.

Questions

1. List the factors on which the stability of an organic ion depend. How do they differ from those affecting the stability of a radical?

2. In a famous experiment, Paneth inferred the presence of methyl radicals produced in the gas phase by the thermal decomposition of lead tetramethyl, by their ability to remove a lead or tellurium mirror further along the flow system. Suggest how this equipment could be modified to measure the lifetimes of aliphatic free radicals in the gas phase.

3. Explain the following observations: the dye rosaniline, is bleached by

$$\left(H_2N-\!\!\left\langle\bigcirc\right\rangle\!\!\right)_2\!\!CH-\!\!\left\langle\bigcirc\right\rangle$$
$$\underset{H_3C}{}$$

sulfur dioxide, the resulting solution (Schiff's Reagent) being restored to its original color by addition of an aldehyde. Crystal violet is rapidly and irreversibly bleached by addition of alkali. The structure of crystal violet is,

$$\left(Me_2N-\!\!\left\langle\bigcirc\right\rangle\!\!\right)_3\!\!C^+ \ Cl^-$$

References

1. K. C. Moss, private communication.
2. J. C. Charlton, I. Dostrovsky, and E. D. Hughes, *Nature*, **167**, 986 (1951).
3. M. Gomberg, *Ber.*, **33**, 3150 (1900); *J. Amer. Chem. Soc.*, **22**, 757 (1900).
4. D. J. E. Ingram, *Free Radicals as Studied by Electron-Spin Resonance*, Butterworth, London, 1958, p. 160.
5. N. C. Deno, *Progress in Physical Organic Chemistry*, Vol. 2, Interscience, New York, 1964, p. 129.

Nonbenzenoid Aromatic
Compounds

The characteristic stability associated with benzene and its derivatives is shown by other completely conjugated cyclic systems which possess six π-electrons. The rings may be five-membered as in the cyclopentadienyl anion (III) or seven-membered, as in the tropyllium cation (V). In III one carbon has to contribute two π-electrons and V one contributes none, so as to maintain the total of six but, as with benzene, all carbon atoms are equivalent and the charge is shared equally. In the most general sense, Hückel [1] has defined an aromatic ring as a planar system of trigonally-hybridized carbon atoms possessing a total of $(4n + 2)$ π-electrons, n being integral. Systems which conform to this definition with 2 $(n = 0)$, 6 $(n = 1)$, 10 $(n = 2)$ etc. π-electrons may be classed as aromatic and are found to possess considerably greater stability than structures with any other number of electrons in the π-orbitals.

Other examples of aromatic compounds [7] include the cyclopropenium system (I [2]) and the cyclobutadiene dication (tetraphenyl derivative, II [3]) for which $n = 0$, the three systems mentioned above (III, IV, V) for which $n = 1$, and the cyclononatetraenyl (VI) anion [4], with 10 π-electrons $(n = 2)$. Larger systems, (annulenes) are known up to $n = 5$ or 6 [8]. Systems other than the six-membered ring are known as nonbenzenoid aromatics [5]. The stability of aromatic rings arises from the fact that the π-electrons are sufficient to fill all the bonding π-orbitals (without any being left over in non-bonding or antibonding orbitals [6]), and these may be considerably more stable than the orbitals associated with isolated double bonds (Table 32–1). In the experiments which follow, the preparations and properties of sodium cyclopentadienide and tropyllium fluoborate are described. Sodium cyclopentadienide (VII) is prepared by the action of sodium on cyclopentadiene (VIII) in which the acidity of the methylene group is unusually high on account of the aromatic stability of the anion. Cyclopentadiene is first prepared by thermal decomposition of dicyclopentadiene (XI)—a reverse Diels–Alder reaction (see Experiment 5, 39).

TABLE 32-1   Scheme of Occupation of Orbitals in Aromatic Systems

	π-Electrons					
	2			6		10
	I	II	III	IV	V	VI
Anti-bonding orbitals			—	— —	— / — —	— —
↑ E 0	— —	— —			— —	
Bonding orbitals	⇅	⇅	⇅	⇅ ⇅ / ⇅ ⇅	⇅ ⇅ / ⇅ / ⇅	⇅ ⇅ / ⇅ ⇅ / ⇅

If the cyclopentadienide ion is allowed to react with Fe^{++} (eg., anhydrous ferrous chloride), it forms the extraordinarily stable "sandwich" compound, ferrocene, bis(cyclopentadienyl)iron^{II}, (X):

$$XI \quad \overset{140°}{\underset{25°}{\rightleftharpoons}} \quad + \quad VIII$$

$$VIII \quad + \quad Na\cdot \quad \longrightarrow \quad VII \quad + \quad Na^+ \quad + \quad \tfrac{1}{2}H_2$$

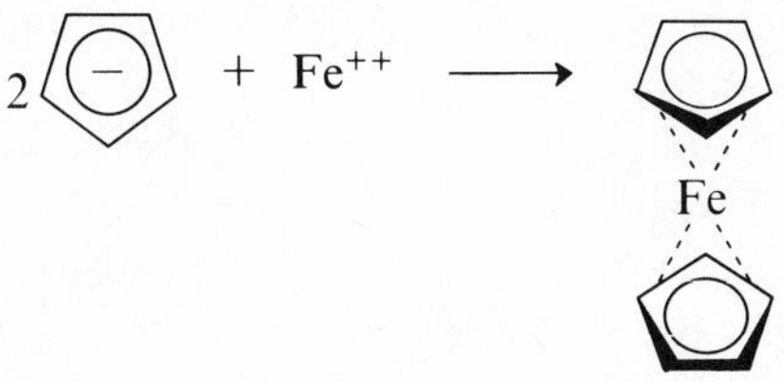

The cyclopentadienide rings in ferrocene still show aromatic character and undergo, for example, the Friedel–Crafts reaction, forming acetylferrocene (XI):

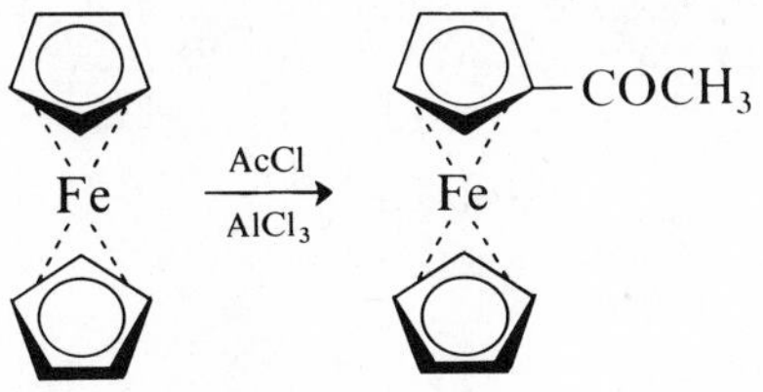

The tropyllium ion is prepared by hydride removal from cycloheptatriene (XII) by phosphorus pentachloride, and may be isolated as the stable fluoborate (XIII):

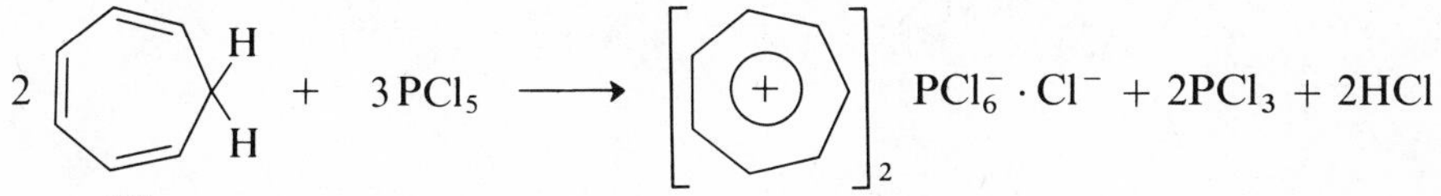

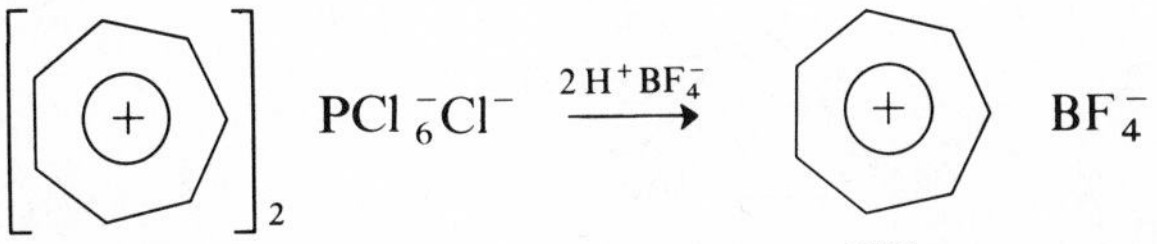

Experimental

PREPARATION OF CYCLOPENTADIENYL SODIUM

Materials Required

Dicyclopentadiene	Xylene
Sodium	Ferric chloride, anhydrous
Tetrahydrofuran, sodium-dried	

Place 2.3 g (0.1 mole) sodium in a 100 ml 3 necked round-bottomed flask fitted with a mechanical stirrer of the Hershberg type (Figure 32–1), dropping funnel and condenser containing a gas inlet connected to a slow supply of

nitrogen (or natural gas if this is not available, but in this case, the apparatus should be in a well-ventilated fumehood). Cover the sodium with about 10 ml of dry xylene and heat until the sodium melts. Run the stirrer at high speed to disperse the sodium then allow the mixture to cool well below the melting point of sodium before ceasing to stir. When cold, the sodium should be very finely divided. Allow it to settle and decant off the xylene. Wash the sodium free of xylene by adding 5 ml dry tetrahydrofuran and decanting the liquid off once more. Dispose of the washings after adding methanol to destroy particles of sodium present. Now add 25 ml of sodium-dried tetrahydrofuran followed by 6.6 g (0.1 mole) cyclopentadiene[1] added over a period of 15–20 min; maintain the stirring and inert atmosphere for a further 15 min, or until the sodium has dissolved. More solvent may be added if excessive evaporation occurs. The resulting solution contains cyclopentadienyl sodium.

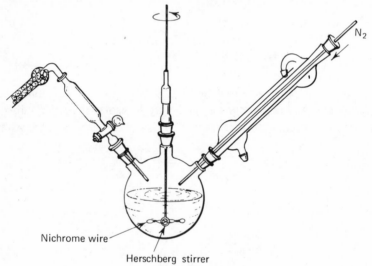

Nichrome wire

Herschberg stirrer

FIGURE 32–1

PROPERTIES OF THE CYCLOPENTADIENYL ANION

Preparation of Ferrocene. Add to the solution of cyclopentadienyl sodium a 5.4 g (0.033 mole) of anhydrous ferric chloride[2] in portions as a slurry in tetrahydrofuran, cooling the solution if the reaction appears too vigorous. When all has been added, heat the mixture under reflux for a further 15 minutes. Add a little methanol to destroy any unreacted sodium and, when this has been

[1] Cyclopentadiene is prepared immediately prior to use by distilling commercial dicyclopentadiene at atmospheric pressure with rapid boiling, through a short fractionating column, collecting the distillate coming over at 40–42°C.

[2] The preparation of ferrocene requires ferrous chloride which may be substituted for the ferric chloride using 0.1 mole with consequent doubling of the yield of ferrocene. In the present method one half of the cyclopentadienyl sodium is used to reduce ferric chloride to ferrous, thus illustrating its reducing properties.

removed wash the contents of the flask into 200 ml water and extract three times with 50 ml petroleum ether, bp 40°–60°. Combine the petroleum extracts, dry over a little sodium sulfate and remove the solvent on the rotary evaporator. Collect the orange crystals of ferrocene which remain and recrystallize from cyclohexane, mp 173°C.   Yield, 4.5 g, 75%

ACETYLFERROCENE

Materials Required

> Ferrocene
> Acetic anhydride
> Boron trifluoride etherate

The stability and aromatic character of ferrocene are illustrated by its acetylation in a Friedel–Crafts reaction. Place 2.0 g ferrocene in a flask and dissolve it in 10 ml dry dichloromethane. Add 1.2 g acetic anhydride, stopper, cool to 0° and add 2 ml boron trifluoride etherate[3]. The initial blue color which forms is due to the ferrocene cation. Allow the mixture to stand at room temperature for 30 min, then add sodium acetate solution and shake well to remove acetic acid. Separate off the dichloromethane (lower) layer, dry over anhydrous sodium sulfate and remove the solvent to obtain red crystals of acetylferrocene, mp 80–82°.   Yield, about 1.7 g, 70%

PREPARATION OF TROPYLLIUM TETRAFLUOBORATE

Materials Required

> Cyclohepta-1,3,5-triene
> Phosphorus pentachloride
> Fluoboric acid (50% aqueous solution)

Place in a fumehood a 250 ml three-necked flask equipped with mechanical stirrer, condenser with calcium chloride drying tube, and dropping funnel, ensuring that all the glassware is dry. Place 80 ml carbon tetrachloride in the flask and suspend in it 10 g (0.05 mole) of phosphorus pentachloride. Add 2.65 g (0.025 mole) cycloheptatriene and stir the mixture until it becomes viscous and then mobile again, and the evolution of HCl gas from the condenser ceases (2–3 hours). Filter the precipitate of the mixed tropyllium hexachlorophosphate-chloride, wash briefly with a little carbon tetrachloride and dissolve immediately in 40 ml absolute ethanol in a clean flask immersed in ice. Cool the reddish solution and add 5 ml 50% aqueous fluoboric acid while swirling the solution vigorously. Filter by suction the white precipitate of tropyllium tetrafluoborate which separates, wash with cold ethanol and dry in the air.

Yield, 3 g, 75%

---

[3] Great care must be taken when handling BF_3Et_2O not to inhale the vapor nor spill any on the skin.

Spectroscopic Properties of the Products. Compare the ultraviolet spectra of benzene ($10^{-3}M$ in ethanol) and tropyllium tetrafluoroborate ($10^{-4}M$ in 0.1 MHCl).

Measure the nuclear magnetic resonance spectrum of tropyllium fluoborate using dimethyl sulfoxide as solvent and show that the ring protons are all equivalent. Compare the spectrum with that of cycloheptatriene.

Measure the nuclear magnetic resonance spectrum of the cyclopentadienyl sodium solution in tetrahydrofuran as solvent and show the equivalence of the ring protons. Compare the spectrum with that of cyclopentadiene in the same solvent, and with that of benzene. Observe the progression of the chemical shift of the protons with increasing charge on the adjacent carbon atoms.

Measure the nuclear magnetic resonance spectrum of ferrocene in carbon tetrachloride solution and show the equivalence of all the protons.

Questions

1. Explain the following observations:

    a. The cyclopropenone system is much more stable than the cyclopentadienone system.

    b. Cyclobutadiene appears to be highly unstable, the following reactions fail to give cyclobutadiene systems:

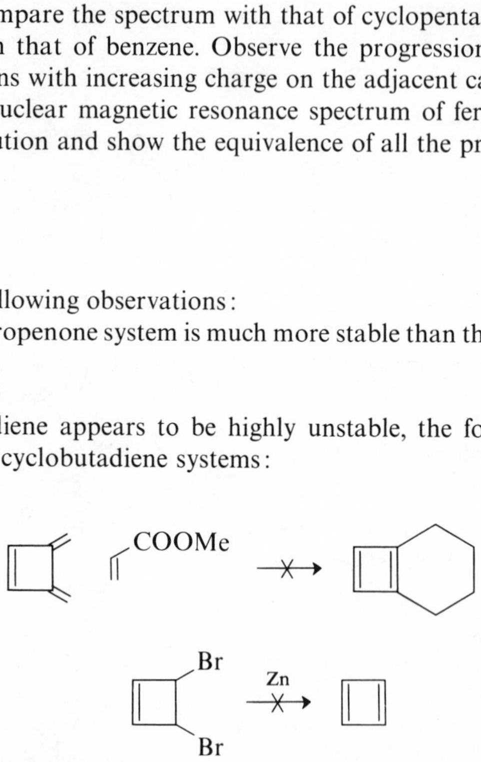

    c. Cationic 1,2-migrations of alkyl groups are very frequently encountered but the anionic counterpart to this reaction is very rare:

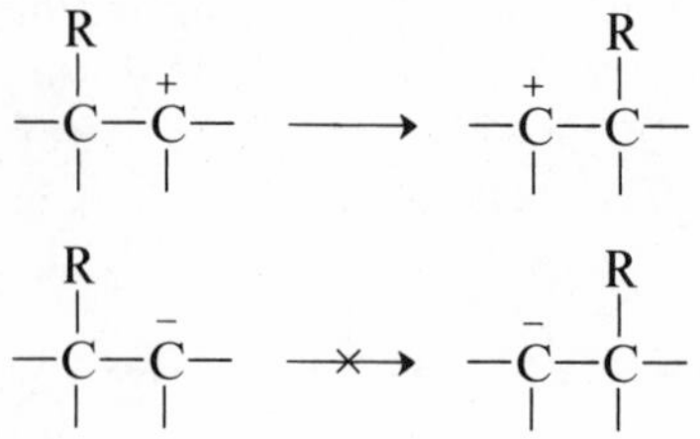

2. Which of the following conjugated systems would you expect to show *aromatic* character, and why?

References

1. E. Hückel, *Z. Physik*, **70**, 204 (1931); *Ibid*, **76**, 628 (1932).

2. R. Breslow and C. Yuan, *J. Amer. Chem. Soc.*, **80**, 5991 (1958).

3. H. H. Freedman, *J. Amer. Chem. Soc.*, **84**, 4165 (1962).

4. T. J. Katz and P. J. Garratt, *J. Amer. Chem. Soc.*, **85**, 2852 (1963); E. A. LaLancette and R. E. Benson, *J. Amer. Chem. Soc.*, **85**, 2853 (1963).

5. K. Hafner, *Angew. Chem.* (Internatl. Ed.), 165 (1964).

6. Streitwieser, *Molecular Orbital Theory for Organic Chemists*, Wiley, New York, 1961, Chapter 10.

7. D. Ginsberg, Ed., *Non Benzenoid Aromatic Compounds*, Interscience, New York, 1959.

8. F. Sondheimer, *Aromaticity*, Chemical Society Special Publication No. 21, 1967.

Reductions with
Alkali Metals

The alkali metals on account of their low ionization potentials are powerful reducing agents. Sodium and lithium are particularly valuable in organic chemistry and can be used under appropriate conditions to reduce a variety of functions including carbonyl and ester groups and aromatic systems:

$$Li \longrightarrow Li^+ + e^-$$

$$Na \longrightarrow Na^+ + e^-$$

Since the metals are one electron donors, the initial products of reduction can be considered anion radicals whose subsequent fate depends on the solvent.

The reduction of a carboxylic ester to a primary alcohol by sodium in boiling alcohol (Bouveault-Blanc reaction) has been long known and probably occurs by the following sequence of reactions:

In the absence of a hydroxylic solvent, no proton is available for transfer to the anion radical and instead, dimerization of this species by radical coupling occurs leading to an α-hydroxyketone or acyloin:

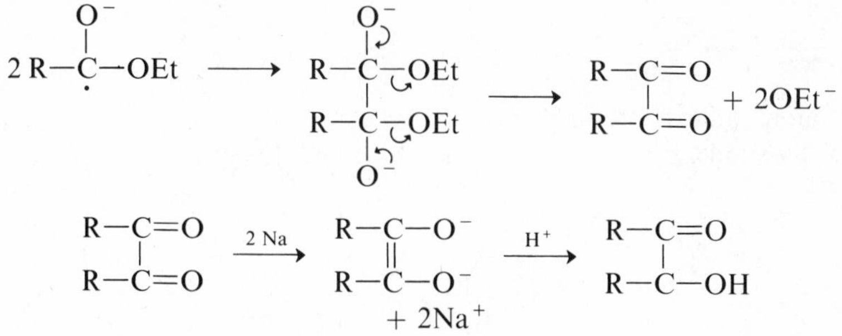

This is a particularly useful synthesis for preparing cyclic acyloins [1] from dibasic esters and provides a route to the rather difficultly accessible medium ring (nine- and ten-membered) systems. The reason why intramolecular dimerization is favored rather than intermolecular, is that the reaction occurs on the surface of the molten sodium at effectively *high dilution* so that the ends of the molecule have a good chance of interacting before another molecule can collide effectively, for example,

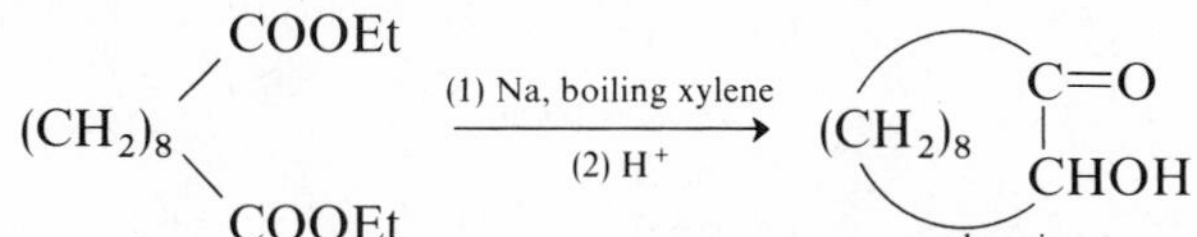

Solutions of the alkali metals may be made in liquid ammonia and anhydrous amines from which the metal may be recovered on evaporation. These solutions may be considered to contain the metal ions and electrons, both solvated:

$$Na \quad \underset{\longleftarrow}{\overset{liq\ NH_3}{\rightleftharpoons}} \quad Na^+_{solv} + e^-_{solv}$$

Such a solution is highly reducing and is capable of adding electrons to aromatic systems leading to partial reduction (Birch Reduction). For instance, benzene is reduced smoothly to 1,4-dihydrobenzene by lithium in liquid ammonia, a reaction which cannot be accomplished by conventional catalytic methods because reduction proceeds to completion:

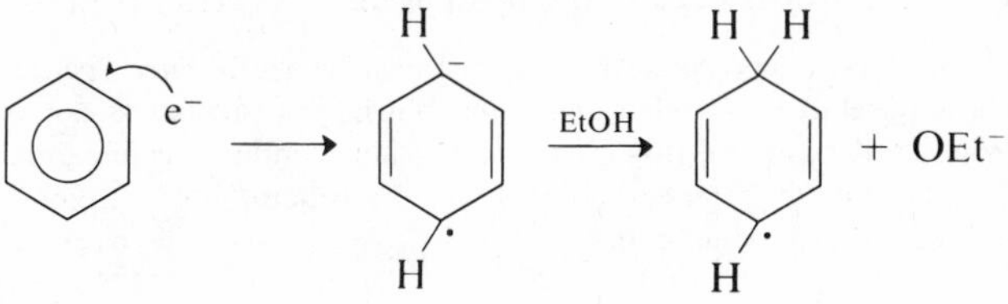

The anion radical intermediate may be detected in some cases where it is especially stable, such as that from naphthalene (Experiment 24):

dark green

PREPARATION OF SEBACOIN

$$(CH_2)_8 \underset{CHOH}{\overset{C=O}{|}}$$

Materials Required

Diethyl sebacate[1]
Sodium
Xylene

Place 120 ml of xylene and 10 g clean sodium in a 500 ml three-necked flask equipped with reflux condenser, dropping funnel and high speed stirrer of the Hirshberg type (Figure 32–1). Pass a slow stream of nitrogen or other inert gas through the flask and heat until the sodium is completely molten. Start the stirrer and run it at full speed until the sodium is very finely dispersed. Allow the xylene to boil gently and introduce slowly a solution of 23 g diethyl sebacate in 100 ml xylene, continuing stirring although the speed may be reduced a little if desired. The rate of addition of the ester is very important from the point of view of the yield of cyclic acyloin and should be as slow as possible, to maintain high-dilution conditions. With addition of the diethyl sebacate over 24 hours, the yield can reach 60–70% while this drops to about half if addition is completed over 8 hours. The latter is acceptable if the longer reaction is inconvenient. Fit

[1] Diethyl sebacate may be prepared from sebacic acid by the Fischer–Speier method. Allow 25 g of sebacic acid to reflux in 200 ml absolute ethanol while passing in a stream of dry hydrogen chloride gas. When all the solid has dissolved (about 15 min) continue heating for a further 30 min then remove the solvent on the rotary evaporator, wash the residual ester with sodium bicarbonate solution, dry over anhydrous sodium sulfate and distill, collecting diethyl sebacate at (308°/60 mm), 160°/7.5 mm.   Yield, 30 g, 98%.

a short piece of capillary tubing on to the dropping funnel to control the addition to a rate of about one drop every 5 seconds and allow the addition to proceed all day, heating for a further 30 min after the addition is complete. Cool the flask and contents in water and finally ice, and gradually add a solution of 28 ml acetic acid in an equal volume of xylene followed by 100 ml water. Filter the reaction mixture and separate the xylene layer containing the product. Wash with a further two portions of water, dry over sodium sulfate and remove the xylene under vacuum on the rotary evaporator over a steam bath. Distill the residue collecting sebacoin at 130–140°/15 mm, as an oil which solidifies on standing and cooling. If desired it may be recrystallized from petroleum ether at low temperature, mp 38°.   Yield, about 5 g, 35%

PREPARATION OF 5,8-DIHYDRO-1-NAPHTHOL

Materials Required

Liquid ammonia[2]	*tert*-Butanol
Sodium	Dewar flask
1-Naphthol	

In a fumehood or in the open air tilt the tank of ammonia so that the valve is lowest and, with a piece of tubing attached to the outlet open the valve and allow 75 ml of the liquid ammonia to flow into a Dewar flask of about 250 ml capacity. Place a piece of cotton wool in the neck of the flask and carry out the rest of the experiment in the fumehood.

Clamp the flask and fit it with a stirrer (NOT a steel paddle since catalytic traces of iron cause sodium and liquid ammonia to react together with the formation of sodamide and hydrogen). Add 5.5 g of finely powdered 1-naphthol, and 3 g *tert*-butanol and follow this while stirring with 2 g sodium cut into small pieces and added over a period of 30–40 minutes. Allow the solution to stand for a further 10 min when the blue color should have been discharged and replaced by a greyish turbidity. Allow the ammonia to evaporate then cautiously add methanol then ice water and finally dilute hydrochloric acid. Extract the solution with petroleum ether, bp 40–60°. After drying the solution over anhydrous sodium sulfate and filtering, concentrate it and allow the product to crystallize. 5,8-Dihydro-1-naphthol forms colorless prisms, mp 74°.

Yield, 3 g 55%

---

[2] Provided eye protection is worn and precautions taken against inhaling ammonia gas, there are no great difficulties in using liquid ammonia as a reaction medium.

Questions

1. Make space-filling models of the cyclooctane, cyclononane and cyclodecane systems and sketch the stablest configurations (ie., those with the least interactions between hydrogen atoms).
2. Suggest syntheses of the following compounds:

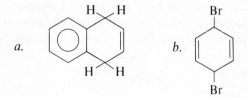

a. *b.*

c. cyclodecane from cyclohexanone   *d.* 1,6-hexanediol from cyclohexanone

References

1. N. L. Allinger, *Org. Syn.*, **36**, 79 (1956).
2. A. Birch, *Quart. Revs.*, **12**, 17 (1958).

Markownikoff's Rule
and Its Modification

Olefins are capable of adding certain polar molecules such as HCl across the double bond. An unsymmetrically substituted ethylene can, and often does, give rise to two products differing in the direction of the addition but one is usually in considerable excess:

$$RCH=CH_2 + HCl \xrightarrow[\delta+\ \delta-]{} \begin{cases} [R\overset{+}{C}H-CH_3] \longrightarrow RCH-CH_3 \quad \text{major product} \\ \qquad \text{I} \qquad\qquad\qquad\ | \\ \qquad\qquad\qquad\qquad\quad\ Cl \\[2mm] [RCH_2-\overset{+}{C}H_2] \longrightarrow RCH_2CH_2Cl \\ \qquad \text{II} \end{cases}$$

The major product is predictable from Markownikoff's Rule (1870) which states that *the major product results from the attachment of the positive part of the addend (here, H^+) to the carbon bearing the greater number of hydrogen atoms.* Some examples of such additions follow:

$$Ph-CH=CH_2 + \overset{\longmapsto}{HBr} \longrightarrow \underset{100\%}{PhCHBr-CH_3} + \underset{0\%}{PhCH_2CH_2Br}$$

$$Me_2C=CHMe + \overset{\longmapsto}{HBr} \longrightarrow \underset{75\%}{Me_2CBr-CH_2Me} + \underset{25\%}{Me_2CHCHMeBr}$$

$$Me_2C=CH_2 + \overset{\longleftarrow}{HOCl} \longrightarrow \underset{80\%}{Me_2C\underset{|}{C}H_2Cl} + \underset{20\%}{Me_2C\underset{|}{C}H_2OH}$$
$$\qquad\qquad\qquad\qquad\qquad\quad OH \qquad\quad Cl$$

Examination of many such additions has shown that the predicted product is indeed formed in major yield at least, while the isomer (anti-Markownikoff product) often occurs to a relatively minor extent.

The explanation of this specificity lies in the detailed mechanism of the reaction which is initiated by attack of the positive or electrophilic part of the addend on the π-electrons of the olefin to give an intermediate carbonium ion which may be written in various ways:

The olefinic carbons now have carbonium ion character, the positive charge being mainly carried by the most highly substituted one since the stabilities of carbonium ions increase in the order: primary < secondary < tertiary (Experiment 4) ie., I > II. The reaction is completed by attachment of the nucleophilic part of the addend (Cl^-) to the positive carbon, forming here, the predicted or Markownikoff product (the other isomer is sometimes referred to as the anti-Markownikoff product):

Thus the important factor in determining the orientation of addition is the relative stabilities of the intermediate [1] carbonium ions I and II.

The Markownikoff Rule might be rewritten in modern terms as follows: *the electrophilic (positive) part of the addend attacks the olefinic double bond such as to produce the more stable ion (or radical) intermediate.* We will examine some examples of additions for which Markownikoff's Rule fails, in the light of this new definition:

a. Addition to an olefin bearing a strongly electron-withdrawing group, such as $-\overset{+}{N}R_3$, $-CF_3$ [2].

$$Me_3\overset{+}{N}-CH=CH_2 + HI \longrightarrow Me_3\overset{+}{N}-\underset{\underset{0\%}{\overset{|}{I}}}{\overset{|}{C}}H-CH_3 + Me_3\overset{+}{N}-CH_2-CH_2I$$
$$100\%$$

Clearly the proximity of the positively-charged nitrogen will destabilize the secondary carbonium ion, $Me_3\overset{+}{N}-\overset{+}{C}HCH_3$ relative to the primary, $Me_3\overset{+}{N}-CH_2\overset{+}{C}H_2$ in which the like charges are further apart.

b. Additions of HBr in the presence of peroxides.

$$PhCH{=}CH_2 + HBr \xrightarrow{\text{lauroyl peroxide}} \underset{\text{20–35\%}}{PhCHBrCH_3} + \underset{\text{65–80\%}}{PhCH_2CH_2Br}$$

Reactions catalyzed by peroxides are typically those of free radicals [3]. Here, a bromine atom produced in a radical chain process attacks the olefin to give the more stable radical according to the same principles which govern the stability of a carbonium ion. The addition is then completed by hydrogen atom abstraction from another HBr molecule thus keeping the chain going:

initiation $\begin{cases} RO{-}OR \xrightarrow{\Delta} 2 \cdot OR \\ \cdot OR + HBr \longrightarrow ROH + \cdot Br \end{cases}$

propagation $\begin{cases} RCH{=}CH_2 + \dot{B}r \longrightarrow R{-}\dot{C}H{-}CH_2Br\,(+\,R{-}CHBr\dot{C}H_2) \\ R{-}CH{-}CH_2Br + HBr \longrightarrow \underset{\text{main product}}{R{-}CH_2{-}CH_2Br} + \cdot Br \end{cases}$

termination $\qquad\qquad 2\ \cdot Br \longrightarrow Br_2$ etc.

c. Hydrations via boron hydrides, (hydroborations). In recent years a new and highly specific method for adding the elements of water to an olefin to give the anti-Markownikoff product has been discovered and investigated by H. C. Brown [4]. The hydrides of boron such as diborane, B_2H_6, (which may be considered to react as BH_3) are electron deficient and act as Lewis acids. The boron will therefore accept an electron pair from a π-bond to give the more stable carbonium ion to which a hydride ion is then transferred. All three hydrogens of the borane are replaceable to give a trialkylborane:

(+ mixed boranes)

On oxidation with alkaline hydrogen peroxide, the alkylboranes give alcohols, predominantly the Anti-Markownikoff product:

$$Ph-CH_2CH_2-B \xrightarrow{\;H_2O_2,\,OH^-\;} Ph-CH-CH_3 + Ph-CH_2CH_2OH$$

$$+$$

$$Ph-CHCH_3$$
$$\underset{B}{|}$$

under Ph—CH—CH₃: OH

20%
1-phenylethanol

80%
2-phenylethanol

Even greater specificity may be achieved as follows. The borane (generated *in situ* from sodium borohydride and boron trifluoride) is first allowed to react with two moles of an olefin such as 2-methyl-2-butene (amylene) to give a di-isoamylborane. This still has one hydride left to react with another mole of olefin such as styrene but now the steric effects of the isoamyl groups reinforce the electronic effects in directing the attack almost exclusively to the terminal carbon atom:

$$2\,Me_2C{=}CHMe + BH_3 \longrightarrow (Me_2CH-CH)_{\overline{2}}BH \equiv Am^i_2BH$$

with Me above the CH; di-isoamylborane

$$Ph-CH{=}CH_2 \xrightarrow[\;(2)\,H_2O_2,\,OH^-\;]{(1)\,Am^i_2BH} Ph-CH-CH_3 + Ph-CH_2-CH_2OH$$
$$\underset{OH}{|}$$

2%   98%

In the following experiments, specific additions to styrene to give both the Markownikoff and anti-Markownikoff products illustrate the principles discussed.

Experimental

Materials Required

Styrene	Diglyme (ethylene glycol dimethyl ether)
Sodium bromide	2-Methyl-2-butene[2]
Sodium borohydride	Hydrogen peroxide, 30%
Boron trifluoride etherate[1]	

PREPARATION OF 1-PHENYLETHYL BROMIDE [5]–MARKOWNIKOFF ADDITION
TO STYRENE

$$PhCH{=}CH_2 + HBr \longrightarrow PhCHBrCH_3$$

Arrange an HBr generator using a Buchner flask containing sodium bromide and dropping in conc. sulfuric acid. An alternative source of the gas which is more convenient for large quantities is provided by dropping bromine slowly

[1] Handle with care and avoid splashing on the skin or inhaling vapor.

[2] Readily made by distilling *tert*-amyl alcohol with a little sulfuric acid.

into hot decalin (decahydronaphthalene), washing the hydrogen bromide evolved by passing through conc sulfuric acid. Fit a 100 ml flask with gas delivery tube or dispersion stick reaching to the bottom. Weigh the apparatus and weigh in 10 g of styrene. If the styrene is not stabilized, add a few crystals of hydroquinone or diphenylamine to minimize the radical reaction. Pass in a rapid stream of hydrogen bromide gas until the theoretical quantity has been absorbed as determined by weighing, maintaining the temperature around 20–25°. Allow the mixture to stand for a further 15 min to complete the reaction then transfer the product to a separating funnel. Wash thoroughly with water and sodium bicarbonate solution until the washings are no longer acidic, dry the organic layer over calcium chloride and distill, collecting 1-phenylethyl bromide at 200–205° (760 mm) or 85–90° (15 mm), $n_D^{25} = 1.5595$.

Yield, 16 g, 90%

PREPARATION OF 2-PHENYLETHANOL BY HYDROBORATION [6]

Arrange a 250 ml three-necked flask equipped with dropping funnel, condenser and stirrer (a magnetic stirrer may be used). Place in the flask 50 ml diglyme (dried by standing over sodium), 11.6 g 2-methyl-2-butene and 2.35 g finely crushed sodium borohydride. Cool the mixture by means of an ice-bath, commence stirring and add, over a period of about 30 min, 12.0 g boron trifluoride etherate. Allow the solution to stand at room temperature for 30 min to complete the formation of di-isoamylborane.

Cool the mixture again in the ice-bath and add 7.1 g styrene. Allow the solution to warm to room temperature and stand for 1 hour then add a mixture of 25 ml 3 M sodium hydroxide and 25 ml 30% hydrogen peroxide slowly and with cooling. Follow this by a further 25 ml of hydrogen peroxide. Extract the solution with three portions of ether, combine the ethereal layers and wash them with four lots of water to remove diglyme. Dry the ethereal solution over anhydrous sodium sulfate and remove the ether on the rotary evaporator. Distill the residue and obtain 2-phenylethanol, bp 220° (760 mm), 110° (15 mm), $n_D^{25} = 1.5240$.   Yield, 6.0 g, 70%.

In order to compare the product with that obtained in part 1, it may be converted to 2-phenylethyl bromide by treating 5.0 g of the alcohol with 3.7 g bromine in the presence of 0.35 g red phosphorus. When the reaction is complete the product is washed with water, filtered, extracted with ether, dried and distilled, bp 210° (760 mm), 100° (15 mm).

Run infrared spectra on the two isomeric bromides and show that they are not identical.

Questions

1. Predict the products formed in major yield in the following reactions:

a.

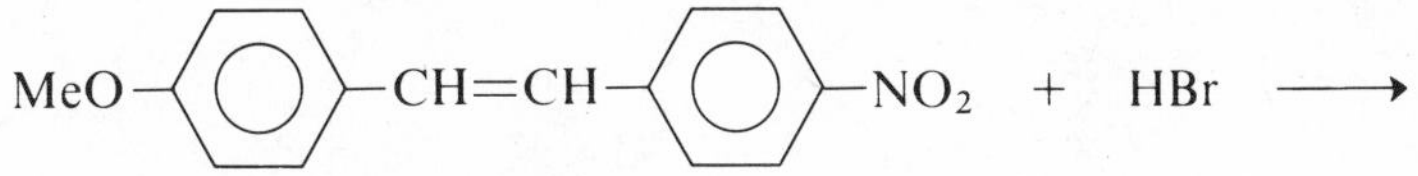

$$MeO-\langle\bigcirc\rangle-CH{=}CH-\langle\bigcirc\rangle-NO_2 \quad + \quad HBr \quad \longrightarrow$$

b. $\qquad$ MeCH=CH$_2$ + ICl $\longrightarrow$

c. $\qquad$ Ph$_3$C—CH=CH$_2$ + Br$_2$ + MeOH $\longrightarrow$
$\qquad\qquad\qquad\qquad\qquad$ (solvent)

d. $\qquad$ MeCH—CH$_2$ + N$_3^-$ $\xrightarrow[\text{H}_2\text{O}]{\text{H}^+}$ $\longrightarrow$
$\qquad\qquad\quad$ \diagdown O \diagup

e.

f. $\quad$ + EtO$_2$C—C≡C—CO$_2$Et $\longrightarrow$

g. $\qquad$ + HI $\longrightarrow$

h. $\qquad$ + HI $\longrightarrow$

i. $\qquad$ CH$_3$—C≡C—COOH + HCl $\longrightarrow$

j. $\quad$ + Br$_2$ $\xrightarrow{\text{H}_2\text{O}}$ C$_5$H$_4$O$_4$Br

k. $\qquad$ Me$_2$C=CH$_2$ + H$_2$S $\xrightarrow{\text{H}^+}$

l. $\xrightarrow[\text{(2) H}_2\text{O}_2]{\text{(1) NaBH}_4, \text{BF}_3, \text{Ether}}$

m. $\qquad$ CH$_2$=CH$_2$ + Al(CH$_2$CH$_3$)$_3$ $\longrightarrow$

n.
$$CH_3CH_2CH{=}CH_2 + \underset{\underset{OEt}{|}}{\overset{\overset{O}{\|}}{HP}}{-}OEt \xrightarrow{\text{Bu}_2^t\text{O}_2}$$

o.
$$+ CCl_4 \xrightarrow{h\nu}$$

p.
$$+ 2NOCl \longrightarrow$$

References

1. J. Hine, *Physical-Organic Chemistry*, McGraw-Hill, 1962, Chapter 9.
2. A. L. Henne and S. Kaye, *J. Amer. Chem. Soc.*, **72**, 3369 (1950).
3. C. Walling, *Free Radicals in Solution*, Wiley, New York, 1957.
4. H. C. Brown, *Hydroboration*, Benjamin, 1962.
5. C. Walling, M. S. Kharasch, and F. R. Mayo, *J. Amer. Chem. Soc.*, **61**, 2696 (1939).
6. H. C. Brown and G. Zweifel, *J. Amer. Chem. Soc.*, **83**, 1241 (1961).

A Topochemical
Experiment

Topochemistry is the name given to reactions occurring in the solid phase, either in crystals or frozen solutions. In such media there can be none of the random movement between reactants which is characteristic of the liquid or gaseous state and reaction can only occur between centers which lie in close proximity in the crystal. Hertel [1] has stated as a general premise in topochemistry, *reactions in the solid state occur with a minimum of molecular displacement*. It follows that the crystal lattice is of crucial importance in determining which or whether a topochemical reaction will occur (crystal lattice control). In practice, the reactions are initiated by irradiation of the crystal with light which, when absorbed by a molecule may activate it to attack a suitably situated neighboring molecule leading to dimerization as one of the principal topochemical reactions. Three principles have been suggested by Cohen and Schmidt [2] as constituting the characteristics of topochemical reactions:

a. A series of closely related compounds may manifest considerable differences in their solid state chemistry. Small changes in size and shape of the molecule, even if remote from the reaction center may cause a profound change in lattice geometry.

b. Different reactions may be observed to occur in solid and in disperse (fluid) phases. For example, a given reaction observed to occur in the crystal because of the peculiar orientation of the molecules may be prevented from taking place by unfavorable entropy considerations when the molecules are free.

c. Polymorphic modifications of the same compound may differ in their topochemistry for reasons set out in *a.* Some examples of topochemical reactions follow which illustrate these principles.

Trans cinnamic acid I crystallizes in two modifications. Crystals of the α- or stable form (II) on irradiation with ultraviolet light give rise to the centro-symmetric dimer, α-truxillic acid (III) whereas the β- or metastable form V, gives mainly β-truxinic acid (IV). No dimerization occurs on irradiation of either molten or dissolved cinnamic acid.

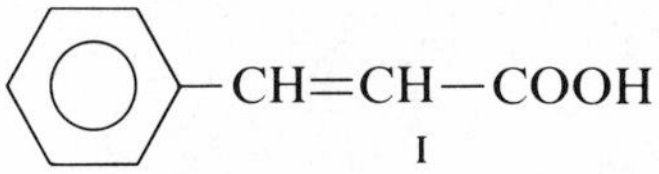

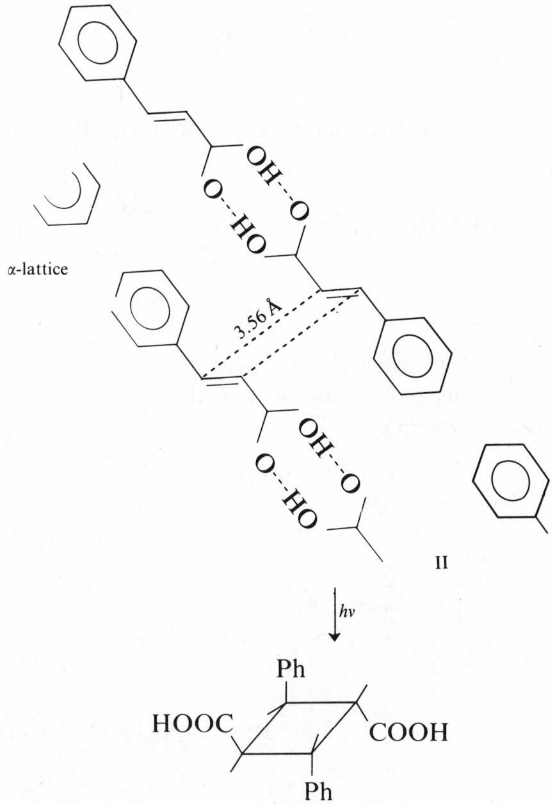

β-lattice

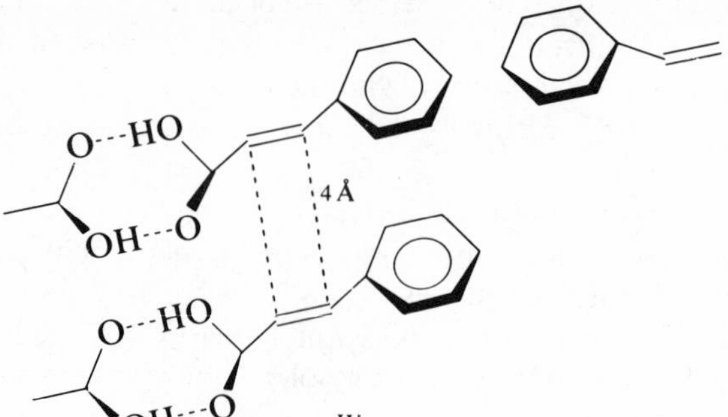

IV

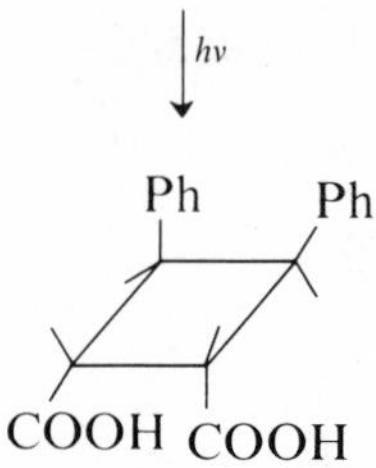

↓ hv

IV

Cinnamylidineacetic acid (VI) dimerizes unsymmetrically to form (VII):

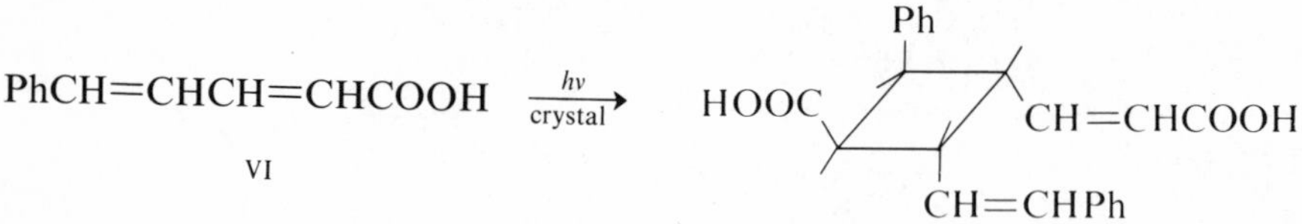

$$PhCH{=}CHCH{=}CHCOOH \xrightarrow[\text{crystal}]{hv}$$

VI

VII

Irradiation of the methyl ester (VIII where R = Me) gives a cyclobutane derivative (IX) analogous to truxillic acid while the ethyl ester (VIII, where R = Et) gives a linear dimer (XI):

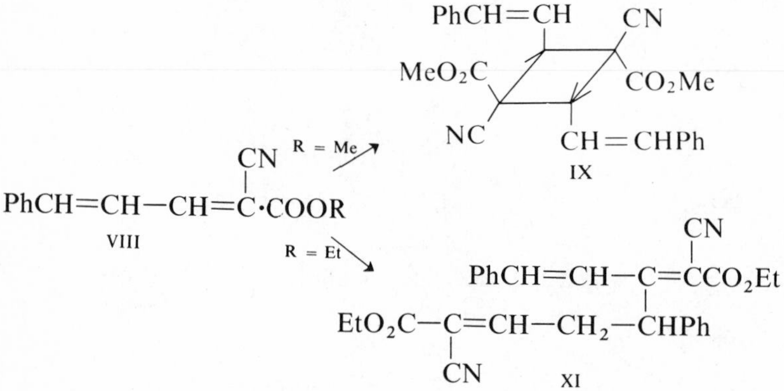

IX

$$PhCH{=}CH{-}CH{=}\overset{\overset{\displaystyle CN}{|}}{C}{\cdot}COOR$$

VIII

R = Me ↗

R = Et ↘

$$PhCH{=}CH{-}\overset{\overset{\displaystyle CN}{|}}{C}{=}CCO_2Et$$
$$EtO_2C{-}\underset{\underset{\displaystyle CN}{|}}{C}{=}CH{-}CH_2{-}CHPh$$

XI

The reactions are rather slow (up to 20 days irradiation) but otherwise afford useful syntheses of cyclobutane derivatives of high stereospecificity.

A topochemical reaction which may more easily be observed is the internal rearrangement of salicylidineaniline (XII). Irradiation of the yellow crystals with ultraviolet light converts them to an orange product (a phototropic change) which may be the quinoid compound (XIII):

yellow   ? orange

XII   XIII

On standing in the dark, warming, melting or dissolving the orange solid, it reverts to the original yellow anil.

Experimental

Materials Required

Salicylaldehyde
Aniline
Mercury vapor lamp

PREPARATION OF SALICYLIDINEANILINE (XII)

Dissolve 6.0 g salicylaldehyde and 4.5 g aniline in 20 ml of ether and allow the solution to stand until a heavy precipitate of yellow crystals forms. Filter off the salicylidineaniline and recrystallize from ethanol, mp 51°C.

Yield, 10 g, 95%

A Topochemical Reaction. Dissolve about 0.1–0.2 g of salicylidineaniline in a little ether and evaporate the solution all over the wall of a 100 ml Pyrex flask using the rotary evaporator. When thoroughly dry, set up an ultraviolet lamp (100–500 Watt) above the flask and a Pyrex Petri dish containing $\frac{1}{2}$-inch of water to act as a heat shield in between. Shield the lamp so that no ultraviolet light shines directly into the laboratory and wear protective glasses while working near the lamp. Continue to rotate the flask and irradiate for 30 min–1 hour or until the crystals in the flask become noticeably orange.

Allow some of the orange product to stand in the dark overnight and compare the color with unirradiated material.

Dissolve some of the irradiated crystals in ether and note the instantaneous color change.

Dissolve a little salicylidineaniline in heavy petroleum oil (nujol) and freeze it slowly in a Pyrex testtube by cooling in dry ice. Suspend the tube in a non-silvered Dewar flask so that it lies against the inner wall half-immersed in ethanol containing some lumps of dry ice, or, better still, liquid nitrogen. Irradiate the frozen material with ultraviolet light and observe the color change after about an hour. Allow the tube to warm until the *glass* of nujol becomes fluid and observe the color change.

Chemiluminescence

While many reactions are exergonic—ie., proceed with the evolution of energy, this energy nearly always appears in a degraded form as heat. Certain reactions, however, produce energy in the form of light with a negligible amount of heat giving rise to the phenomenon of chemiluminescence [1,4]. Reactions which exhibit chemiluminescence are nearly always oxidations, the most familiar being that of the firefly glow—the enzymatic oxidation of luciferin (I):

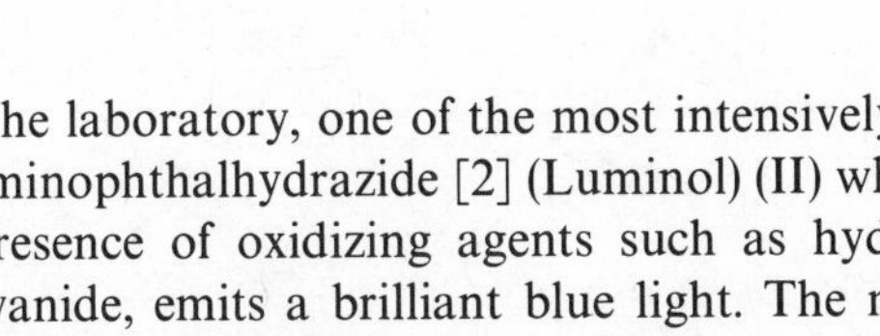

I

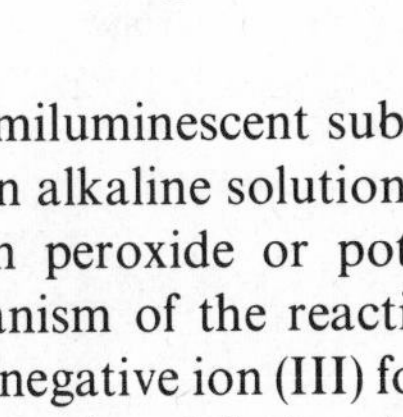

II

In the laboratory, one of the most intensively chemiluminescent substances is 3-aminophthalhydrazide [2] (Luminol) (II) which in alkaline solution and in the presence of oxidizing agents such as hydrogen peroxide or potassium ferricyanide, emits a brilliant blue light. The mechanism of the reaction has recently been shown [3] to involve formation of the dinegative ion (III) followed by reaction with oxygen or an equivalent to give the aminophthalate ion (IV).

$$II \xrightleftharpoons{2\,OH^-} \quad \longleftrightarrow \quad etc.$$

$$\downarrow 2\,(0)$$

IV singlet $+ h\nu \longleftarrow$ IV triplet $+ N_2$

$$\downarrow oxidation$$

degradation products.

Moreover the aminophthalate ion is produced in an excited electronic state which happens to be a triplet state[1] and hence its transition to the singlet[2] ground state is 'forbidden'. Thus, this transition occurs at a slow rate, one quantum of light energy being emitted per molecule. The process is, in effect, a phosphorescence phenomenon (Experiment 37).

It is tempting to speculate that coordination between III and molecular oxygen (which is itself a triplet) is occurring and leading to a species which is in a triplet state because of spin conservation.

Experimental

PREPARATION OF LUMINOL

Materials Required

3-Nitrophthalic acid	Ammonium sulfide
Hydrazine sulfate	Sodium acetate

[1] Has two unpaired electrons.
[2] No unpaired electrons.

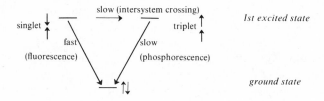

Luminol is prepared by heating 3-nitrophthalic acid with hydrazine, followed by reduction of the nitro group by sulfide ion:

Dissolve 6.5 g hydrazine sulfate and 13.6 g sodium acetate in hot water, add the solution to 10.6 g 3-nitrophthalic acid in an evaporating basin and heat to dryness while stirring. Alternatively, the mixture may be dried on a rotary evaporator the purpose being to ensure good mixing. Grind the solid residue, place in a wide-necked flask and heat in an oil bath at 160° for 3 hours, stirring at intervals. Grind the solid product with two 20 ml portions of water to remove inorganic matter, filter and dry the residual 3-nitrophthalhydrazide, V.

Dissolve 21 g ammonium sulfide in 40 ml water and gradually add 10 g of the crude 3-nitrophthalhydrazide with stirring, cooling the solution in ice during the addition. Boil the mixture for 1 hour after addition bubbling a slow stream of hydrogen sulfide through it meanwhile. Cool the solution well and filter the yellow precipitate of luminol containing some free sulfur. More product may be obtained by acidifying the filtrate with glacial acetic acid. To purify the product, dissolve the yellow solid in 5% sodium hydroxide (note the acidity of the imine hydrogen), filter off undissolved sulfur and reprecipitate luminol by acidification with glacial acetic acid.

Yield, 6.5 g, 75%

Demonstration of chemiluminescence.   Take two liter beakers; in one, place a solution of 0.1 g luminol in 10 ml 5% sodium hydroxide diluted to about 1 liter with water, and in the other, 0.25 g potassium ferricyanide and 5 ml 10% hydrogen peroxide in 1 liter water. In a dark room arrange a large funnel to drain into a 2 liter beaker. Pour the two solutions simultaneously into the funnel and observe the emission of light from the liquid.

a. Insert a thermometer and determine whether any heat is evolved.

b. Divide the luminescent solution into three parts. To one add more potassium ferricyanide, to another add more hydrogen peroxide and to the remainder add both oxidizing agents. Compare the effects on the light emission of the three solutions.

c. To a part of the solution add dilute HCl slowly and note the effect on the luminescence. Raise the pH again by adding NaOH solution.

References

1. K. D. Gundermann, *Angew. Chem.* (Internatl. Ed.) **4**, 566 (1965).
2. E. H. Huntress, L. N. Stanley, and A. S. Parker, *J. Chem. Ed.*, 142 (1934).
3. E. H. White, O. Zofirion, H. H. Kagi, and J. H. M. Hill, *J. Amer. Chem. Soc.,* **86**, 940, 941 (1964).
4. F. McCapra, *Quart Rev.*, 485 1966.

Photochemistry

Frequently, quite novel reactions of organic compounds are observed when they are converted to electronically excited states by the absorption of visible or ultraviolet light. Generally, excitation of a molecule from the ground electronic state, S_0, in which all electron spins are paired (singlet) leads to promotion of an electron from the highest filled orbital to a vacant orbital of higher energy (frequently antibonding). This state, S_1, is also a singlet[1] since processes in which spin orientation are conserved are much more probable than those in which they are changed. The excited singlet molecule may have a lifetime of only 10^{-8} sec during which it will either return to the ground state with the emission of a quantum of light (fluorescence) or, less efficiently may be converted to a triplet state, T_0, by a process of spin inversion (intersystem crossing). T_0 will revert to the ground state by the much slower process of phosphorescence (10^{-4} sec or more), or may undergo reaction or other processes which are indicated in Figure 37–1 in which transitions between several electronic levels and their associated vibrational and rotational sublevels are shown. It should also be noted that electronic transitions occur so rapidly that the shapes of the excited molecules may be considered to be the same as the ground state (Franck–Condon Principle). It is only when considering the relatively stable triplet states that *relaxation* of the molecule to other geometries is possible and in

---

[1] A molecule in which all electron spins are paired, even though two orbitals each contain a single electron is called *singlet* since the state is nondegenerate and in a magnetic field is not separated into further levels. A *triplet* state, containing two electrons with spins parallel (and necessarily in different orbitals) is degenerate and splits into three different levels in a magnetic field (cf. page 244).

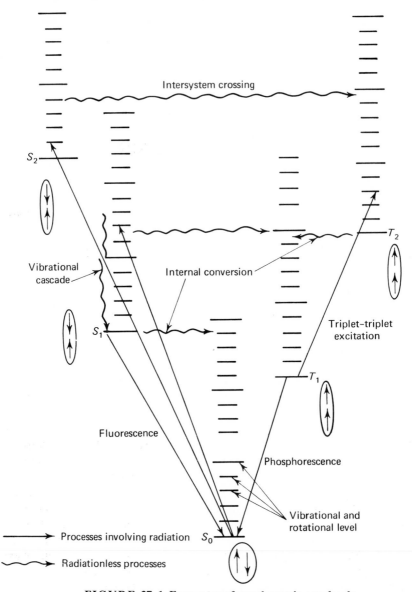

FIGURE 37–1 Energy-transfer pathways in a molecule.

these configurations reactions occur. Some examples of photochemical reaction types follow [2]:

1. *Cis-trans* isomerism [3]

2. Valence isomerism, isomerizations involving ring opening or closure [4, 5]

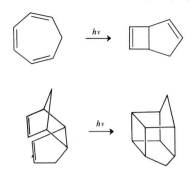

3. Double bond migration [6, 7]

4. Molecular rearrangements [8, 9]

5. Additions [10, 11, 12]

6. Sensitized reactions. A sensitizer such as benzophenone will absorb a quantum of light (wavelength around 330 mμ) and may then pass the energy on to another molecule which is not able to absorb in that region but, thus activated, may undergo photochemical reaction [13]:

7. Expulsion of a small stable molecule [14, 15]

For further details of these and other photochemical reactions, the reviews quoted in Reference 2 may be consulted. The following preparations are illustrative of the principles discussed.

Note that photochemical reactions often lead to the less thermodynamically stable products, eg., (1) and (3).

Experimental

PHOTOADDITION OF CYCLOOCTENE TO CHLORANIL

Materials Required

> Maleic anhydride   Chloranil
> Benzene   *p*-Benzoquinone
> *cis*-Cyclooctene   500 W Medium pressure mercury lamp[1]

Dissolve chloranil (I, 2.0 g) in a mixture of cyclooctene (20 ml) and benzene (150 ml). Place the mixture in a Pyrex or other borosilicate glass tube or flask and immerse this in a beaker full of a solution containing potassium hydrogen phthalate (5 g/liter), ethylene glycol (200 ml/liter), and saturated aqueous sodium nitrite (250 ml/liter) with pH adjusted to 11.

This solution acts as a filter permitting only light of wavelength greater than 410 mμ to pass. Arrange the flask so that it is within 2 cm of the beaker containing the filter solution and irradiate from that side with a 500 W mercury arc lamp for 2 hours (Figure 37–2). Remove the solvents on a rotary evaporator and crystallize the residual oil from either methanol or carbon tetrachloride. The product, the 1:1 adduct (II) forms pale yellow crystals, mp 105°.

Yield, 2–2.5 g, (80–90%)

---

[1] NOTE: It is essential that the eyes be shielded at all times from ultraviolet light.

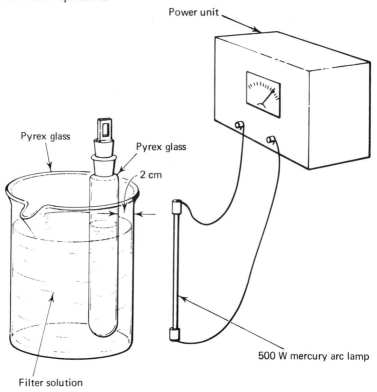

FIGURE 37–2

FORMATION OF THE $1:2$ ADDUCT (III)

Place 2 g of the previous product (II) in a Pyrex flask and dissolve it in cyclo-octene (20 ml) and benzene (150 ml); immerse the solution this time in a Pyrex beaker of water which will permit the passage of light of wavelength above about 320 mμ. Irradiate as before for 2 hours and remove the solvents on the evaporator. Dissolve the residual oil in 20 ml of ether and leave to crystallize in a refrigerator overnight. Filter the white crystalline $1:2$ adduct (III) and dry in the air, mp 233°.

Yield, 2–2.5 g, (80–90%)

PHOTOADDITION OF *p*-BENZOQUINONE TO CYCLOOCTENE

Dissolve 2 g of *p*-benzoquinone (IV) in 100 ml dry benzene and add 20 ml of cyclooctene. Place the solution in a Pyrex tube immersed in a Pyrex beaker of water (Figure 37–2) and irradiate with a 500 W mercury arc lamp. A high power tungsten filament lamp may also be used for this experiment, but appreciably longer reaction times are necessary. At time intervals of approximately 30 min take samples of the solution and measure the spectrum between 350 and 500 mμ, diluting each by the same factor (as found by experiment) in order to observe the intensity of the absorption due to benzoquinone (430–540 mμ). When this band has disappeared, which usually takes between 3 and 4 hours depending somewhat on the arrangement for the irradiation, switch off the lamp and remove the solvents on the rotary evaporator. Distill the residual oil *in vacuo* to obtain a pure sample of the spiro-oxetan, V.   Yield, 2–2.5 g, (80–90%)

THE PHOTOCHEMICAL REACTION BETWEEN BENZENE AND MALEIC ANHYDRIDE

Prepare two solutions of 7 g maleic anhydride in 100 ml benzene and place in identical 250 ml conical flasks. In one, dissolve in addition 3 g of benzophenone. Stopper the flasks and allow them to stand in daylight, under as near as possible identical conditions of light intensity, for about 14 days. Observe any changes noted during this period.

Filter off and weigh the crystalline products from these reactions. Carry out the following tests on them.

1. Determine the melting points of each product and perform a mixed melting point determination to check their identity.
2. Measure the infrared spectra of each product and interpret them.
3. Measure the NMR spectrum of the product dissolved in conc. sulfuric acid.
4. Measure the ultraviolet spectrum of the product in conc. sulfuric acid solution.

Suggest a structure for the product of this reaction whose elemental analysis is; C, 61.3%; H, 3.65% and suggest what function the benzophenone has in this reaction.

Questions

1. Suggest mechanisms for the following photochemical transformations:

a.

hv

b.

COOEt
|
C
|||
C
|
COOEt

$\xrightarrow{hv}$

COOEt

COOEt

c.

CH=NPh

NO$_2$

$\xrightarrow{hv}$

O

NH

+ PhNO

d.

$\xrightarrow{hv}$

O

e.

$\xrightarrow{hv}$

f.   PhN$_3$ $\xrightarrow{hv}$ PhN=NPh

2. What products would you expect from irradiation of the following compounds:

a.

b.

c.

O

d.

O   O

e. (PhCOO)$_2$ in benzene.

f.

g.

R

ONO

References

1. F. Wilkinson, *Quart. Rev.*, **403** (1966).

2. G. Hammond and N. Turro, *Science*, **142**, 1541 (1963). For an extensive bibliography in this subject, see also the list of references in this review.

3. G. S. Hammond and J. Saltiel, *J. Amer. Chem. Soc.*, **85**, 4983 (1962).

4. W. G. Dauben and R. L. Cargill, *Tetrahedron*, **12**, 186 (1961).

5. D. De Mayo and S. T. Reid, *Quart Rev.*, **15** (1961) 393.

6. N. C. Yang and M. J. Jorgenson, *Tetrahedron Letters*, 1203 (1964).

7. N. C. Yang and C. Rivas, *J. Amer. Chem. Soc.*, **83**, 2213 (1961).

8. H. E. Zimmerman and D. I. Schuster, *J. Amer. Chem. Soc.*, **83**, 4486 (1961); *ibid*, **84**, 4527 (1962).

9. P. J. Kropp, *J. Amer. Chem. Soc.*, **85**, 3779 (1963).

10. G. S. Hammond, N. J. Turro, and R. S. H. Liu, *J. Org. Chem.*, **28**, 3297 (1963).

11. J. G. Atkinson, D. E. Ayer, G. Buchi, and E. W. Robb, *J. Amer. Chem. Soc.*, **85**, 2257 (1963).

12. E. J. Corey, R. B. Mitra and H. Uda, J., *Amer. Chem. Soc.*, **86**, 485 (1964).

13. Reference 2., see Reference 43 therein.

14. D. M. Lemal and K. S. Shim, *J. Amer. Chem. Soc.*, **86**, 1550 (1964).

15. N. J. Turro, G. W. Byers, and P. A. Leermakers, *J. Amer. Chem. Soc.*, **86**, 955 (1964).

Stereochemistry of the
Diels-Alder Reaction

EXPERIMENT 38

The Diels–Alder Reaction is the name given to a remarkably facile cycloaddition of a 1,3-diene (in a cisoid configuration) to an olefin, usually activated by electron-withdrawing groups, the product being a cyclohexene derivative.

The mechanism is believed to involve the simultaneous attachment of both ends of the diene in a concerted rearrangement of the π-electron systems as shown (the directions of the arrows have no significance; they could all be reversed). Thus, six electrons are involved and the process is one of a group of cycloadditions permitted to occur by the Hoffmann–Woodward Rules [1] which are based on a correlation of the orbital symmetries between the starting materials and the product (see Table 38–1).

With suitably substituted reagents, stereoisomerism of the products is possible, [2]. For instance, furan (I) and maleic anhydride (II) may add to give the *exo*[1] adduct (III) or the *endo* adduct (IV):

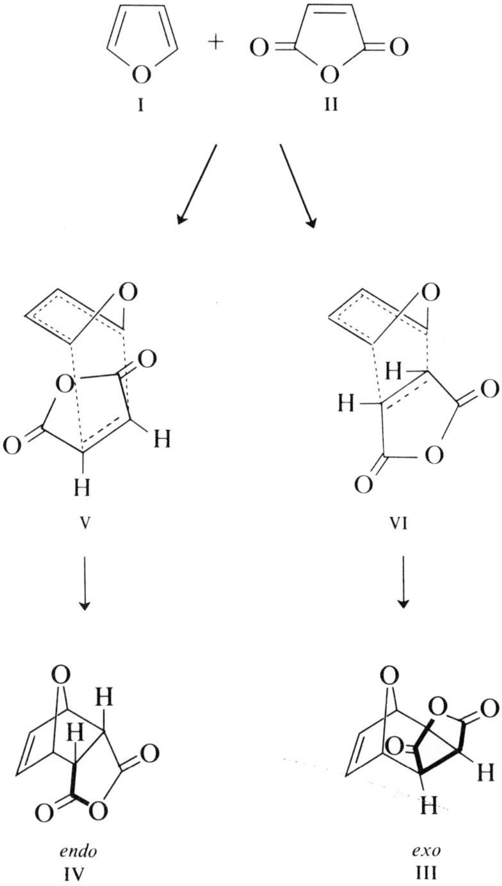

As a rule, the *endo* isomer is formed the more rapidly, at least at low temperatures and short reaction times. This is a result of the more favorable overlap between the two π-systems in the transition state leading to *endo* product (V) compared with that leading to *exo* (VI) with consequent lowering

[1] This terminology is applicable to boat forms of cyclohexane rings (as in this case on account of the methylene oxide bridge) and indicates the substituent to be on the inside (convex side)—*endo* or outside (concave side)—*exo* of the boat.

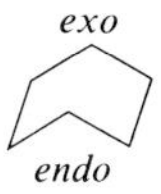

TABLE 38–1. Cycloaddition Reactions

1.		Carbene additions to olefins (Experiment 30)
2.		Photodimerization of alkenes (Experiments 35, 37)
3.		1,3-Dipolar cycloadditions (Experiment 39)
4.		Diels-Alder reaction (Experiment 38)

of activation energy in the former case. This property is quite solvent dependent, however, and *endo–exo* ratios have been used as a measurement of solvent polarity (see Experiment 25).

The *exo* isomer may, in some instances, be inaccessible by the Diels–Alder route [3], although it is usually the more stable of the two by virtue of reduced steric interactions (in the above example, repulsive forces between the anhydride ring and the ethylenic double bond in IV are greater than those between the anhydride ring and the oxygen bridge in III). If the *endo-exo* transition energy is sufficiently low (10–20 cal per mole), the *exo* isomer may be obtained by carrying out the reaction at a sufficiently high temperature. The furan–maleic anhydride adduct is one of the most labile; the initial product at 25°, which contains both *endo* and *exo* in the ratio 1:2, reverts entirely to *exo* on standing. The mechanism of this isomerization has been shown in at least one instance [4] to proceed by dissociation and recombination, IV → V → VI → III. This is a further example of kinetic and thermodynamic control of reaction products (Experiment 26).

In the following experiment, the preparations of *endo* (VIII) and *exo* (IX) adducts of maleimide (VII) and furan are described:

endo
VII

exo
VIII

Experimental

ENDO Δ⁴-TETRAHYDROPHTHALIMIDE-3,6-OXIDE (VII)

Materials Required

Maleimide
Furan
Ethylacetate

In a small sample ampoule with screw-cap, place 100 mg maleimide and dissolve it in 3 ml furan. Stopper tightly and cover the tube with aluminum foil to exclude all light, and allow the mixture to stand for 24 hours. Evaporate the excess furan by blowing in a gentle stream of dry nitrogen and recover the product which is nearly pure *endo* adduct (VII) and melts around 120°. Recrystallize from a little chloroform, precipitating the material with hexane, mp 131°.

Yield, 130 mg, 85%

EXO Δ⁴-TETRAHYDROPHTHALIMIDE-3,6-OXIDE (VIII)

Dissolve 90 mg of the *endo* adduct (VII) in 10 ml dry ethyl acetate and reflux gently for 45 minutes. Concentrate the solution carefully on a steam bath to 2 ml and cool when the *exo* isomer (VIII) separates. Filter and dry, mp 165–170°.

Yield, 80 mg, 90%

Questions

1. Suggest syntheses for the following compounds:

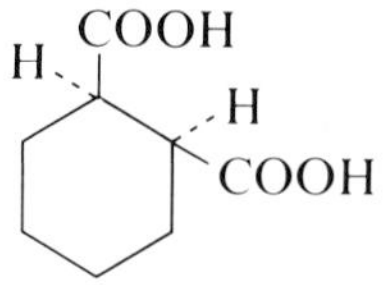

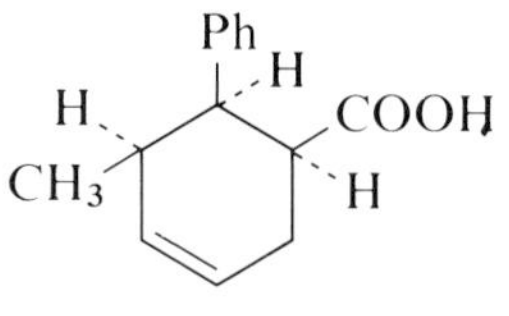

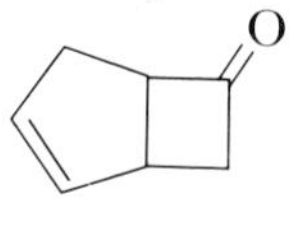

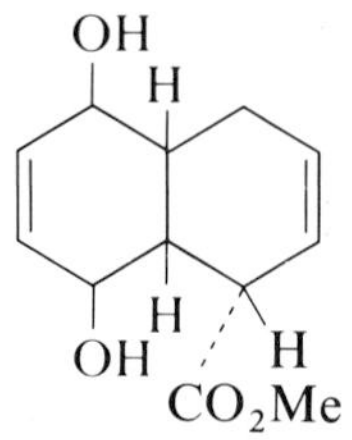

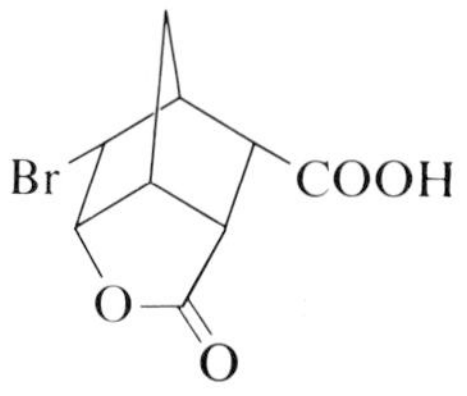

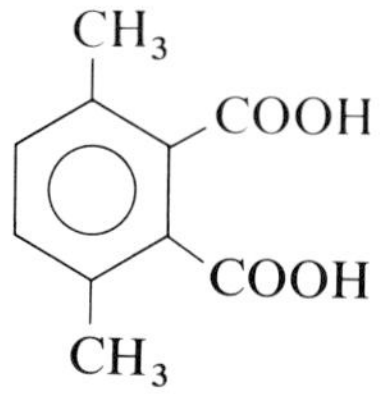

2. What products would you expect to obtain from the reaction between tetra-cyanoethylene and *trans, trans* hexa-2,4-diene? What difference would it make if you used the *cis, trans* diene?

References

1. R. Hoffman and R. B. Woodward, *J. Amer. Chem. Soc.*, **87**, 2046 (1965); R. B. Woodward, *Aromaticity*, Chemical Society (London) Special Publication No. 21, p. 217, (1967).
2. J. G. Martin and R. K. Hill, *Chem. Revs.*, **61**, 537 (1961).
3. H. Kwart and L. Kaplan, *J. Amer. Chem. Soc.*, **75**, 3356 (1953).
4. H. Kwart and I. Burchuk, *J. Amer. Chem. Soc.*, **74**, 3094 (1952).

Dipolar Cycloadditions

Somewhat similar to the Diels–Alder reaction (Experiment 38) is the addition to a double bond of a three atom species bearing opposite charges (or partial charges) at either end, thus:

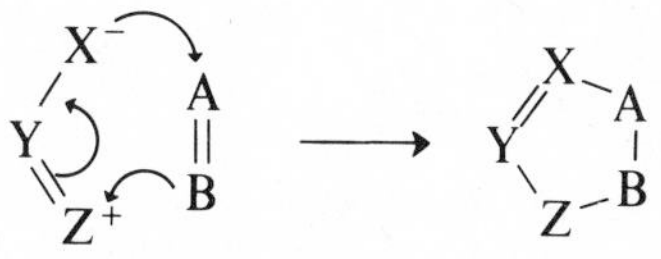

The species $X^- — Y — Z^+$ takes the place of the diene and a five-membered ring is formed. This type of reaction is known as a dipolar cycloaddition and has been extensively investigated especially by Huisgen at Munich and Quilico in Milan. Some typical examples are shown in Table 39–1.

In the following preparations, phenyl cyanate (benzonitrile N-oxide) PhCNO, is prepared *in situ* from phenylhydroxamic acid chloride (II). It is difficult to isolate pure since it readily adds to itself with the formation of diphenylfuroxan (III) but, prepared in the presence of phenyl cyanide, adds to the latter with the formation of diphenyl-1,3,4-dioxazole (IV). Addition to maleic anhydride occurs yielding the isoxazoline derivative (V).

TABLE 39–1. 1,3-Dipolar Cycloadditions

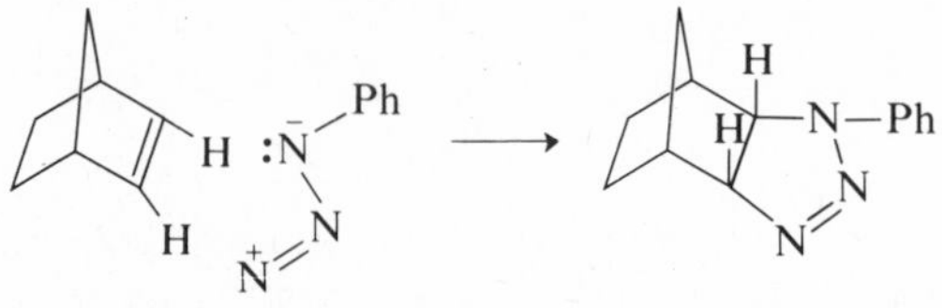

phenylazide

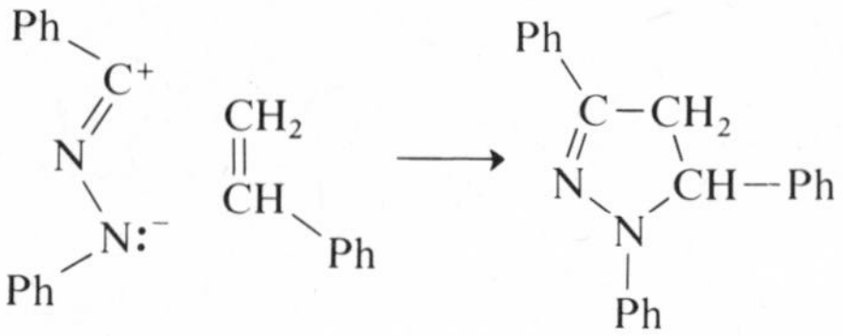

diphenylnitrilimine

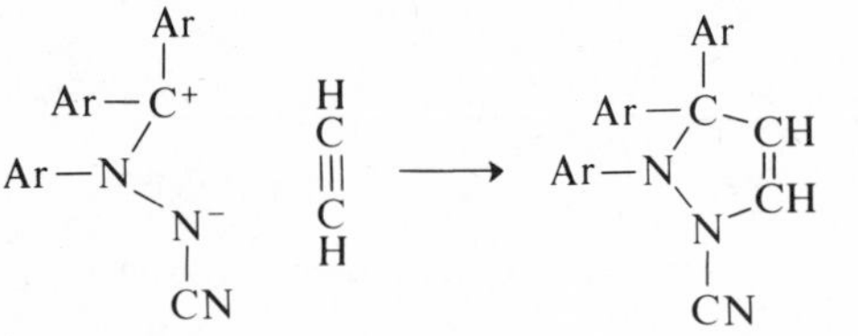

an azomethineimine

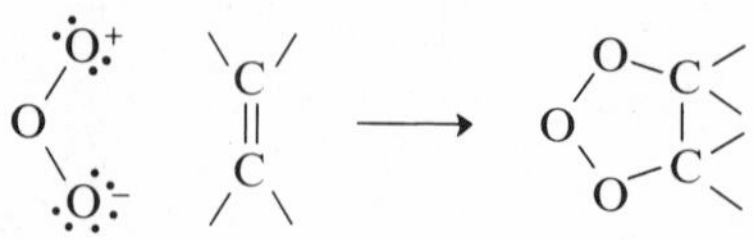

ozone   an ozonide

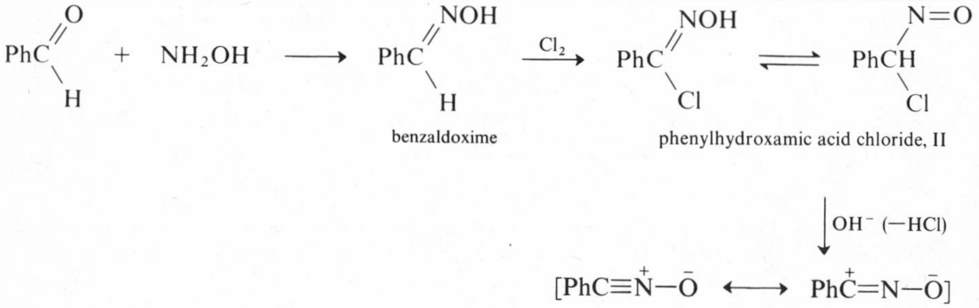

benzaldoxime   phenylhydroxamic acid chloride, II

$$OH^- \ (-HCl)$$

$$[PhC{\equiv}\overset{+}{N}-\bar{O} \longleftrightarrow Ph\overset{+}{C}{=}N-\bar{O}]$$

benzonitrile oxide, I

TABLE 39–1. (Continued)

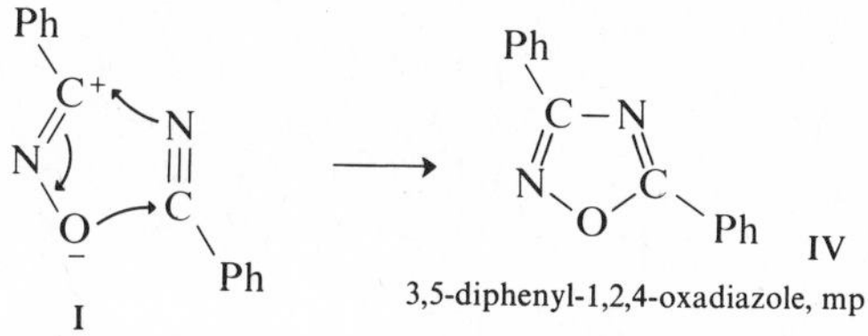

3,5-diphenyl-1,2,4-oxadiazole, mp 107°

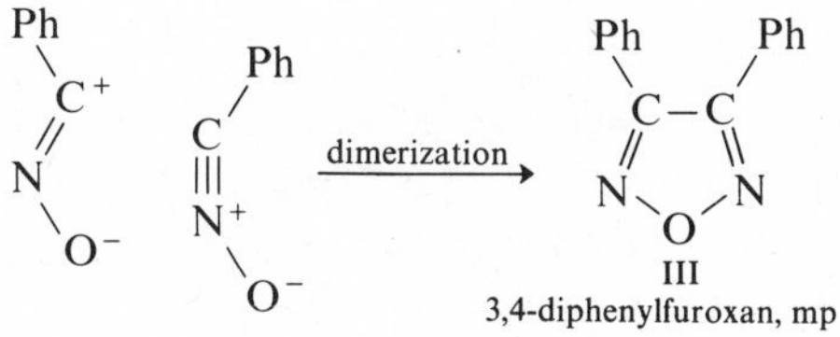

3,4-diphenylfuroxan, mp 114°

maleic anhydride

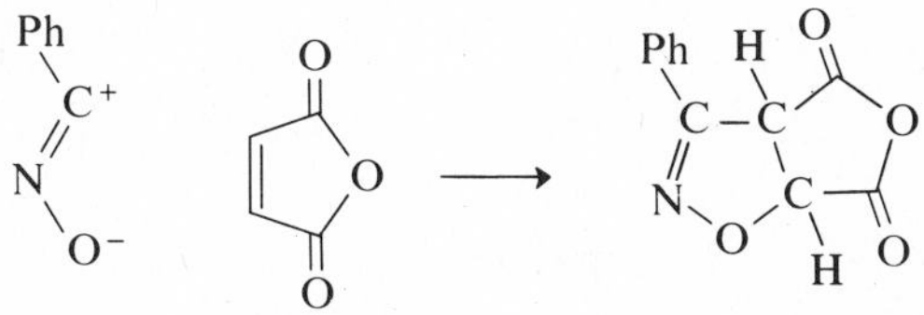

Experimental

Materials Required

Benzaldehyde	Triethylamine
Hydroxylamine hydrochloride	Phenyl cyanide (benzonitrile)
Chlorine	

PREPARATION OF BENZALDOXIME

Prepare a cooled solution of 15 g sodium hydroxide in 50 ml water and add 20 ml benzaldehyde. Stir or shake the mixture while adding, in small portions, 15 g hydroxylamine hydrochloride cooling the solution from time to time. Continue stirring until all the benzaldehyde has gone into solution. Solid benzaldoxime hydrochloride may crystallize out at this stage. Now add several lumps of solid CO_2 (dry ice) or cool well and pass in a stream of CO_2 gas. Filter off the solid benzaldoxime which forms and use without further purification.

Yield, 20 g 90 %

PREPARATION OF PHENYLHYDROXAMIC ACID CHLORIDE (II)

Place 20 g benzaldoxime in a 250 ml conical flask and suspend it in 100 ml ice-cold 8 *M* hydrochloric acid. Pass in a rapid stream of chlorine gas keeping temperature of the mixture around 0°. A yellow oil quickly forms which re-solidifies on passage of further chlorine. Filter the solid crystalline precipitate of the hydroxamic acid chloride, wash free of acid with ice water and dry in a desiccator. This compound is stable and may be stored for use as a source of benzonitrile oxide.

Yield, about 25 g, 90%

PREPARATION OF 3,4-DIPHENYLFUROXAN (III)

Dissolve 2.0 g of the phenylhydroxamic acid chloride in 20 ml ether and add gradually with vigorous shaking 10 ml of 10% sodium hydroxide keeping the flask cool by occasional immersion in an ice bath. Separate off the ethereal layer which contains phenyl cyanate, dry over anhydrous sodium sulfate and allow the solution to stand in a warm water bath for 30 min. Remove the ether on the rotary evaporator and isolate the white crystalline residue of the furoxan, mp 114°.

Yield, 1 g, 70%

PREPARATION OF 3-PHENYLISOXAZOLINE-4,5-DICARBOXYLIC ANHYDRIDE (V)

Prepare a solution of 3.0 g maleic anhydride in 20 ml of ether. In another flask place 20 ml of 10% sodium hydroxide and 20 ml of ether. Cool the flask well in an ice bath. Add 5.0 g of the hydroxamic acid chloride in small portions, shaking well between each addition and keeping the temperature at 0°. After addition, which should take about 10 min, separate off the ethereal layer, dry by swirling with a little anhydrous sodium sulfate and quickly transfer the solution to the flask containing the maleic anhydride. Allow the mixture to stand at room temperature for about 30 min then filter off the white crystalline precipitate of 3-phenylisoxazoline-4,5-dicarboxylic anhydride, mp 162°.

Yield, 5 g, 80%

Questions

1. Give formulae and names to the products obtained from *a.* styrene and *b.* acetophenone with the following 1,3-dipolar compounds:

    Phenyl azide, $PhN^- - N = N^+$

    Benzonitrilemethylimine, $Ph - C^+ = N - N^- - Me$

    Benzophenonephenylnitrone, $Ph_2C^+ - NPh - O^-$

    Phenyl benzoyl carbene, $Ph - C^+ = C - O^-$
    $\quad\quad\quad\quad\quad\quad\quad\quad\quad\quad\quad | $
    $\quad\quad\quad\quad\quad\quad\quad\quad\quad\quad\quad Ph$

2. Diphenyldiazomethane, $Ph_2C^- - N = N^+$ adds to olefins with the formation

of pyrazolines. The rates of formation of products with some olefins are given below:

$$H_2C=CHC_4H_9 \qquad \frac{10^5\,k_2}{\text{v. slow}}$$

$H_2C=CHPh$	1.40
$H_2C=CHCN$	434
$H_2C=CHCOOEt$	707
$H_2C=CMeCOOEt$	51
$MeCH=CHCOOEt$	2.5
$Ph-CH=CHCOOEt$	1.3
Dimethyl maleate	69
Dimethyl fumarate	2450
Dimethyl dimethylmaleate	1.6
Dimethyl dimethylfumarate	13.9

Comment on the factors which affect the reaction rates, drawing a transition state which accords with these facts. What are the expected structures of the products in each case?

Reference

1. R. Huisgen, *Angew. Chem.* (Internat. Ed.), **2**, 565, (1963); **3**, 135, (1964); R. Huisgen and W. Mack, *Tet. Letters*, 585, (1961); 917, (1967).

Electrochemical Reactions

An electrolytic cell is a device in which electrons may be moved from the anode and its environment to the cathode region. Oxidation therefore occurs at the anode and reduction at the cathode. Electrolytic oxidations and reductions of inorganic materials are commonplace and include all metal electrodepositions, the electrolysis of water and of hydrochloric acid and so on.

Electrochemical oxidation and reduction of organic compounds is less well-known as a preparative method although polarographic studies of many organic compounds have been carried out at the dropping mercury cathode or anode. However, certain organic electrode reactions were known to Michael

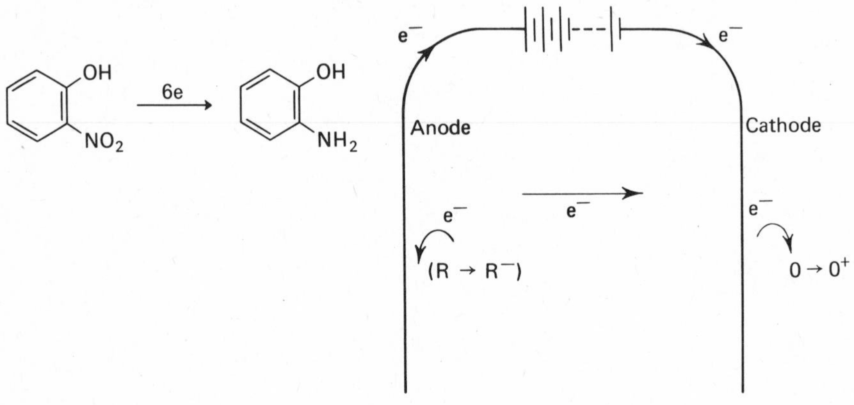

FIGURE 40–1

266

Faraday who reported the formation of hydrocarbons from the electrolysis of acetate solutions as long ago as 1834, while in 1849 the Kolbe electrosynthesis of hydrocarbons was first published [1]. This remained for many years the best-known example of an organic electrolytic reaction and involves the oxidation at the anode of a carboxylate anion to give CO_2 and an alkyl radical which then dimerizes. The product isolated is the symmetric hydrocarbon:

$$2\,R-CO_2^- \xrightarrow[\text{anode}]{-2e^-} 2\,R\cdot + CO_2 \longrightarrow R-R$$

Some examples of the Kolbe synthesis are:

a.
$$2n\text{-}C_7H_{15}CO_2^- \xrightarrow[\text{anode}]{} n\text{-}C_{14}H_{30} + 2\,CO_2$$

b.
$$\begin{array}{l} CH_2-COOH \\ | \\ CH_2-COOH \end{array} \xrightarrow[\text{anode}]{KOH} \underset{\text{very little}}{H_2C{=}CH_2} + CH_3CH_2COOH + CH_3CH_2OH$$

c.

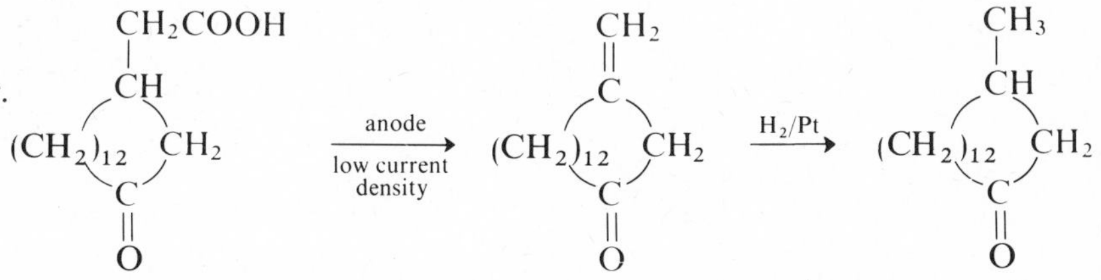

$\pm$-muscone

d.
$$RO_2C(CH_2)_n COOH \xrightarrow{\text{anode}} RO_2C(CH_2)_{2n}CO_2R$$

e.

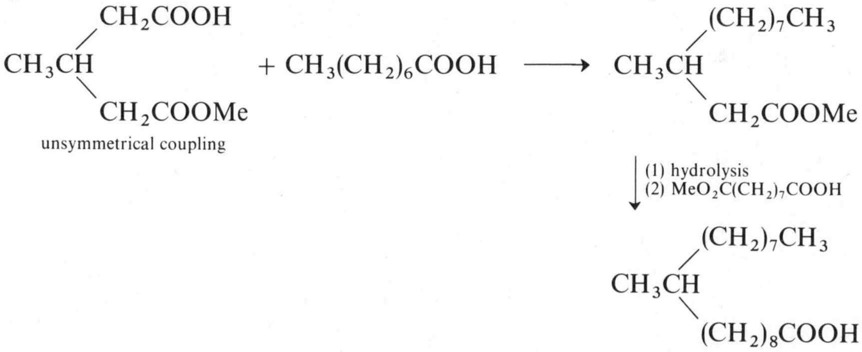

unsymmetrical coupling

(1) hydrolysis
(2) $MeO_2C(CH_2)_7COOH$

$(-)$ tuberculostearic acid

In recent years increasing interest in electrochemical reactions has arisen and a variety of new reactions other than the Kolbe synthesis shown to occur, for example:

a.

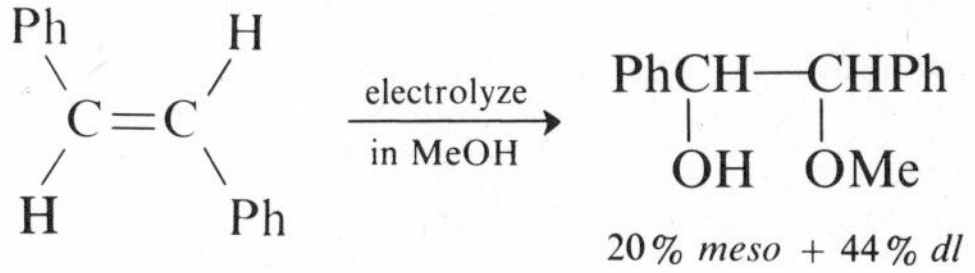

20% *meso* + 44% *dl*

b. $CH_3CH_2NO_2$ $\xrightarrow[\text{NaNO}_2]{\text{electrolyze}}$ $CH_3CH(NO_2)_3$

c.

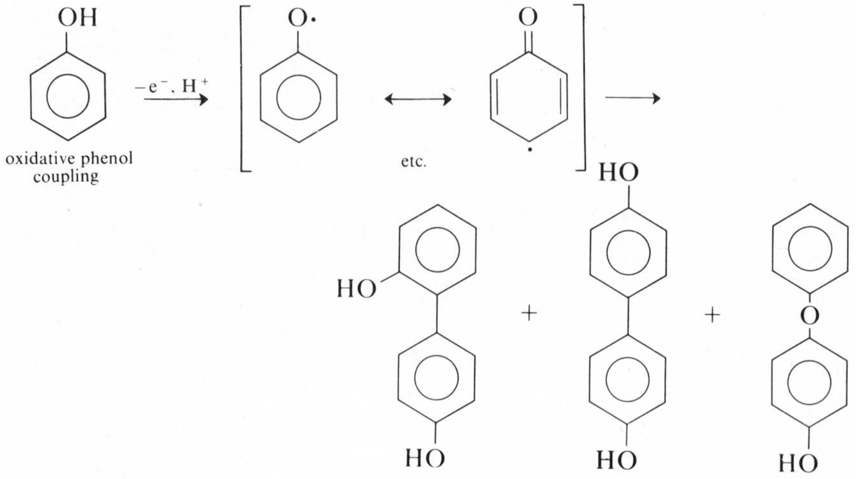

oxidative phenol
coupling

etc.

d.

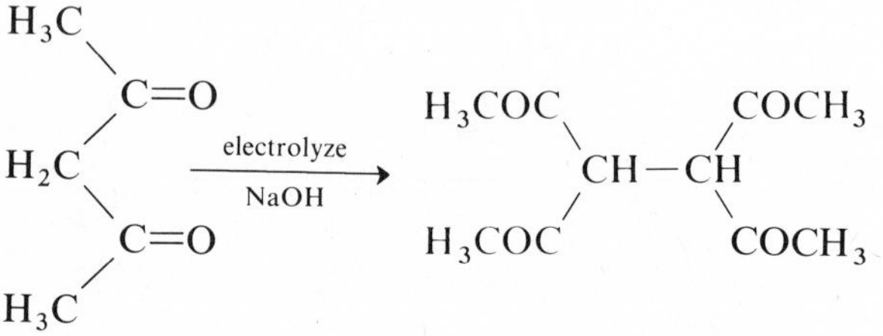

e.

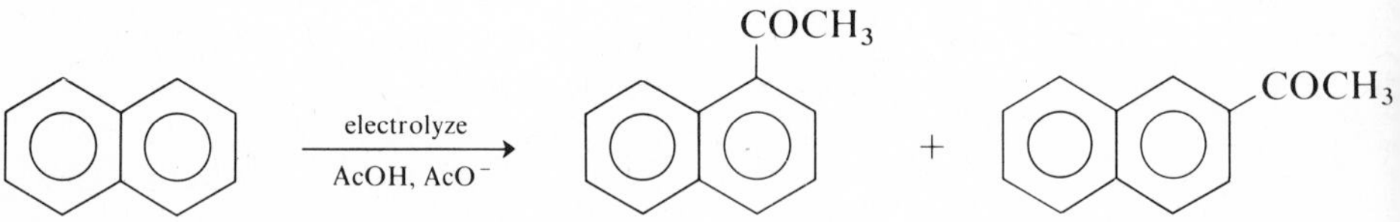

f.

+   polychlorobenzenes

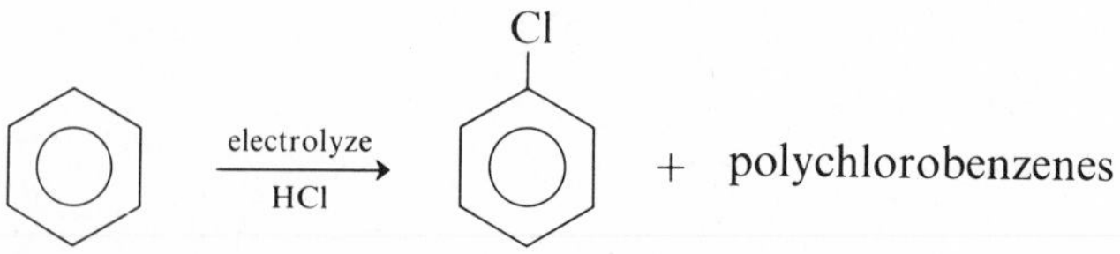

g.

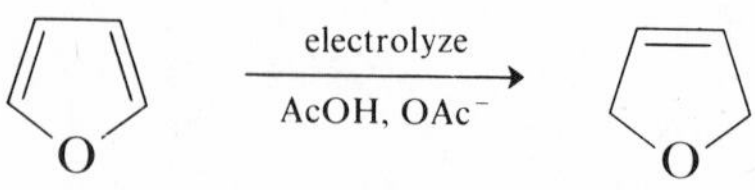

h. C_2H_5MgCl $\xrightarrow[\text{with Pb anode}]{\text{electrolyze}}$ $(C_2H_5)_4Pb$

Commercial process for lead tetraethyl for use in gasoline.

Nitro compounds can also be conveniently reduced to amines, and this reaction is examined in Experiment 40. *o*-Nitrophenol is used since it is soluble in sodium hydroxide giving a conducting solution. The reduction potential of the nitro group is less than that of the hydrogen ion hence it is preferentially reduced in aqueous solution and no hydrogen is generated until the reduction is complete—a useful indication of when to stop the electrolysis:

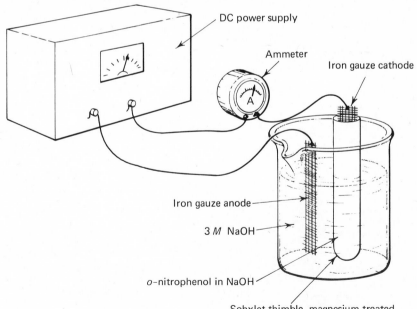

Experimental

Materials Required

o-Nitrophenol   5 A Power supply (DC)

Assemble the apparatus shown in Figure 40–2. A 43×123 mm Sohxlet thimble is used as the diaphragm to separate anolyte and catholyte. It should previously be wetted with a conc magnesium chloride solution which, on contact with the alkaline electrolyte forms a coating of magnesium hydroxide. This reduces the permeability of the paper without affecting its conductance. Fill the thimble with a solution of 5 g *o*-nitrophenol in 100 ml 3 *M* sodium hydroxide and the outer vessel to the same level with 3 *M* sodium hydroxide

FIGURE 40–2 Apparatus for electrolytic reduction.

solution. Insert an electrode into either compartment; strips of iron gauze serve very well. Connect these to a dc source capable of an output of 4–5 amps making the center electrode the cathode. The source of current may be an electronic power supply or a 6 V storage battery equipped with rheostat and ammeter.

Pass a current of 4–5 amps until all the nitrophenol is reduced, at which point bubbles of hydrogen will begin to be evolved from the cathode compartment.

Remove the contents of the thimble and make the solution slightly acidic with glacial acetic acid. Cool the solution in ice and filter the crude *o*-aminophenol which separates. This may be recrystallized from a little hot water to form brown rhombic plates, mp 173°.

Yield, about 3 g, 80%

Preparation of 2-Methylbenzoxazole

To 2 g *o*-aminophenol add 5 ml acetic acid and 5 ml acetic anhydride. Reflux gently together for 30 min then slowly distill the liquid at atmospheric pressure collecting the distillate boiling at 190–200°, which is 2-methylbenzoxazole.

Measure the ultraviolet spectrum in the region 250–350 mμ. Does this give any evidence of conjugation between the heterocyclic and aromatic rings?

Yield, 1.8 g, 80%

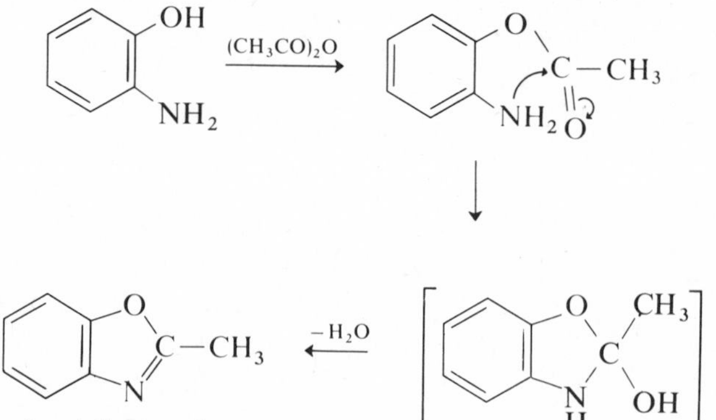

2-methylbenzoxazole

Questions

Suggest syntheses of the following compounds:

a.

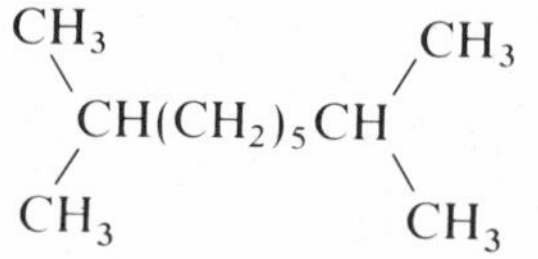

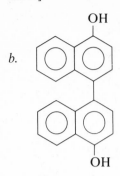

b.

References

1. H. Kolbe, *Annalen*, **33**, 438 (1834).
2. A. P. Tomilov, *Russian Chem. Rev.*, 30 (1963).
3. K. M. Johnston, *Educ. Chem.*, 299 (1963); 15 (1968).

Mesoionic Compounds

Preparation of a Sydnone

In 1935, workers [1] in the University of Sydney, Australia, were examining analogies between the properties of carbonyl (I) and nitroso (II) groups:

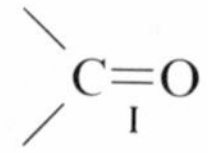

$$\diagdown C{=}O \qquad\qquad -N{=}O$$
$$\text{I} \qquad\qquad\qquad\qquad \text{II}$$

A γ-keto acid cyclizes under the action of acetic anhydride giving either an O-acetylhydroxylactone (III) or an unsaturated lactone (IV):

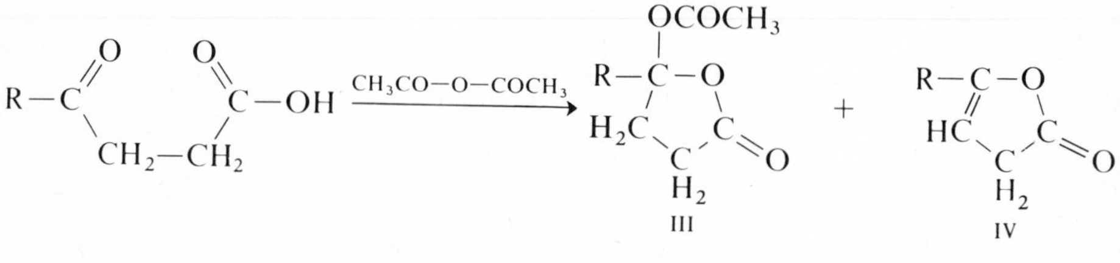

The same reaction was tried with a γ-N-nitroso acid (V) expecting to obtain a product analogous to III, (namely, VI) an unsaturated compound like IV not being possible on account of the tervalency of nitrogen.

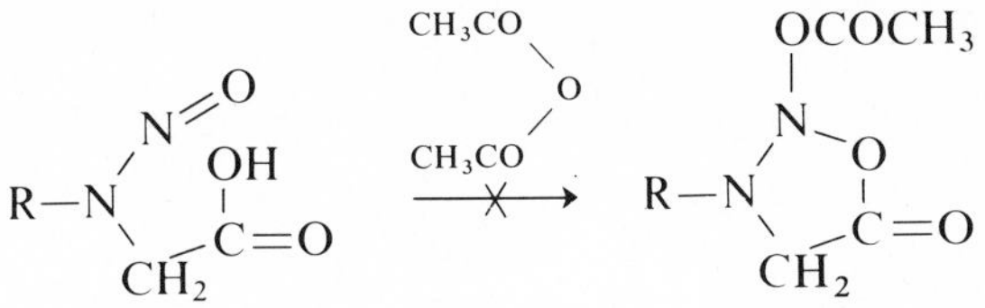

The product, however, contained one molecule of acetic acid less than VI and the formula was accommodated by a bicyclic structure (VII):

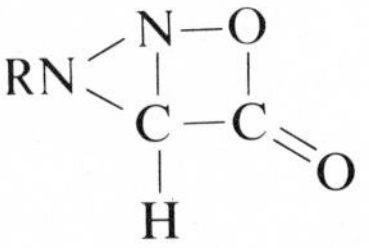

and named a *sydnone* after the city of origin. Later workers [2] showed that the bicyclic formulation was incorrect and that the sydnones contained only one ring. In order to take account of valence requirements, positive and negative charges must be inserted. There is still some uncertainty as to the location of some of the electrons but various attempts at formulation include such structures as VIII, IX and X:

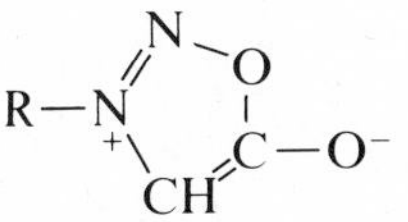

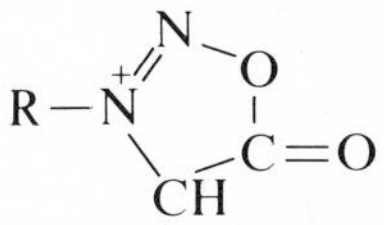

The zwitterion (VIII) puts all the positive charge on N-3 and the negative charge on carbonyl oxygen, but the infrared spectrum of the carbonyl region is not wholly in agreement nor is the ready solubility in organic solvents and relative insolubility in water. Formula IX delocalizes six π-electrons (one unshared pair from each nitrogen and one *p*-electron from each carbon) in the positively charged ring in a structure which is analogous to tropone (XI) (Experiment 32), with aromatic character in the tropyllium ring; neither the ultraviolet nor infrared spectra are in agreement with this representation [3]:

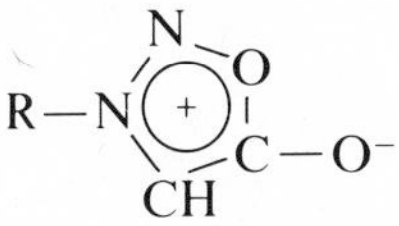

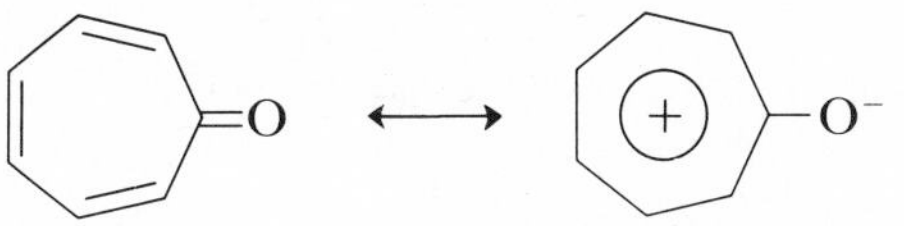

The sydnones are best described as resonance hybrids of all the possible valence tautomers (there are twelve; check.) with various weights assigned to each canonical structure. The noncommittal representation (XII) in which only single bonds are indicated and the distribution of the delocalized charges not specified, is commonly employed:

$$\text{R}-\text{N}\underset{\underset{\text{CH}}{\diagup}}{\overset{\text{N}_{\diagdown \text{O}}}{\underset{\diagdown}{\boxed{\pm}}}}\overset{\text{O}}{\underset{\diagdown}{}}\text{C}-\text{O}$$

XII

The sydnones are the most familiar examples of *mesoionic* compounds [4], a term coined to describe compounds whose structures must be represented as a hybrid of several dipolar forms.

The following preparation of 3-phenylsydnone illustrates the general method of synthesis [4] via an N-alkyl (or aryl)-α-amino acid:

$$\text{PhNH}_2 + \text{ClCH}_2\text{COOH} \longrightarrow \text{PhNHCH}_2\text{COOH}$$

$$\text{PhNHCH}_2\text{COOH} + \text{HNO}_2 \longrightarrow \underset{\underset{\text{N}=\text{O}}{|}}{\text{PhNCH}_2\text{COOH}}$$

$$\underset{\underset{\text{N}=\text{O}}{|}}{\text{PhNCH}_2\text{COOH}} + (\text{CH}_3\text{CO})_2\text{O} \longrightarrow \text{Ph}-\text{N}\underset{\underset{\text{CH}}{\diagup}}{\overset{\text{N}_{\diagdown \text{O}}}{\underset{\diagdown}{\boxed{\pm}}}}\overset{\text{O}}{\underset{\diagdown}{}}\text{C}-\text{O}$$

Experimental

Materials Required

Aniline	Sodium nitrite
Chloracetic acid	Acetic anhydride

N-PHENYLGLYCINE

Add 21 ml aniline to 5.0 g chloracetic acid in a small flask and heat on a hotplate until solution of the acid occurs. Cool, filter the precipitate of N-phenylglycine, wash out residual aniline with ether and dry.

Yield, 7 g, 83%

N-NITROSO-N-PHENYLGLYCINE

Suspend 5.0 g N-phenylglycine in 120 ml water at 0°C and add a solution of 5 g sodium nitrite in 30 ml water dropwise over a period of 30 min, stirring meanwhile. After adding all the sodium nitrite, stir the mixture for a further hour. Filter off any unreacted material and acidify the filtrate with dilute hydrochloric acid. Filter the N-nitroso-N-phenylglycine which precipitates, wash with a little water and dry, mp 100–102°.

Yield, 4 g, 67%

3-Phenylsydnone

Dissolve 0.1 g N-nitrosophenylglycine in 5 ml acetic anhydride. Allow to stand for a few minutes then pour the solution into 20 ml water and cool in ice. Stir and "scratch" the oily precipitate until it crystallizes. Filter, wash with water and dry the precipitate of 3-phenylsydnone which is frequently light brown at this stage and may be recrystallized from boiling water, mp 135°.

Measure the infrared spectrum. Compare the position of the carbonyl absorption band (between $1650-1800 \text{ cm}^{-1}$) with other types of carbonyl compounds [6] (Experiment 18). What may be inferred about the structure of the sydnone?

Yield, 0.07 g, 75%

Questions

1. Can the sydnones be regarded as "aromatic"? What experiments could be performed to examine this?
2. The dipole moment of N-phenylsydnone is 6.5 D. Which of the possible canonical structures for this compound do you think contributes mainly to the structure?

References

1. J. C. Earl and A. W. Mackney, *J. Chem. Soc.*, 899 (1935).
2. W. Baker and W. D. Ollis, *Nature*, **158**, 703 (1946).
3. T. M. Tien and I. M. Munsberger, *J. Amer. Chem. Soc.*, **83**, 178 (1961).
4. W. Baker and W. D. Ollis, *Quart. Revs.*, **XI**, 15 (1957).
5. F. M. C. Stewart, *Chem. Revs.*, **64**, 129 (1964).
6. A. W. Cross, *An Introduction to Practical Infrared Spectroscopy*, sec. ed., Butterworth, London, 1964.

Radical Bromination with N-Bromosuccinimide

Nitrogen–halogen covalent bonds are relatively weak (30–40 cal/mole) and undergo homolysis at quite low temperatures. N-bromosuccinimide (I) is often used as source of bromine atoms for this reason. The bromine atom is capable of abstracting a hydrogen atom from carbon, particularly in an allylic or benzylic position, and initiating a radical chain reaction, the final products of which are succinimide and an allyl or benzyl bromide:

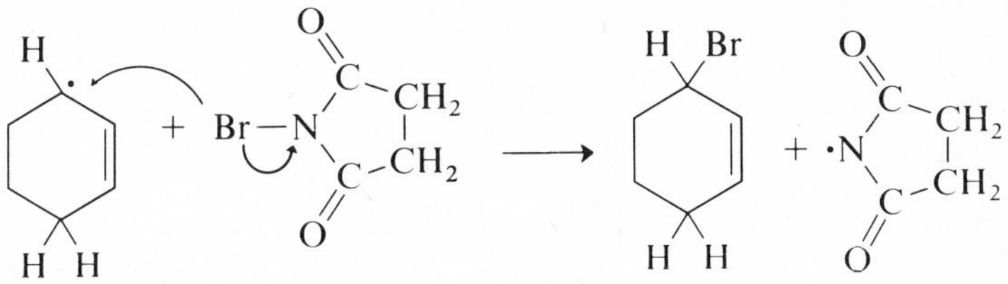

The reaction is best carried out in carbon tetrachloride in which N-bromosuccinimide is virtually insoluble. The reaction is believed to be heterogeneous, occurring on the surface of the reagent. The selective attack on the allylic position is due to the special stability of the radical (II) in which the unshared electron is conjugated with the double bond. This experiment illustrates the use of N-bromosuccinimide in the preparation of 3-bromocyclohexene. The latter compound may be readily dehydrobrominated to cyclohexa-1,3-diene:

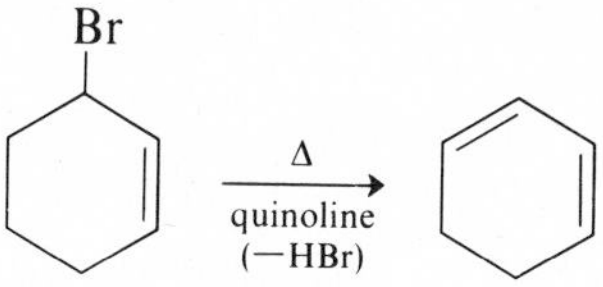

Experimental

Materials Required

N-Bromosuccinimide	Benzene
Cyclohexene	Quinoline

3-BROMOCYCLOHEXENE

Mix 11.5 g N-bromosuccinimide and 6.8 g cyclohexene in 46 ml carbon tetrachloride and reflux the solution for 40 min. Cool and filter the precipitate of succinimide and distill the filtrate, removing benzene at 80° under normal atmospheric pressure, then reducing the pressure to collect 3-bromocyclohexene, bp 68°/15 mm, 44°/2 mm, as a pleasant-smelling oil.

Yield, 9 g, 65%

CYCLOHEXA-1,3-DIENE

Dissolve 5 g 3-bromocyclohexene in 15 ml redistilled quinoline in a flask fitted with a short fractionating column, distillation head with thermometer and condenser set for distillation. Boil the mixture briskly without letting the temperature at the head rise above 80–85°. Collect the distillate of cyclohexa-1,3-diene and dry over calcium chloride if it is turbid. Confirm the identity of the compound by comparing its ultraviolet spectrum with that predicted (Experiment 20) by Woodward's Rules.

Yield, 1.5 g, 60%

Questions

1. Suggest mechanisms for the following reactions:

   a. $PhC(CH_3)_2CH_2CHO \xrightarrow{Bz_2O_2} PhC(CH_3)_3 + PhCH_2C(CH_3)_2$

   What other products might you search for?

   b.

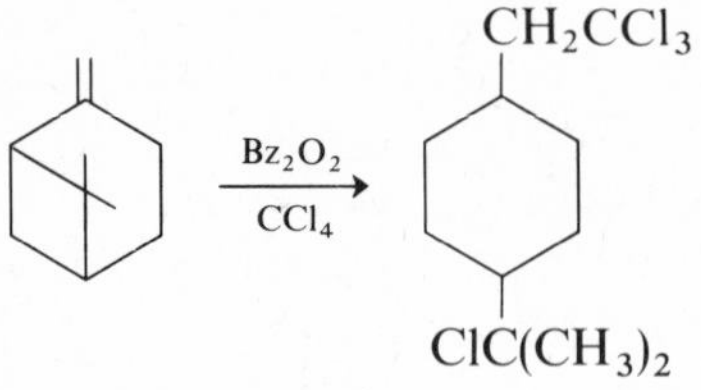

   c.

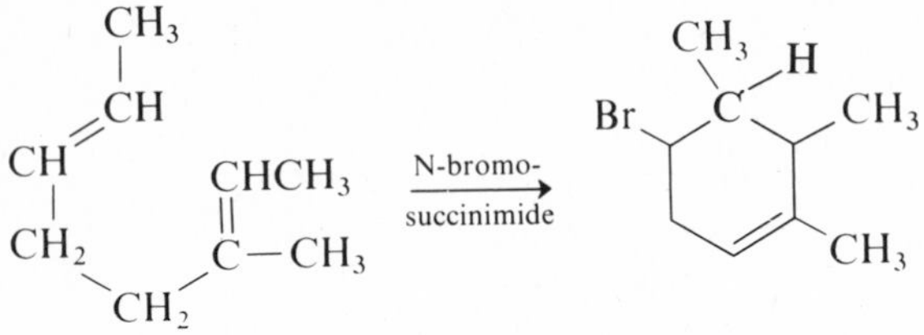

   d.

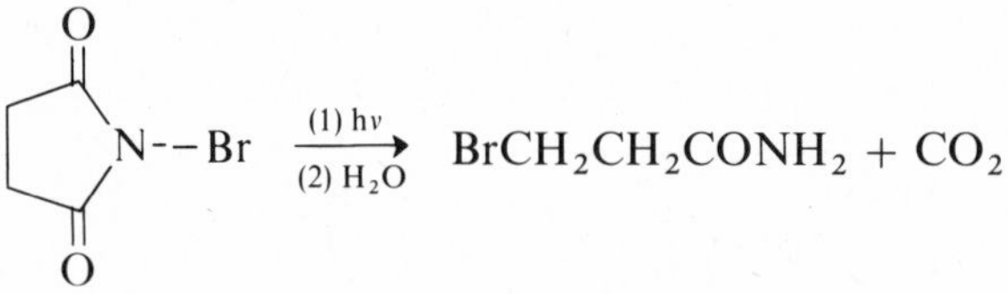

   $\xrightarrow[(2)\ H_2O]{(1)\ h\nu} BrCH_2CH_2CONH_2 + CO_2$

   e.

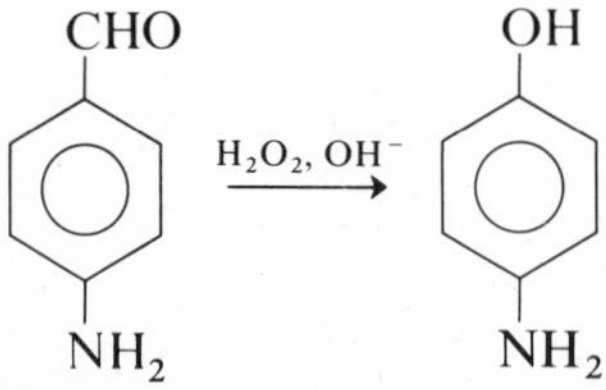

2. Suggest the main products which would be isolated from N-bromo-succinimide reaction with the following compounds:

   a.

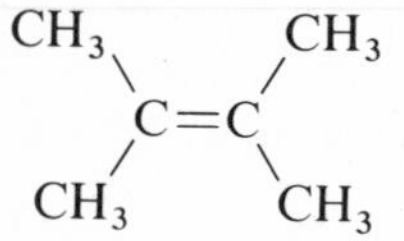

   b.

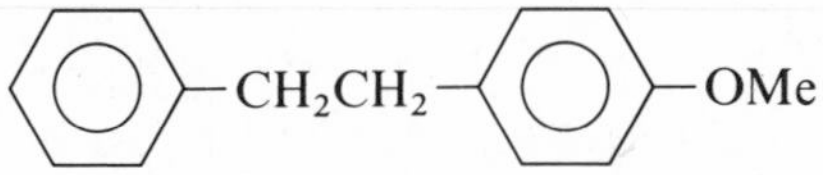

   c.

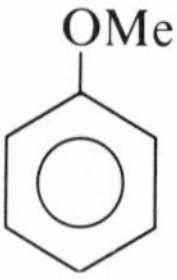

   d.

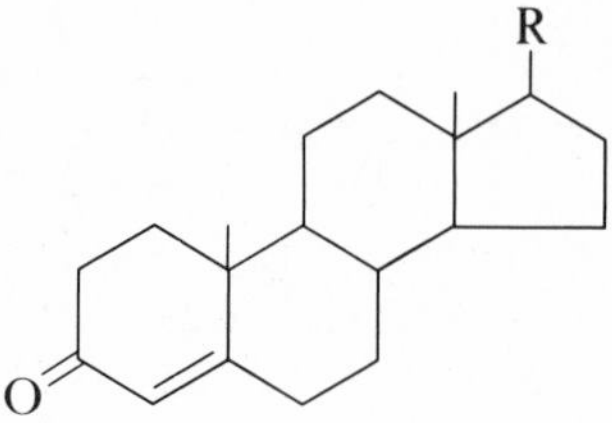

e.

f.

Reference

1. L. Horner and E. H. Winkelmann, (Ed. W. Foerst) *Newer Methods of Preparative Organic Chemistry*, Vol. 3, Academic Press, New York, 1964.

Preparations Using
Enamines

EXPERIMENT **43**

Although the hydrogen atoms adjacent to a carbonyl group are quite acidic owing to stabilization of the carbanion by the carbonyl oxygen (I):

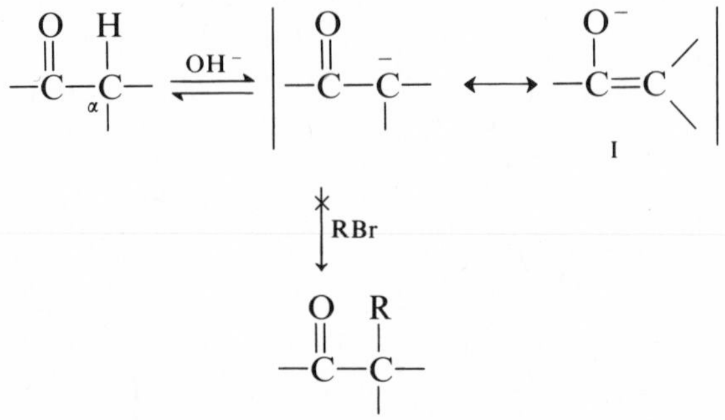

$$-\overset{\overset{\displaystyle O}{\|}}{C}-\overset{\overset{\displaystyle H}{|}}{\underset{\underset{\displaystyle \alpha}{|}}{C}}- \xrightleftharpoons{\text{OH}^-} \left| -\overset{\overset{\displaystyle O}{\|}}{C}-\overset{-}{\underset{|}{C}}- \longleftrightarrow -\overset{\overset{\displaystyle O^-}{|}}{C}=C\overset{/}{\diagdown} \right|$$

I

$$\Big\uparrow \text{RBr}$$

$$-\overset{\overset{\displaystyle O}{\|}}{C}-\overset{\overset{\displaystyle R}{|}}{\underset{|}{C}}-$$

α-alkylation of aldehydes and ketones is not often achieved in good yield owing to side reactions such as aldol condensations which occur under basic conditions. An important modification of the carbonyl function, introduced by Gilbert Stork [1] in 1954 is the enamine (II)—the nitrogen analog of the enol—formed by condensation with a secondary amine:

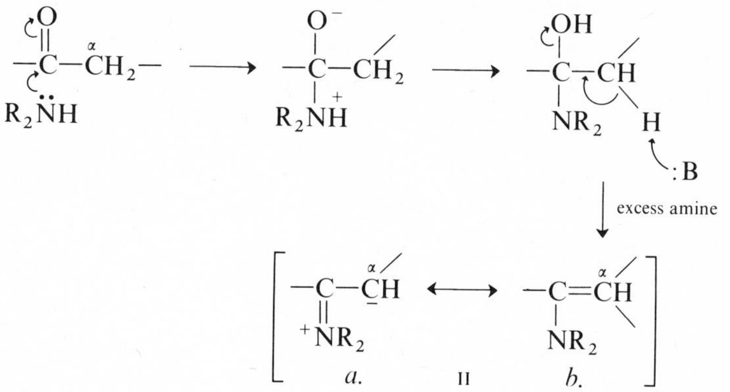

The partial carbanion character of the α-carbon (IIa) renders it capable of displacing halide from an alkylhalide thus bringing about α-alkylation (III) (Stork reaction):

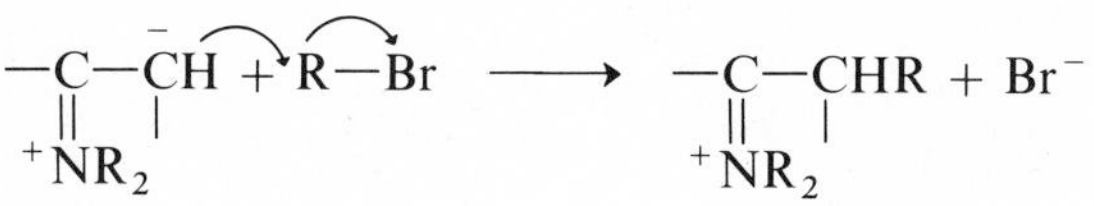

III

Basic hydrolysis of the product now restores the carbonyl function:

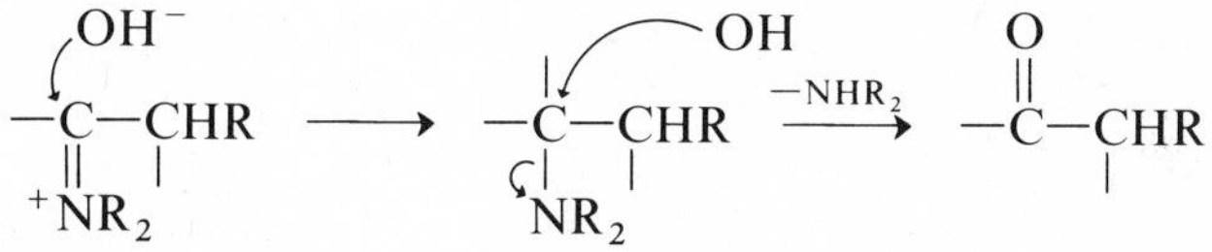

The bases used are customarily piperidine, morpholine and pyrrolidine in order of increasing ease of formation of the enamine. In addition to C-alkylation as above, a certain amount of N-alkylation (IV) also occurs which reduces the yields somewhat:

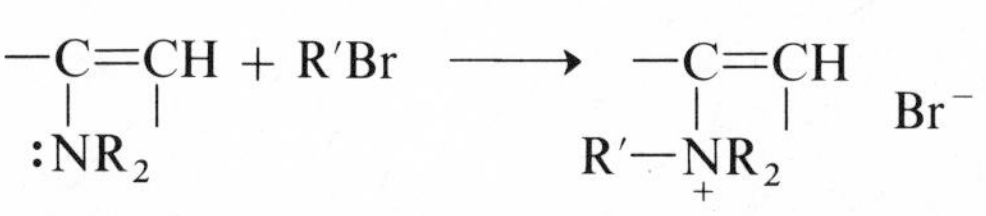

IV

Stork has shown, however, that electrophilic olefins such as α,β-unsaturated ketones, nitriles, esters and aldehydes can be used for alkylation. In this case the N-alkylation reaction is reversible so that the equilibrium is displaced towards the C-alkyl product (V) an example of thermodynamic control, (Experiment 26).

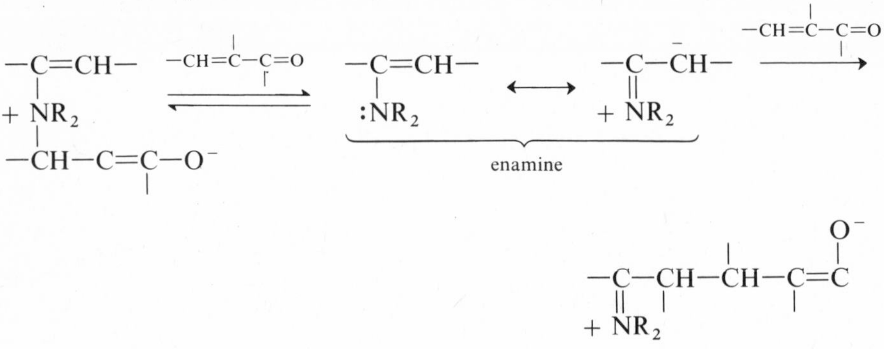

$$-C=CH- \atop +NR_2 \atop -CH-C=C-O^-} \quad \underset{\longleftarrow}{\overset{-CH=C-C=O}{\longrightarrow}} \quad -C=CH- \atop :NR_2} \quad \longleftrightarrow \quad -C-CH- \atop +NR_2} \quad \overset{-CH=C-C=O}{\longrightarrow}$$

enamine

$$-C-CH-CH-C=C \atop +NR_2} \quad O^-$$

V

Enamines will attack many other electrophilic systems [2] including isocyanates, from which carboxylamides (VI) result:

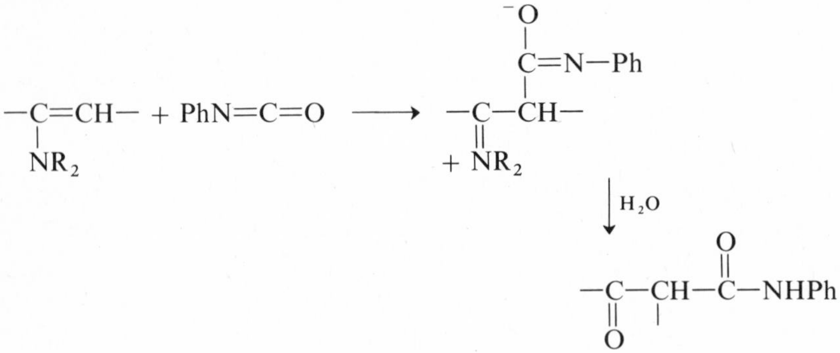

$$-C=CH- + PhN=C=O \longrightarrow \quad -C-CH- \atop +NR_2} \quad \overset{O^-}{\underset{C=N-Ph}{}}$$

$$\downarrow H_2O$$

$$-C-CH-C-NHPh \atop O}$$

VI

Experimental

Materials Required

Pyrrolidine	Methyl vinyl ketone
Cyclohexanone	

CYCLOHEXANONE PYRROLIDINE ENAMINE

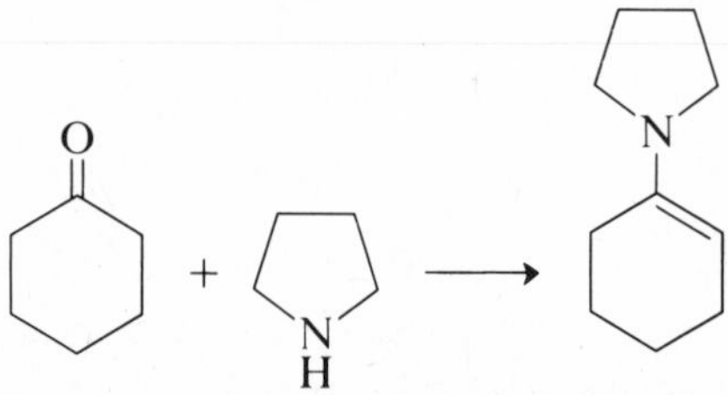

Dissolve 49 g (0.5 mole) cyclohexanone and 39 g (0.5 mole) pyrrolidine in 50 ml benzene in a 250 ml round bottomed flask and allow the mixture to boil under reflux through a Dean Stark water trap (Experiment 27). Continue boiling until the aqueous layer in the trap ceases to rise further (approximately 10 ml is collected). Remove the benzene in the rotary evaporator. The crude cyclo-hexanone pyrrolidine enamine may be used directly or may be purified by distillation under reduced pressure collecting at 120–125°/10 mm.

Yield, 53 g, 70% purified

PREPARATION OF $\Delta^{1,9}$-OCTALONE-2

In a 100 ml Erlenmeyer flask, place 20 g (0.06 mole) cyclohexanone pyrrolidine enamine and 50 ml dry dioxane. Add slowly 9.2 g (0.06 mole) methyl vinyl ketone. Stopper and warm the mixture at 55° for 30 min or leave at room tem-perature for 4–6 hours, agitating occasionally. A slight precipitate may form after this period. Add 30 ml 5 M hydrochloric acid to the mixture and reflux for 1 hour, after which two layers may be apparent. Add 100 ml water and extract the product with two 50 ml portions of ether. Combine the ethereal extracts and dry with anhydrous sodium sulfate. Remove the ether in the rotary evaporator and distill the residual liquid under reduced pressure. Collect $\Delta^{1,9}$-octalone-2 at 125–130°/8–10 mm.

Measure the ultraviolet spectrum of the product and compare the spectrum with that calculated by Woodward's Rules (Experiment 20). Suggest a mech-anism for the formation of this product.

Yield, 10 g, 50%

Questions

1. Suggest syntheses of the following compounds:

a.
$$CH_3COCHCOOEt$$
with substituent $CH_2C{\equiv}CH$

b.

c.

d.

e.

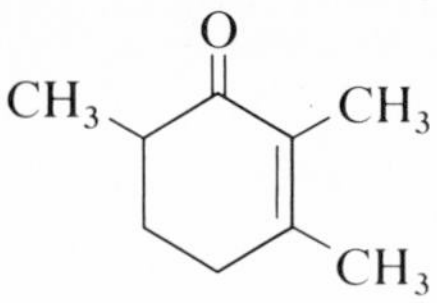

f.

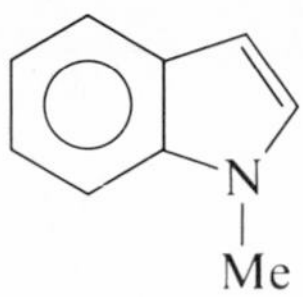

g.

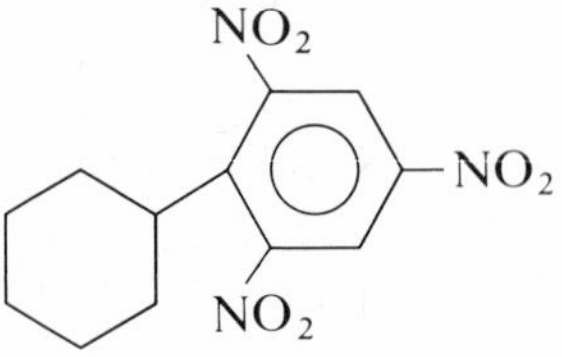

h.

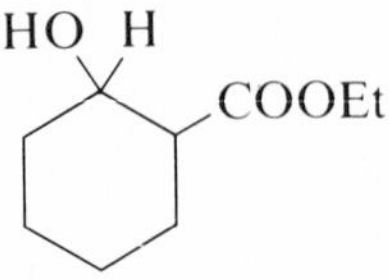

2. Suggest mechanisms for the following enamine reactions:

a.

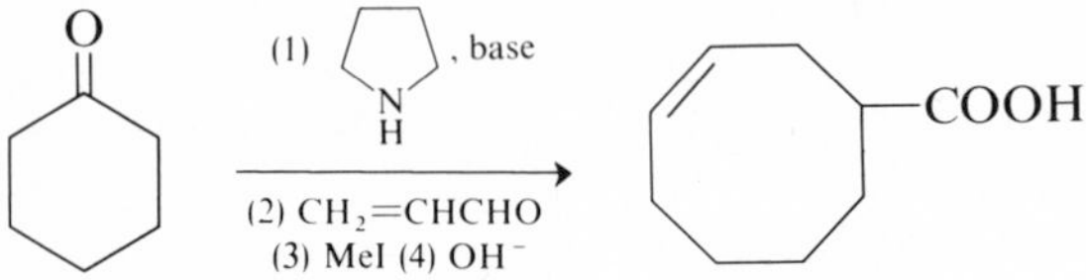

b. 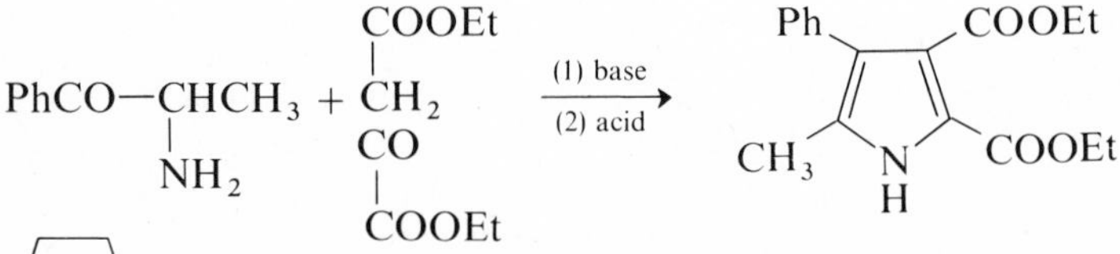 PhCO—CHCH$_3$ + $\xrightarrow[\text{(2) acid}]{\text{(1) base}}$

c. 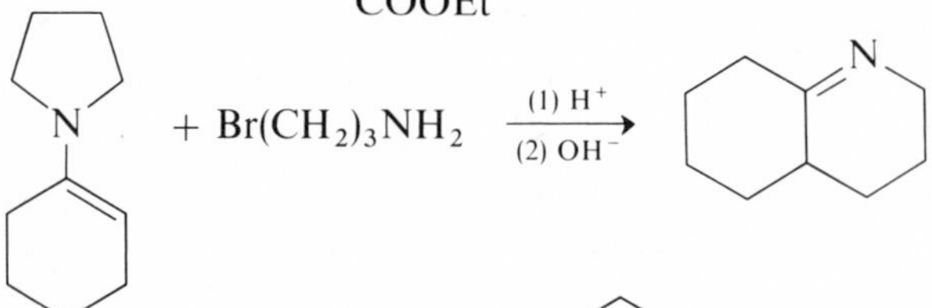 + Br(CH$_2$)$_3$NH$_2$ $\xrightarrow[\text{(2) OH}^-]{\text{(1) H}^+}$

d. 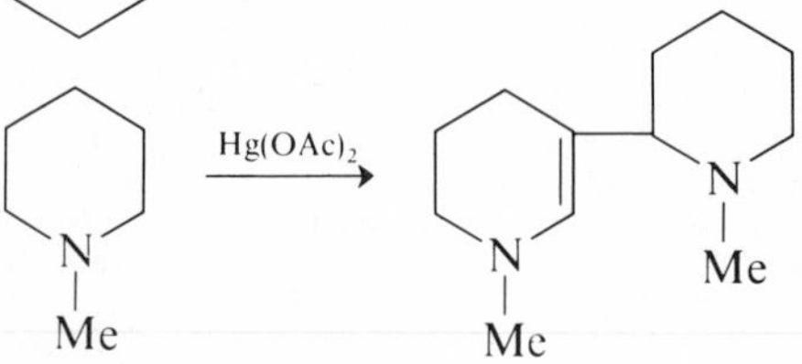 $\xrightarrow{\text{Hg(OAc)}_2}$

References

1. G. Stork, R. Terrell, and J. Szmuszkovicz, *J. Amer. Chem. Soc.*, **76**, 2029 (1954).
2. J. Szmuszkovicz, *Adv. Org. Chem.*, Vol. 4, Interscience, New York, 1963, pp. 1–113.
3. G. Stork and H. K. Landesman, *J. Amer. Chem. Soc.*, **78**, 5128 (1956).
4. G. Berchtold, *J. Org. Chem.*, **26**, 3044 (1961).
5. S. Hünig, E. Lücke, and W. Brenninger, *Org. Syn.*, **41**, 65 (1961).

Small Ring Compounds

Preparation of Cyclobutanecarboxylic Acid

Diethyl malonate (I) is a versatile reagent for the synthesis of carboxylic acids (II). The methylene group is highly acidic on account of inductive electron withdrawal from two flanking carboxylate groups and may readily be alkylated in two stages via the stable carbanion (III). After hydrolysis of the ester functions, the malonic acid (IV) is readily decarboxylated by heat:

$$
\begin{array}{c}
R' - \underset{\underset{\underset{O}{\parallel}}{\underset{COEt}{|}}}{\overset{\overset{R}{|}\ \overset{O}{\parallel}}{C} - COEt} \quad \xleftarrow[\text{(2) R)Br}]{\overset{\text{repeat}}{\underset{\text{(1) EtO}^-}{}}} \quad \underset{H}{\overset{R}{\diagdown}} C \overset{\overset{O}{\parallel}}{\underset{\underset{O}{\parallel}}{\diagup}}\overset{COEt}{\diagdown}\underset{COEt}{} \quad + \; Br^-
\end{array}
$$

$$\big\downarrow \text{hydrolysis}$$

$$
\underset{\underset{COOH}{|}}{R' - \overset{\overset{R}{|}}{C} - COOH} \quad \xrightarrow{\;\;\Delta\;\;} \quad \underset{\underset{COOH}{|}}{R' - \overset{\overset{R}{|}}{C} - H} \; + \; CO_2
$$

$$\qquad\quad \text{IV} \qquad\qquad\qquad\qquad \text{V}$$

Experiment 44 utilizes this sequence of reactions in preparing a cyclic system from an α,ω-dibromoalkane. The earliest synthesis of the cyclobutane system was achieved by William Perkin, Jr., using the condensation of 1,3-dibromo-propane with diethyl malonate to give diethyl cyclobutane-1,1-dicarboxylate (V). This he hydrolyzed and decarboxylated to cyclobutanecarboxylic acid (VI) but was unable to decarboxylate further to give the parent cyclobutane since ring fission occurred under the conditions used:

$$
\underset{CH_2Br}{\overset{CH_2Br}{H_2C\diagup\diagdown}} \quad + \; CH_2(COOEt)_2 \quad \xrightarrow{\; 2\,EtO^-\;} \quad \underset{CH_2}{\overset{CH_2}{H_2C\diagup\diagdown}}C\overset{COOEt}{\diagup\diagdown}\underset{COOEt}{}
$$

$$\big\downarrow 2OH^-$$

$$
\underset{CH_2}{\overset{CH_2}{H_2C\diagup\diagdown}}CHCOOH \quad \xleftarrow{\;\Delta\;} \quad \underset{CH_2}{\overset{CH_2}{H_2C\diagup\diagdown}}C\overset{COOH}{\diagup\diagdown}\underset{COOH}{}
$$

$$\qquad\quad \text{VI} \qquad\qquad\qquad\qquad\qquad \text{V}$$

Decarboxylation was later achieved by the Hunsdiecker reaction in which the silver salt of the acid is treated with bromine to yield bromocyclobutane (VII) which is readily reduced via the Grignard reagent or hydride to the parent hydrocarbon:

$$
\underset{CH_2}{\overset{CH_2}{H_2C\diagup\diagdown}}CHCOO^-Ag^+ \quad \xrightarrow{\;Br_2\;} \quad \underset{CH_2}{\overset{CH_2}{H_2C\diagup\diagdown}}CHBr \; + \; CO_2 \; + \; AgBr
$$

$$\text{VII}$$

$$\underset{\text{LiAlH}_4}{\diagup} \qquad\qquad\qquad \underset{\text{Mg, Ether}}{\big\downarrow}$$

$$
Mg(OH)Br + \underset{CH_2}{\overset{CH_2}{CH_2\diagup\diagdown}}CH_2 \quad \xleftarrow{\;H_2O\;} \quad \underset{CH_2}{\overset{CH_2}{CH_2\diagup\diagdown}}CHMgBr
$$

Experimental

Materials Required

Anhydrous ethanol   1,3-Dibromopropane
Diethyl malonate   Sodium

Cyclobutane-1,1-Dicarboxylic Acid

A semimicro apparatus as shown in Figure 44–1 may be conveniently used; care should be taken to ensure all glassware is scrupulously dry.

Place 12.5 ml anhydrous ethanol[1] in the flask and add 0.6 g of clean sodium. Allow the sodium to dissolve completely, warming and stirring, if desired, to

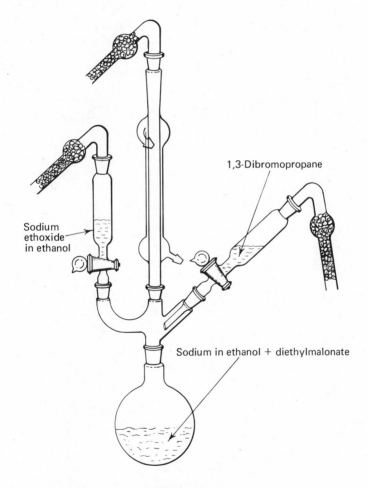

Sodium ethoxide in ethanol

1,3-Dibromopropane

Sodium in ethanol + diethylmalonate

FIGURE 44–1

[1] Dried by distillation over sodium or by the magnesium method of Lund and Bjerrum (A. Vogel, *Practical Organic Chemistry*, Longmans, Green & Co., New York, 1948).

hasten the process of dissolution. A 5 ml portion of the solution is now removed by pipet and placed in one of the tap funnels while into the other, 2.43 ml (2.4 g, 0.015 mole) diethylmalonate is added and run into the flask, swirling to mix the components. To the empty tap funnel now add 1.3 ml (2.5 g, 0.012 mole) of 1,3-dibromopropane.[2] Bring the solution in the flask to the boiling point by using an electric heating mantle or a boiling water bath and add the contents of the two funnels simultaneously over 10–15 minutes. Continue refluxing for 30 min after addition, when the mixture should be neutral.

Arrange the apparatus for distillation by inserting a distillation head. Remove about 10 ml of the alcohol. Pour the residue into a separatory funnel and wash it in with about 10 ml of water. Shake and separate the organic layer. Extract the aqueous layer with two 5 ml portions of benzene and combine the benzene extracts with the previous organic layer. If care is taken to separate off the water, no drying is necessary since water is removed azeotropically with the benzene.

Set up an apparatus for vacuum distillation (Figure 44–2). Place about 15 ml of the product in the flask and distill off the benzene at atmospheric pressure on a boiling water bath adding more solution as the space in the flask becomes available. When all has been added and no further benzene is distilling, dis-

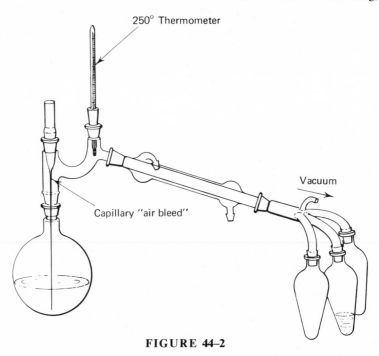

250° Thermometer

Vacuum

Capillary "air bleed"

FIGURE 44–2

[2] 1,3-Dibromopropane may be prepared from 1,3-propanediol (Experiment 13) by treatment concentrated HBr or HBr gas; bp 167°.

continue heating and cautiously lower the pressure using a water aspirator or mechanical vacuum system capable of working at 10–20 mm pressure.

Avoid a too sudden drop of pressure at this point since traces of benzene remaining will foam and cause the whole charge to be carried over. When the full vacuum is finally applied gently heat using the small flame from a micro-burner, which permits greater control of the heating than a heating mantle or bath. Collect the distillate coming over between 110–115° at 15 mm. High boiling material may be left in the flask and contains tetraethylpentane-1,1,5,5-tetracarboxylate formed in a side reaction. Record the boiling-range, pressure, refractive index and yield of the product.

Cyclobutane-1,1-Dicarboxylic Acid

To 2 g diethyl cyclobutane-1,1-dicarboxylate add 5 ml 30% aqueous sodium hydroxide and gently reflux for about 1–1½ hours. Cool the solution and extract any unchanged ester with ether. Acidify the aqueous layer by adding the minimum of concentrated hydrochloric acid and extract with five 5 ml portions of ether. After combining the extracts and drying over sodium sulfate remove the ether on the rotary evaporator and isolate the crude *cyclobutane-1,1-dicarboxylic acid*. This may be recrystallized from ethyl acetate, mp 156°.

Yield, 1.5 g, 85%

Cyclobutanecarboxylic Acid

Construct a distillation tube as shown in Figure 44–3. Place 0.5 g cyclobutanedicarboxylic acid in the bulb and place it in an oil bath. Raise the temperature to 160–170° where decomposition sets in quite rapidly, carbon dioxide being evolved. Raise the temperature of the bath to 210–220° at which point the *cyclobutanecarboxylic acid* distills and condenses into the bulbs in the tube which may be sealed off to preserve the specimen, bp 195°.

Yield, 0.3 g, 80%

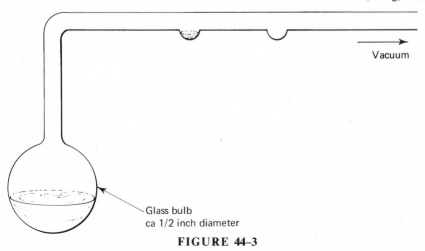

Vacuum

Glass bulb
ca 1/2 inch diameter

FIGURE 44–3

Questions

1. Suggest methods for the preparation of the following compounds,

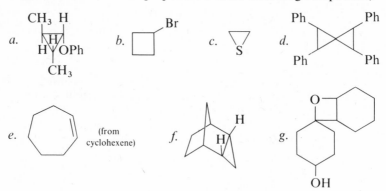

2. Cyclopentane is a more stable compound than cyclopropane but it appears from the properties of derivatives that cyclopropenone is more stable than cyclopentadienone. Explain this.

3. A model of cyclopropane which has been proposed utilizes a three center σ-bond with the remaining 6 electrons in a π-system. This would imply that the cyclopropane system should possess *double bond* character. Suggest experiments which you would perform in order to test this hypothesis.

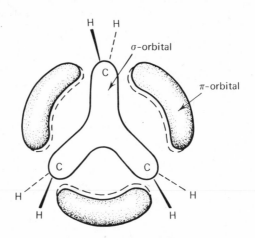

References

1. G. B. Hersig and F. H. Stodola, *Org. Syn.*, Coll. Vol. III, Wiley, New York, 1955, p. 213.

2. L. F. Fieser and M. Fieser, *Advanced Organic Chemistry*, Reinhold, New York, 1961, p. 241.

Synthesis of Alkenes by the Wittig Reaction [1]

EXPERIMENT 45

In 1954, G. Wittig announced a new and versatile synthesis of olefinic compounds by way of pentavalent phosphorus intermediates known as triarylalkylidinephosphoranes,

$$Ar_3P{=}C\begin{matrix} R_1 \\ R_2 \end{matrix}$$

When triphenylphosphine reacts with a primary or secondary alkyl halide, a quaternary phosphonium salt is formed (see the Menshutkin reaction, Experiment 5) which is isolated. The α-proton is fairly acidic and may be removed on treatment with a suitable base, since phosphorus may expand its valence shell from 8 to 10 electrons, to give the phosphorane (III):

$$Ph_3P^{III} + RCH_2Br \longrightarrow Ph_3\overset{+}{P}{-}CH_3R \quad Br^-$$

$$Ph_3\overset{+}{P}{-}\underset{\underset{:B}{H}}{CHR} \quad Br^- \longrightarrow \underset{a}{Ph_3P^{V}{=}CHR} \longleftrightarrow \underset{b}{Ph_3\overset{+}{P}{-}\overset{-}{C}HR}$$

III

This compound has a considerable amount of dipolar (*ylid*) character and can also be written as a phosphonium methylide (IIIb); as such, the anionic carbon may add to a carbonyl function in a similar fashion to an aldol condensation. The dipolar intermediate (IV) then rapidly loses the very stable molecule triphenylphosphine oxide with the formation of an olefin (V):

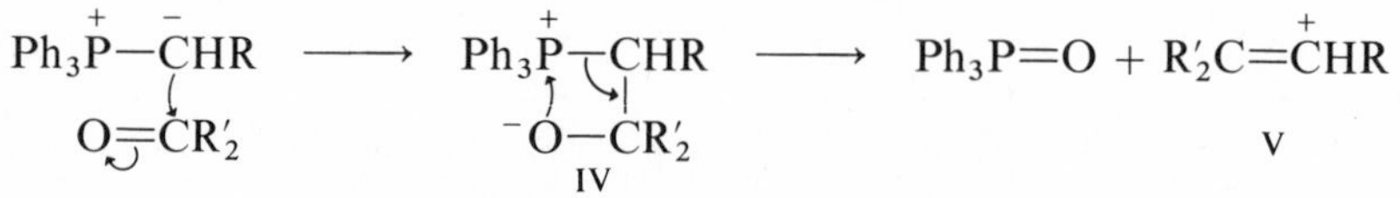

$$\overset{+}{Ph_3P}-\overset{-}{CHR} \longrightarrow \overset{+}{Ph_3P}-CHR \longrightarrow Ph_3P=O + R'_2C=\overset{+}{CHR}$$
$$O=\overset{\cdot}{C}R'_2 \qquad\qquad ^-O-CR'_2$$
$$\qquad\qquad\qquad IV \qquad\qquad\qquad\qquad V$$

Effectively, the alkylidine group replaces the carbonyl oxygen. The Wittig reaction has been used successfully to prepare a variety of interesting olefins including steroids, carotenoids, vitamins and the otherwise difficultly accessible exocyclic olefins [2]. The conditions vary according to the acidity of the phosphonium ion, frequently alkoxide in alcohol is used. In the following experiments, the highly basic system dimethyl sulfoxide—sodium hydride is used:

$$Na^+H^- + CH_3SOCH_3 \longrightarrow Na^+\bar{C}H_2SOCH_3 + H_2$$

Dimethyl sulfoxide is a polar but nonhydrogen bonding solvent and its anion a strong base; the combination of these factors produces a system eight to ten orders of magnitude more basic than hydroxide ion and capable of ionizing a methyl phosphonium salt:

$$\overset{+}{Ph_3P}-CH_3 + \bar{C}H_2SOCH_3 \rightleftharpoons Ph_3P=CH_2 + CH_3SOCH_3$$

The following experiments exemplify the Wittig synthesis in the preparation of β,β-dimethylstyrene (VI) and dicyclohexylidine (VII) according to the following schemes:

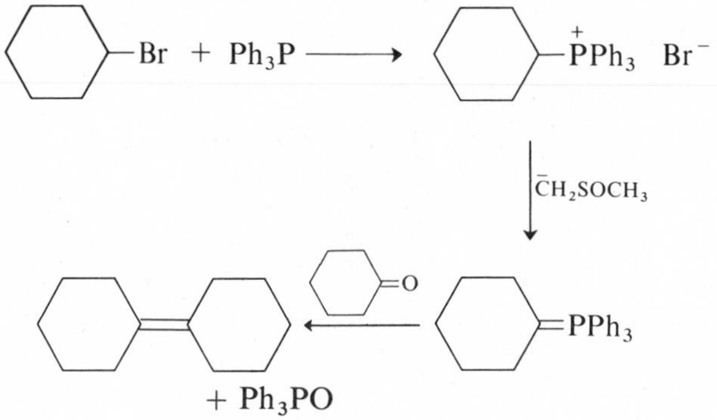

VII

$$PhCH_2Br + Ph_3P \longrightarrow PhCH_2\overset{+}{P}Ph_3 \quad \overset{-}{Br}$$

VIII

$$\downarrow \bar{C}H_2SOCH_3$$

$$PhCH=C\underset{Me}{\overset{Me}{\diagup}} + Ph_3PO \xleftarrow{Me_2C=O} PhCH=\dot{P}Ph_3$$

VI   IX

Experimental

PREPARATION OF β,β-DIMETHYLSTYRENE (VI)

Materials Required

Benzyl bromide	Dimethylsulfoxide
Triphenylphosphine	Acetone
Sodium hydride (50% suspension in oil)	

Place 8.5 g (0.05 mole) benzyl bromide (CAUTION: lachrymatory) and 13.1 g (0.05 mole) triphenylphosphine in a stoppered flask and heat on a hot water bath until the reaction mixture turns solid (about 10 min). Remove the product from the flask and grind in a mortar with several portions of benzene until all unreacted starting material has been removed. Filter and dry the white crystalline product of triphenylbenzylphosphonium bromide (VIII).

Yield, 21 g, 97%

Place 2.3 g sodium hydride[1] (50% suspension in oil), (0.05 mole) in a small flask fitted with reflux condenser and nitrogen[2] delivery tube, all previously dried thoroughly. Add about 20 ml of dry petroleum ether (bp 40–60°), swirl to dissolve the oil, allow the solid matter to settle and decant off the liquid. Destroy any particles of hydride carried over by adding a little methanol to the liquid.

Pass a slow stream of dry nitrogen through the flask and add 20 ml of sodium-dried dimethylsulfoxide, swirling to dissolve the sodium hydride. When the evolution of hydrogen is complete add 20 g (0.05 mole) triphenylbenzylphos-phonium bromide in portions down the condenser, shaking the liquid after each addition. The mixture turns bright orange due to the formation of the phosphorane (IX). When all the phosphonium salt has been added, wash down any solid material adhering to the inside of the condenser with a little dimethyl-sulfoxide and allow the mixture to stand for five minutes. Add dropwise 5 ml of acetone and then warm the mixture gently until the reaction has subsided. Pour the product into 250 ml of water and extract three times with petroleum

---

[1] Sodium hydride reacts violently with water. Great care should be taken to ensure the apparatus and reagents are dry and eye protection should be worn.

[2] Or other inert gas.

ether (bp 40–60°). Combine the extracts, dry over sodium sulfate and remove the solvent on the rotary evaporator. Transfer the residue to a small vacuum distillation apparatus and add a few crystals of hydroquinone to prevent polymerization. Distill, collecting β,β-dimethylstyrene, VI at 60–65°/1–2 mm.

Yield, 4 g, 60%

a. Check the infrared spectrum (thin film) of the product and try to identify the following features:

aromatic C—H stretch	3030–3080 cm^{-1}	3.30–3.25 μ
aliphatic C—H stretch	2850–2975 cm^{-1}	3.53–3.36 μ
absence of carbonyl (C=O stretch)	1700–1720 cm^{-1}	5.80–5.88 μ
ethylenic C=C stretch	1620–1680 cm^{-1}	5.95–5.88 μ
aromatic C=C stretch	ca. 1500 and 1600	6.2, 5.6 μ
methyl bend, *anti* symmetric	1420–1450	6.90–7.05 μ
symmetric	1300–1320	7.58–7.70 μ

b. Test the product for unsaturation by bromine in carbon tetrachloride.

PREPARATION OF DICYCLOHEXYLIDINE (VII)

Materials Required

Cyclohexyl bromide[3]   Dimethyl sulfoxide
Triphenylphosphine   Sodium hydride (50% suspension in oil)
Cyclohexanone

Allow 8.1 g (0.05 mole) cyclohexyl bromide and 13.1 g (0.05 mole) triphenylphosphine to reflux gently on an oil bath in an atmosphere of nitrogen for 1–1$\frac{1}{2}$ hours. Cool the product and pour into benzene in a mortar. Grind the precipitate until granular and repeat with fresh benzene until a white crystalline solid, cyclohexyltriphenylphosphonium bromide, is obtained. Filter and dry the solid.

Yield, 18–20 g, 85–95%

Prepare a solution containing 0.05 mole dimethylsulfoxide anion as in the previous experiment. Add 16 g cyclohexyltriphenylphosphonium bromide in portions keeping the mixture under an inert atmosphere. Warm the mixture gently until the reaction is complete then add 5 ml cyclohexanone and allow the flask to stand for ten min with occasional shaking. Pour the reaction mixture into water, extract the product with four 25 ml portions of petroleum ether (20–40°) and dry the combined extracts over sodium sulfate. Remove most of the solvent on the rotary evaporator and distill the residue, obtaining dicyclohexylidine as an oil, bp 120–130°/1–2 mm which later crystallizes, mp 55°.

[3] Cyclohexyl bromide may be prepared by the dropwise addition of 25 g bromine to a mixture of 10 g cyclohexanol and 3.2 g red phosphorus. After warming for 10 min, the mixture is poured into water, neutralized with sodium bicarbonate, the product extracted with ether, dried and distilled, collecting cyclohexyl bromide at 160–165°.   Yield, 15 g.

Examine the infrared spectrum (thin film) of the product and check its consistency with the assumed structure. Search in *Chemical Abstracts*, 1947–1956 for another synthesis of this compound and compare the two for yields, convenience and cost.

Yield, 4 g, 65%

Questions

1. Suggest syntheses of the following compounds:

a.

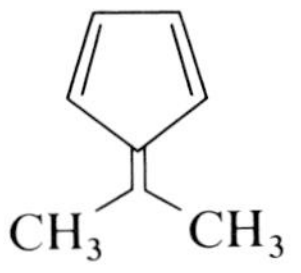

CH$_3$ CH$_3$

b.   Ph$_2$C=C=CPh$_2$

c.   PhCHCH$_3$CHO (from PhCOCH$_3$)

d.   CH$_3$

CH$_3$

CH$_3$

CH$_3$

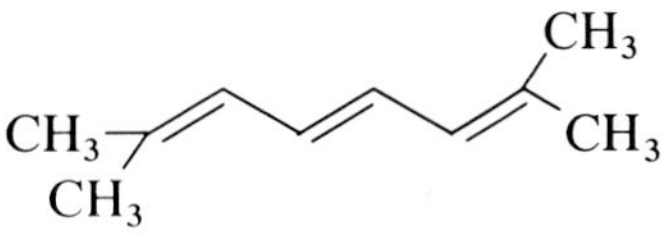

e.

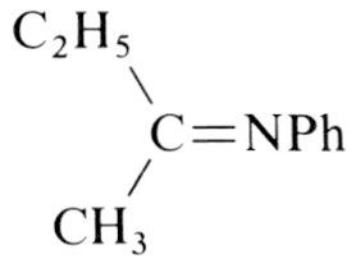

C$_2$H$_5$

C=NPh

CH$_3$

f.

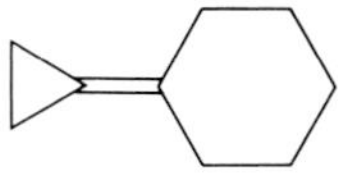

2. Devise an experiment to examine the stereochemistry of the Wittig olefin synthesis.

Reference

1. S. Trippett, *Quart. Rev.*, **17**, 406 (1962).

Reductions with Diimine

EXPERIMENT 46

It was noticed by several workers [1, 2, 3] that hydrazine occasionally brought about reductions of carbon–carbon double bonds such as of oleic acid to stearic:

$$CH_3(CH_2)_7CH{=}CH(CH_2)_7COOH \xrightarrow{N_2H_4} CH_3(CH_2)_{16}COOH$$

   Corey [4] and Hünig [5] independently examined this reaction and produced evidence that the reducing species is not hydrazine itself but an oxidation product, diimine, $HN{=}NH$, hitherto unknown. Diimine may transfer a pair of hydrogen atoms to a double bond by a concerted and considerably exothermic process and may be generated from hydrazine by air oxidation or better, by hydrogen peroxide. The species is not sufficiently stable to be isolated but when generated in the presence of olefins such as maleic or fumaric acids, stilbene (1,2-diphenylethylene), diphenylacetylene and azobenzene gives 80–95% yields of saturated compounds. The oxidation of hydrazine is catalyzed by heavy metal ions, especially copper:

$$H_2N{-}NH_2 + H_2O_2 \xrightarrow{Cu^{++}} HN{=}NH + 2\,H_2O$$

$$\underset{\text{cinnamic acid}}{HN{=}NH + PhCH{=}CHCOOH} \longrightarrow \underset{\text{hydrocinnamic acid}}{PhCH_2CH_2COOH + N_2}$$

Experimental

Materials Required
     Cinnamic acid   Hydrogen peroxide, 30%
     Hydrazine (or hydrazine hydrate)

REDUCTION OF CINNAMIC ACID

Dissolve 2.0 g cinnamic acid in a solution of 2.5 g hydrazine (or 4.0 g hydrazine hydrate), a considerable excess, in 25 ml water. Place the beaker in an ice bath and stir well. Dissolve a few small crystals of cupric sulfate in the solution and add slowly an ice-cold solution of 10 g hydrogen peroxide (30%) in water such that the temperature remains below 25° during this exothermic reaction. After addition, allow the beaker to stand at room temperature for 10 min then cool in ice and acidify with a little 1 : 1 hydrochloric acid. Hydrocinnamic acid separates out, frequently as an oil, which crystallizes on standing in the ice bath, mp 48°.

                     Yield, 1.6 g, 80%

Question

1. Review all the methods available for the preparation of hydrocinnamic acid and compare their convenience.

References

1. J. Hanus and J. Varisek, *Coll. Czech. Chem. Comm.*, **1**, 223 (1929).
2. H. Fischer, *et al.*, *Liebig's Annalen*, **548**, 183 (1941); *ibid.*, **550**, 208 (1942).
3. R. E. Cross, *J. Chem. Soc.*, 3022 (1960).
4. E. J. Corey, W. L. Mock, and D. J. Pasto, *Tetrahedron Letters*, 347 (1961).
5. S. Hünig, H. R. Muller, and W. Thier, *Tetrahedron Letters*, 353 (1961).
6. S. Hünig, *Angew. Chem.* (Int. Edn.), **4**, 271 (1965).

Appendices

Reaction Kinetics
in Solution

APPENDIX A

The *order* of a reaction is a number expressing the total number of powers of concentration terms on which the rate of the reaction is found by experiment to be dependent. Provided the concentrations of all the reagents are of comparable magnitude, the measured order is frequently equated with the *molecularity* of the reaction which is the number of molecules (ions, radicals, etc.) of one sort or another which are actually involved in the transition state of the rate-determining step of the reaction. Information concerning the mechanism of a reaction may then be deduced from the molecularity and thus from the reaction order.

For example, the hydrolysis of ethyl bromide by hydroxide ion in aqueous ethanol is observed to be second-order—first-order in each of ethyl bromide and hydroxide ion,

$$\text{rate} = k_2[\text{ethyl bromide}][\text{OH}^-]$$

where k_2, the constant of proportionality is the second-order *specific rate constant* and the square brackets indicate concentrations. We infer that the reaction is bimolecular—i.e., the molecularity is two—to account for this rate dependence, the mechanism being,

301

$$CH_3CH_2Br + OH^- \longrightarrow CH_3 \longrightarrow products$$

$$\overset{\delta-}{HO}----\overset{|}{C}----\overset{C^{\delta-}}{Br}$$
$$\diagup \quad \diagdown$$
$$H \quad H$$

transition state

Since kinetic methods are required for a number of the experiments in this book both for the purpose of deducing mechanisms and also, providing an index of the reaction rate specific rate constants, the following treatment of the most common cases is given.

REACTIONS OF THE FIRST-ORDER— *Unimolecular*

The rate is dependent on the concentration of one species only:

$$A \xrightarrow{k_1} products$$

initial conc $= a$

conc at time, $t = (a - x)$

$$\text{Rate} = -\frac{d}{dt}(a - x) = k_1(a - x)$$

Integration gives,

$$k_1 = \frac{2.303}{t} \log \frac{a}{(a - x)}$$

Hence the rate constant, invariant with time, is given by insertion of the appropriate values of residual concentration of A, $(a - x)$ at times, t, or from the slope of the straight line plot of $a/(a - x)$ against t. The time required for the concentration of A to fall to half its original value $(a - x = a/2)$ may be readily seen, by application of the above equation to be

$$t_{1/2} = \frac{2.303 \log 2}{k_1} = \frac{0.693}{k_1}$$

The half-life, $t_{1/2}$, may be estimated from the (curved) plot of x or $(a - x)$ against t (Figure A–1). Several values should be measured from different starting points and the results averaged. This procedure is less rigorous but more rapid than the linear plot and is often adequate where relative values of k are needed.

The same kinetic form is exhibited by bimolecular reactions carried out with a large excess of one reagent. For example, the hydrolysis of ethylene oxide (Experiment 6) in water is independent of the concentration of water which changes to a negligible extent during the reaction. Such a reaction is *pseudo-unimolecular* and exhibits first-order kinetics,

$$\text{rate} = k_1 \left[\begin{array}{c} CH_2-CH_2 \\ \diagdown \quad \diagup \\ O \end{array} \right]$$

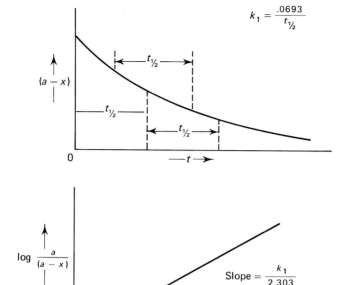

FIGURE A–1 First-order rate plots.

REACTIONS OF THE SECOND-ORDER—*Bimolecular*

The rate is dependent on the product of the concentrations of two species (or a squared term),

$$A + B \xrightarrow{\;k_2\;} \text{products}$$

$$\text{Rate} = -\frac{d[A]}{dt} = -\frac{d[B]}{dt} = k_2[A][B]$$

If the initial concentrations of the two reagents are a and b respectively, they fall to $(a - x)$ and $(b - x)$ after time t since they are consumed at the same rate. Integration then gives,

$$k_2 = \frac{2.303}{t(a - b)} \log \frac{b(a - x)}{a(b - x)}$$

where k_2 is the second-order specific rate constant.

In these circumstances, k may be evaluated from the straight line plot of $\log(a - x)/(b - x)$ against t.

If, however, the reagents are of similar concentration, i.e. $(a - b)$ is small, the above expression reduces to

$$k_2 = \frac{1}{t}\left(\frac{x}{a(a - x)}\right)$$

and k is found by plotting $1/(a - x)$ against t.

With equal initial concentrations, a, the half-life may be shown to be given by

$$t_{1/2} = \frac{1}{k}a$$

Hence it is possible to distinguish a first-order from a second-order reaction by observing whether the half-life is dependent on the initial concentration of the reagents. In the second-order plot of $(a - x)$ against t, this is manifested by the half-life gradually increasing as the reaction proceeds (Figure A–2). This, of

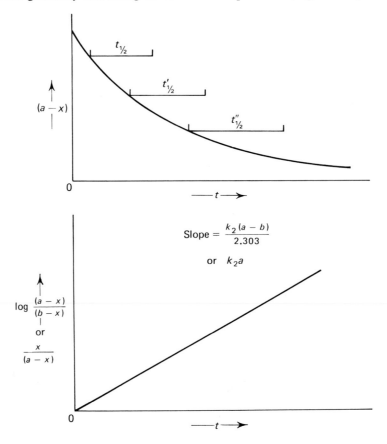

FIGURE A–2 Second-order rate plots.

course, is a reflection on the decreasing probability of collision between the two reagent species as the concentration of each falls.

Other more complicated kinetic laws are frequently encountered. The interested reader is referred to specialized texts such as A. A. Frost and R. G. Pearson, *Kinetics and Mechanism*, Wiley, New York, 1952, for further discussion.

Reaction rates invariably increase with temperature according to the Arrhenius Law,

$$\frac{d}{dt}\log k = Ae^{-E_A/RT}$$

where A is the frequency factor (a measure of the efficiency of the collision process in leading to reaction), R is the gas constant and T the temperature, $K°$. E_A is the Arrhenius activation energy and is a measure of the free energy of activation of the reaction. The reaction parameters may be estimated from the linear plot of $\log k$ against $1/T$; see Figure A–3.

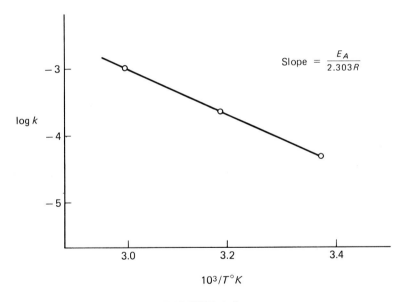

FIGURE A–3

Computer Programs for Kinetic Calculations

First-Order Kinetics, Weighted Least-Square Program. (FORTRAN).

```
   DIMENSION T(20),C(20),Y(20),W(20)
   DIMENSION A1(20), A2(20), A3(20)
24 FORMAT (1X,4(4X,E14.8),F8.2)
 2 FORMAT (12,22X,12)
 3  FORMAT (E15.8,E12.6,F8.2)
77 FORMAT (1X, E14.8, 5X, 12)
 9 FORMAT (1X, 4(4X,E14.8))
30 FORMAT ( 11H SUMS FOLLO, 5(4X,E14.8))
12 READ 2, N, NRUN
   DO 4 1 = 1,N
 4 READ3,T(I),C(I)
   A = 0.
   B = 0.
   D = 0.
   E = 0.
   G = 0.
   DO 5 1 = 1,N
   A = A + C(I)
   B = B + T(.I) * C(I)
   D = D + C(I) * LOGF(C(I))
   E = E + T(I) * T(I) * C(I)
 5 G = G + T(I) * C(I) * LOGF(C(I))
   DET = A*E - B*B
   HA = (D*E -B*G)/DET
   HK = (A*G - B*D)/DET
   HAS = EXPF(HA)
   SUM = 0.
   DO 6 1 = 1, N
   Y(I) = HAS*EXPF(HK*T(I))
   W(I) = Y(I) - C(I)
 6 SUM = SUM + W(I) * W(I)
   PRINT 7, SUM, NRUN
   PRINT 9, HA, HK, HAS
   DO 8 1 = 1,N
```

```
    8 PRINT 9, T(I), C(I), Y(I), W(I)
      DO 25 J = 1, 3
      S1 = 0.
      S2 = 0.
      S3 = 0.
      S4 = 0.
      S5 = 0.
      DO 20  I = 1,N
      A1(I) = EXPF( HK*T(I))
      A3(I) = A1(I) * HAS
      A2(I) = A3(I) *T(I)
      S1 = S1 + A1(I)*A1(I)
      S2 = S2 + A1(I) * A2(I)
      S3 = S3 + A1(I)* (C(I) -A3(I))
      S4 = S4 + A2(I)* A2(I)
   20 S5 = S5 + A2(I) *  (C(I) -A3(I))
      DET = S1*S4 - S2 *S2
      DZ = (S3*S4-S2*S5)/DET
      D1 = (S1*S5 - S2*S3)/ DET
      HAS = HAS + DZ
      HK = HK + D1
      PRINT 30, S1, S2, S3, S4, S5, DET
      PRINT 24, HAS, DZ, HK, D1
      SUM = 0.
      DO 22 I = 1,N
      Y(I) = HAS * EXPF(HK*T(I))

      W(I) = Y(I) - C(I)
   22 SUM = SUM + W(I) *W(I)
      DO 23 I = 1,N
   23 PRINT 24, T(I), C(I), Y(I), W(I)
   25 CONTINUE
      GO TO 12
      END
```

The program is followed by data consisting of (a) the number of readings, N and (b) N cards each bearing a value of t and $(a - x)$.

First–Order Kinetics

Nonlinear Least Squares Programme   (ALGOL).

```
                FIRST ORDER RATE CONSTANTS'
BEGIN REAL K,KP,SUM,SUM1,SUM2,SUM3,SUM4,F,DF,X,X1,A'
INTEGER 1,N,NRUN,N1
ARRAY C,T(1:100)'
SWITCH SS:=S1,S2'
S2:READ NRUN,N,A'
FOR 1:=1 STEP 1 UNTIL N DO READ T(I),C(I)'
K:=(LN(A/C(2)))/T(2)'
S1:SUM1:=0'
SUM2:=0'SUM3:=0'SUM4:=0'
FOR 1:=1 STEP 1 UNTIL N DO BEGIN X:=EXP(-K*T(1))'
X1:=T(1)*X'
SUM1:=SUM1+X1*X'
SUM2:=SUM2+C(1)*X1'
SUM3:=SUM3+X1*X1'
SUM4:=SUM4+C(1)*T(1)*X1'
END
F:=A*SUM1-SUM2'DF:=-2.0*A*SUM3+SUM4'KP:=K'K:=K-F/DF'
IF ABS(K-KP) GREQ 0.000001*ABS(K) THEN GOTO S1'
SUM:=0'X1:=0'N1:=0
FOR 1:=1 STEP 1 UNTIL N DO BEGIN X:=A*EXP(-K*T(1))-C(1)'
X:=X*X'IF X GREQ X1 THEN BEGIN X1:=X'N1:=1'END'
SUM:=SUM+X'
END'
SUM:=(SORT(SUM))/N'
PRINT  L? RUN NUMBER?,SAMELINE,DIGITS(3),NRUN,DIGITS(5),N,   VALUES ?
PRINT  K=?,SAMELINE,FREEPOINT(7), K,  DEVIATION=? SUM, L3??,
MAXIMUM DEVIATION=?,SQRT(X1),  AT VALUE ?, DIGITS(3),N1,  L2??'
GOTO S2'
END'
```

The data are provided in the form (a) run number, (b) number of readings, (c) accuracy value (Delta), e.g. 0.00005, and (d) pairs of values of t and $(a - x)$.

Second-order Kinetics, FORTRAN

```
      WWFORX 2
      *LIST PRINTER
      DIMENSION A(20), T(20)
   99 READ 100,N,NRUN, (T(I),A(I),I = 1,N)
  100 FORMAT (2I3/(E20.0,F10.0))
      ST = 0
      S1A = 0
      STA = 0
      ST2 = 0
      DO20I = 1,N
      ST = ST + T(I)
      S1A = S1A + 1./A(I)
      STA = STA + T(I)/A(I)
   20 ST2 = ST2 + T(I)**2
      XN = N
      RK = (ST*S1A/XN - STA)/(ST**2/XN - ST2)
      PRINT 101,NRUN,RK
  101 FORMAT (1H0,4HRUN ,I3,21H      RATE CONSTANT = ,E14.8)
      G0T099
      END
```

Data Follows, as for the FORTRAN first-order program.

Instruments

It is a necessary part of an organic chemist's training that he become familiar with many physical methods of measurement. It is not the purpose of this book to give a detailed account of instrumental methods since many excellent accounts are already available. The student is recommended to the following sources for accounts of the theory, scope and methods of use for the instruments required in this course:

F. L. J. Sixma and H. Wynberg, *A Manual of Physical Methods in Organic Chemistry*, Wiley, New York, 1964.

E. A. Braude and F. C. Nachod, *Determination of Organic Structures by Physical Methods*, Academic, New York, 1955.

J. C. P. Schwarz, Ed., *Physical Methods in Organic Chemistry*, Oliver and Boyd, London, 1964.

A. Weissberger (Ed.), *Technique of Organic Chemistry*, 11 Vols., Interscience, New York, 1948–65.

Instruments of good quality have been used in checking these experiments. Those described here or others of similar quality, are recommended.

Infrared Spectrophotometers. Moderately good resolution is recommended for measurement of absorbance or small changes in wavelength (Experiments 16, 17, 21, 33): the Beckman IR4, Perkin–Elmer 21 series, Unicam SP 100, and Baird–Atomic 4–55 instruments are more than adequate. For other experiments and routine spectra of products, less expensive models such as the Perkin-Elmer Infracord, Unicam SP 200 or Beckman IR 5A are suitable.

Ultraviolet-Visible Spectrophotometers. Where full spectra are required, a great deal of time is saved by using scanning instruments which should be of good quality for the accurate measurement of absorbances or absorbance maxima, as in Experiments 17, 19, 20 and 24. For all experiments such models as the Beckman DK, Unicam SP 700 and SP 800 or Carey are suitable : Experiments 9, 10, 31, 32 and 45 require only lower resolution instruments such as the Beckman DB, or Perkin–Elmer 137UV while measurements at fixed wavelength as in Experiments 9 or 10 are equally easily made on non-scanning spectrophotometers such as the Beckman DU or Unicam SP 500 or SP 600.

Nuclear Magnetic Resonance Spectrometers. Experiments 22 and 23 are best carried out on 60 mc/sec proton resonance instruments. The Varian A60 (or HR60) and Perkin–Elmer R10 instruments are suitable.

Electron-Spin Resonance. The Varian E3 esr spectrometer has been found suitable for Experiment 24.

Dipole Moment Measurement. A Sargent oscillometer has been used in testing Experiment 14. The apparatus may also be constructed to designs given in the literature, see P. Bender, *J. Chem. Ed.*, **23**, 179 (1946).

Gas-Liquid Chromatography. Many manufacturers supply adequate glc equipment, for instance Varian-Aerograph, Perkin–Elmer, F and M, and Beckman. The instruments used for Experiments 1, 4, and 8 should be capable of use at temperatures up to 200° stable to $\pm 1°$ and have a heated inlet system, and a variety of interchangeable columns ($\frac{1}{8}''$ diameter preferred). The detector may be of the thermal conductivity type, using helium as a carrier gas or hydrogen flame which permits nitrogen to be used and is more sensitive.

pH-Meters. Experiments 2 and 11 require accurate measurement of pH. Instruments giving one pH unit full scale deflection are recommended. The Beckman and Corning instruments have been found suitable.

Polarimeters. A good quality conventional polarimeter reading to $\pm 0.02°$ is recommended for Experiments 3 and 27. Bausch and Lomb and Rudolph instruments have been found suitable. Better, especially for the accurate measurement of low rotations as in Experiments 27 and 13, is an automatic recording polarimeter such as the Bendix 143C.

Refractometers. An Abbé refractometer, reading to 0.0001 is suitable for Experiment 29 and is available from most scientific suppliers.

Interpretation of
Organic Spectra

APPENDIX C

Average positions of infrared absorption bands are given in Table C–1 and of proton resonance lines in Table C–2 with typical coupling constants listed in Table C–3. Ultraviolet spectral correlations are given in Experiment 20.

TABLE C-1 N.M.R Spectral Assignments

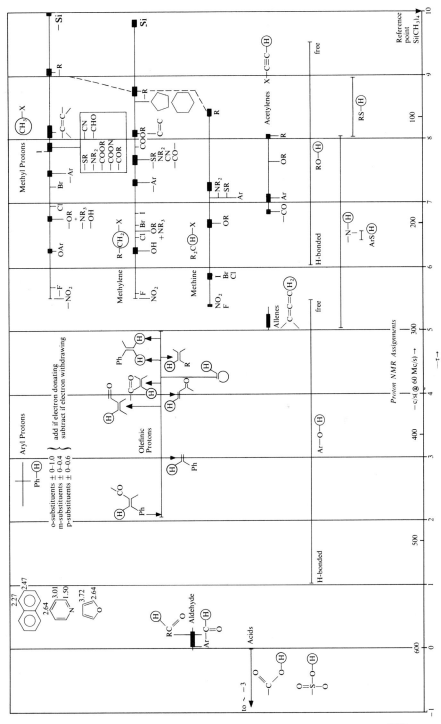

TABLE C-2 Infrared Spectral Assignments

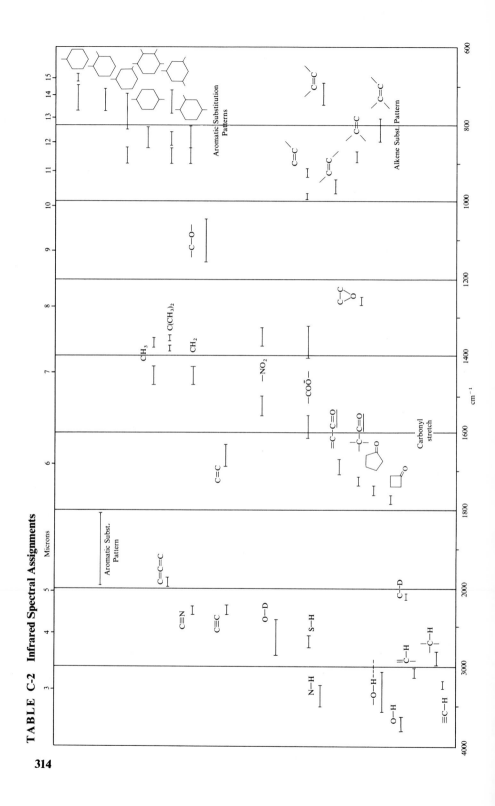

314

TABLE C-3

Spin–Spin Coupling Constants, J_{AB}	(60 Mc/s spectra)

	J_{AB} c/s
C with two H (non-identical protons)	12–15
C—C with H H	2–9
C—(C)$_n$—C with H, H	~0
CH_3—CH_2	6.5–7.5
$(CH_3)_2 \cdot CH$	~6.0
cyclohexane ring (aa / ae / ee)	aa 5–10 / ae 2–4 / ee 2–4
C=C with two H (geminal)	0.5–3
H, H on C=C (cis)	7–12
H and H on C=C (trans)	13–18
C=C—C—H	0.5–2.5
H, C=C, C—H	~0
C=C—C=C with H H	9–13

TABLE C-3 **(Continued)**

Spin–Spin Coupling Constants, J_{AB}   (60 Mc/s spectra)

J_{AB} c/s

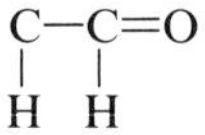

C—C=O   1–3
| |
H   H

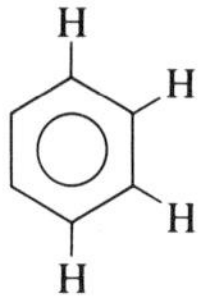

	o	6–9
	m	1–3
	p	~0

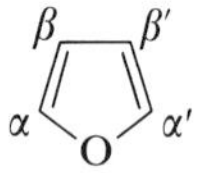

	$\alpha\beta$	1.6–2.0
	$\alpha\beta'$	0.6–1.0
	$\alpha\alpha'$	1.3–1.8
	$\beta\beta'$	3.2–3.8

Coupling to Fluorine

	$J_{HF}(X{=}H)$	$J_{FF}(X{=}F)$
	40–80	~160
	7–13	20–80
o	6–10	20
m	6–7	2–4
p	2	12–15
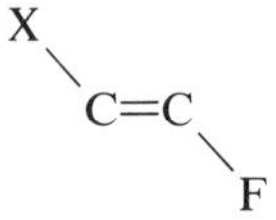	12–40	115–125
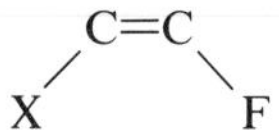	1–8	33–60

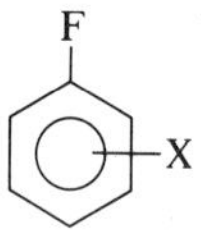

Dihedral Angle Dependence

θ	J
0	8.2
30	6.0
60	1.7
90	−0.28

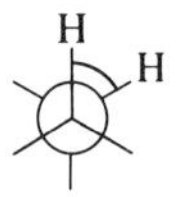

Linear Free
Energy Parameters

APPENDIX **D**

The first two columns in Table D–1 list accepted values for the Hammett substituent constant, σ, as defined in Experiment 2, for substituents located in the *para* and *meta* positions respectively with respect to the site of reaction.

TABLE D-1 Substituent Constants

	σ_p	σ_m	σ^+ p	σ^+ m	σ_p^-	σ^*
NMe$_2$	-0.83	-0.21	-1.7			
NH$_2$	-0.66	-0.16	-1.3			
OH	-0.37	$+0.12$	-0.92			
OMe	-0.27	$+0.11$	-0.77	$+0.05$		
OEt	-0.24	$+0.10$	-0.5			
Me	-0.17	-0.07	-0.31	-0.06		0
Et	-0.15	-0.07				-0.10
Pr^i	-0.15	-0.07				-0.19
Bu^t	-0.20	-0.10	-0.26			-0.30
H	0	0	0	0		$+0.49$
Ph	-0.01	$+0.06$	-0.18			$+0.60$
Cl	$+0.23$	$+0.37$	$+0.11$	$+0.39$	$+0.26$	
I	$+0.28$	$+0.35$	$+0.13$	$+0.35$	$+0.32$	
COOEt	$+0.45$	$+0.37$			$+0.73$	$+2.0$
COCH$_3$	$+0.50$	$+0.38$			$+0.87$	$+1.65$
NO$_2$	$+0.78$	$+0.71$			$+1.27$	
NMe$_3{}^+$	$+0.82$	$+0.88$				

The third and fourth columns, listed σ^+, contain amended values of σ for certain substituents which should be used when, in the transition state of the reaction, the aromatic ring is becoming positively charged. In these circumstances, greatly enhanced interactions between the aromatic nucleus and $+M$ (electron-donating by a mesomeric mechanism) substituents is found to occur and hence σ^+ values apply only to strongly $+M$ substituents such as $-OMe$ particularly in the *para* position. For example, in electrophilic substitution,

use σ^+, -0.77 OMe   OMe $_+$OMe   products

a much better correlation of measured rates is obtained using σ^+ values rather than σ.

The fifth column contains values of σ^-, another modified σ this time to be used when the reaction center or the aromatic nucleus is becoming negatively charged in the transition state. Under these circumstances, the effect of strongly $-M$ groups will be greatly enhanced. For example, the dissociation of phenols,

use σ^-, $+1.27$

The final column lists values of σ^*, the Taft substituent constants which may be used in an expression entirely analogous to the Hammett expression, $\log(k/k_0) = \sigma^*\rho^*$, for aliphatic systems in which steric interactions are relatively unimportant. Some representative values of ρ are given in Table D–2.

For further discussion of this topic, the reader is referred to the books of Hine or Ferguson and for further values of ρ to Jaffé's review, as listed in the bibliography to Experiment 2.

TABLE D-2 Representative Reaction Constants ρ[1]

	$T°C$	*Solvent*	ρ
Equilibria			
Acid dissociation constants of Benzoic acids	25	water	1.000
			(standard)
	15	water	0.954
	25	methanol	1.537
	25	95% EtOH	1.890
Acid dissociation, phenylboronic acids, $ArB(OH)_2$	25	25% EtOH	2.146
Acid dissociation, phenols	25	water	2.113
Acid dissociation, anilinium ions	25	water	2.767
$ArCHO + HCN \rightleftharpoons ArCH(OH)CN$	20	95% EtOH	-1.492
$ArCOMe + H_2 \rightleftharpoons ArCH(OH)Me$	25	water	1.630
Rates			
Esterification of $ArCOOH$ $(MeOH + H^+)$	25	MeOH	-0.229
$ArCOOEt + PhNH_2 \rightarrow ArCONHPh$	80	$PhNH_2$	0.518
$ArCH_2Cl + I^- \rightarrow ArCH_2I + Cl^-$	0	Me_2CO	0.809
$Ar_2Hg + H^+ \rightarrow ArH + ArHg^+$	30	dioxan	2.282
$(ArCOO\text{-})_2 \rightarrow 2\,ArCOO \cdot$	80	dioxan	-0.374
Styrenes, copolymerized with maleic anhydride	60	—	-0.612

[1] *Jaffé, Chem. Rev.*, 191, (1954).

Index